Mind and Machine

Palgrave Philosophy Today
Series Editor: **Vittorio Bufacchi**, University College Cork, Ireland

The *Palgrave Philosophy Today* series provides concise introductions to all the major areas of philosophy currently being taught in philosophy departments around the world. Each book gives a state-of-the-art informed assessment of a key area of philosophical study. In addition, each title in the series offers a distinct interpretation from an outstanding scholar who is closely involved with current work in the field. Books in the series provide students and teachers with not only a succinct introduction to the topic, with the essential information necessary to understand it and the literature being discussed, but also a demanding and engaging entry into the subject.

Titles include

Pascal Engel
PHILOSOPHY OF PSYCHOLOGY

Shaun Gallagher
PHENOMENOLOGY

Simon Kirchin
METAETHICS

Duncan Pritchard
KNOWLEDGE

Mathias Risse
GLOBAL POLITICAL PHILOSOPHY

Joel Walmsley
MIND AND MACHINE

Forthcoming Titles

Helen Beebee
METAPHYSICS

James Robert Brown
PHILOSOPHY OF SCIENCE

Neil Manson
ENVIRONMENTAL PHILOSOPHY

Chad Meister
PHILOSOPHY OF RELIGION

Matthew Nudds
MIND AND THOUGHT

Lilian O'Brien
PHILOSOPHY OF ACTION

Don Ross
PHILOSOPHY OF ECONOMICS

Nancy Tuana
FEMINISM AND PHILOSOPHY

Palgrave Philosophy Today
Series Standing Order ISBN 978-0-230-00232-6 (hardcover)
Series Standing Order ISBN 978-0-230-00233-3 (paperback)
(*outside North America only*)

You can receive future titles in this series as they are published by placing a standing order. Please contact your bookseller or, in case of difficulty, write to us at the address below with your name and address, the title of the series and the ISBN quoted above.

Customer Services Department, Macmillan Distribution Ltd, Houndmills, Basingstoke, Hampshire RG21 6XS, England

Mind and Machine

Joel Walmsley
University College Cork, Ireland

palgrave
macmillan

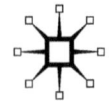

© Joel Walmsley 2012

All rights reserved. No reproduction, copy or transmission of this publication may be made without written permission.

No portion of this publication may be reproduced, copied or transmitted save with written permission or in accordance with the provisions of the Copyright, Designs and Patents Act 1988, or under the terms of any licence permitting limited copying issued by the Copyright Licensing Agency, Saffron House, 6–10 Kirby Street, London EC1N 8TS.

Any person who does any unauthorized act in relation to this publication may be liable to criminal prosecution and civil claims for damages.

The author has asserted his right to be identified as the author of this work in accordance with the Copyright, Designs and Patents Act 1988.

First published 2012 by
PALGRAVE MACMILLAN

Palgrave Macmillan in the UK is an imprint of Macmillan Publishers Limited, registered in England, company number 785998, of Houndmills, Basingstoke, Hampshire RG21 6XS.

Palgrave Macmillan in the US is a division of St Martin's Press LLC, 175 Fifth Avenue, New York, NY 10010.

Palgrave Macmillan is the global academic imprint of the above companies and has companies and representatives throughout the world.

Palgrave® and Macmillan® are registered trademarks in the United States, the United Kingdom, Europe and other countries

ISBN: 978–0–230–30293–8 hardback
ISBN: 978–0–230–30294–5 paperback

This book is printed on paper suitable for recycling and made from fully managed and sustained forest sources. Logging, pulping and manufacturing processes are expected to conform to the environmental regulations of the country of origin.

A catalogue record for this book is available from the British Library.

A catalog record for this book is available from the Library of Congress.

10 9 8 7 6 5 4 3 2 1
21 20 19 18 17 16 15 14 13 12

Printed and bound in Great Britain by
CPI Antony Rowe, Chippenham and Eastbourne

For Catherine and Charlotte

Contents

Series Editor's Preface ix
List of Illustrations xi
Acknowledgements xiii

Introduction 1

1 Historical and Theoretical Background 4
  1.1 Early modern roots 5
    1.1.1 Descartes: the ghost in the machine 5
    1.1.2 Hobbes and Hume: mental mechanics 7
    1.1.3 Pascal and Leibniz: mathematical machines 10
  1.2 Turing and the 'Dartmouth Conference' 13
  1.3 Varieties of AI 14
  1.4 Is AI an empirical or *a priori* enterprise? 19
  1.5 AI and the mind-body problem 23

2 Classical Cognitive Science and 'Good Old Fashioned AI' 26
  2.1 Three roots of the classical approach 27
    2.1.1 Logic 27
    2.1.2 Linguistics 30
    2.1.3 Functionalism and the 'Representational Theory of Mind (RTM)' 32
  2.2 Algorithms, Turing Machines and Turing's thesis 35
  2.3 GOFAI's success stories 44
    2.3.1 Reasoning: the logic theory machine 44
    2.3.2 Chess: Deep Blue 48
    2.3.3 Conversation: ELIZA 51
  2.4 GOFAI and the mind-body problem 54

3 Gödel, the Turing Test and the Chinese Room 57
  3.1 Gödel's incompleteness theorem 58
  3.2 The Turing Test 64
  3.3 Searle's Chinese Room 69

4 Connectionism 77
  4.1 Physiological and psychological realism 79
  4.2 Representation reconsidered 83
  4.3 Some connectionist models 88

	4.3.1	Pattern recognition: the mine/rock detector	88
	4.3.2	Language: past-tense learning	90
	4.3.3	Disorders: network models of schizophrenia	93
4.4		Connectionism and the mind-body problem	96

5 Criticisms and Consequences of the Connectionist Approach — **99**
- 5.1 Connectionism, folk psychology and eliminativism — 99
- 5.2 Connectionism and compositionality — 107

6 The Dynamical Approach — **115**
- 6.1 Motivation — 115
- 6.2 Dynamical systems theory — 117
- 6.3 Dynamical cognitive science: time and timing — 120
- 6.4 Dynamical cognitive science in action — 124
  - 6.4.1 Finger wagging: the 'HKB' model — 124
  - 6.4.2 Beer on bugs — 126
  - 6.4.3 Perceptual categorisation — 130
- 6.5 Taking stock: consequences and criticisms of the dynamical approach — 131
  - 6.5.1 Explanation — 132
  - 6.5.2 Situation — 134
  - 6.5.3 Representation revis(it)ed — 138
  - 6.5.4 Incrementalism — 143
- 6.6 The dynamical approach and the mind-body problem — 146

7 The Future: Mind and Machine Merged — **151**
- 7.1 The extended mind hypothesis — 152
- 7.2 Cognitive technology and human-machine hybrids — 160
- 7.3 'The singularity' — 165

Conclusion — **170**

Notes — 173
Suggestions for Further Reading — 176
Works Cited — 179
Index — 189

Series Editor's Preface

It is not easy being a student of philosophy these days. All the different areas of philosophy are reaching ever increasing levels of complexity and sophistication, a fact which is reflected in the specialized literature and readership each branch of philosophy enjoys. And yet, anyone who studies philosophy is expected to have a solid grasp of the most current issues being debated in most, if not all, of the other areas of philosophy. It is an understatement to say that students of philosophy today are faced with a Herculean task.

The books in this new book series by Palgrave are meant to help all philosophers, established and aspiring, to understand, appreciate and engage with the intricacies which characterize all the many faces of philosophy. They are also ideal teaching tools as textbooks for more advanced students. These books may not be meant primarily for those who have yet to read their first book of philosophy, but all students with a basic knowledge of philosophy will benefit greatly from reading these exciting and original works, which will enable anyone to engage with all the defining issues in contemporary philosophy.

There are three main aspects that make the Palgrave Philosophy Today series distinctive and attractive. First, each book is relatively short. Second, the books are commissioned from some of the best-known, established and upcoming international scholars in each area of philosophy. Third, while the primary purpose is to offer an informed assessment of opinion on a key area of philosophical study, each title presents a distinct interpretation from someone who is closely involved with current work in the field.

Joel Walmsley's *Mind and Machine* deals with one of the most exciting puzzles in contemporary philosophy, and modern society more generally: do machines think? The answer to this question tells us something about the technology that surrounds us, but also (and perhaps more crucially) about ourselves as thinking beings.

Contrary to what some younger members of the philosophical community may think, these questions have been around a long time. Walmsley traces the philosophical roots to the mysteries of mentality, intelligence and cognition in the works of the philosophers that shaped modern philosophy in the seventeenth century: Descartes, Pascal, Leibniz and Hobbes. But of course it is in the twentieth century – perhaps starting from Alan Turing's conceptual breakthroughs – that these issues have become a central concern to philosophers of mind.

In a field which requires as much philosophical dexterity as technical (and technological) know-how, Walmsley helps us to make sense of all the theories at the cutting edge of this fast-moving field, including functionalism, connectionism, and the dynamical approach. Walmsley's *Mind and Machine* is an impressive achievement, and a rarity amongst philosophical books: a work that will be of equal interest to philosophers and non-philosophers.

Vittorio Bufacchi
General Editor, Palgrave Philosophy Today
Department of Philosophy
University College Cork

Illustrations

1.1	The seven bridges of Königsberg	20
2.1	A Turing Machine	39
4.1	A schematic connectionist network	81
4.2	The mine/rock detector network	89
6.1	The Centrifugal Governor	116
6.2	Qualitative tools of DST	119
6.3	Trajectory through state space for an artificial insect	128

Acknowledgements

The material in this book has been developed over the course of many years teaching courses in philosophy of AI – "Minds and Machines" at the University of Toronto, and "Philosophy in the 21st Century" at University College Cork – and so I am grateful to the many students on whom this material was given a trial run. I owe a special thanks to the most recent (2011–12) cohort of students at UCC, who subjected an entire draft of the manuscript to the kind of careful scrutiny and helpful discussion that amounts to *pro bono* copy-editing.

The bulk of this book was written during a sabbatical leave in the latter half of 2011, and so I'm grateful both to UCC's College of Arts, Celtic Studies and Social Sciences for granting it, and to my colleagues in the Department of Philosophy for covering my absence. To the following individuals, for various ways in which they helped, I offer particular thanks: Vittorio Bufacchi, Ruud Burke, Des Clarke, Colette Connolly, Dylan Evans, Rob Fehily, James Flynn, Martin Hayes, Brandon Hildreth, Stephen Kavanagh, Lilian O'Brien, Cathal O'Madagain, Robert Parker, Graham Parkes, Sanky Payne, Bill Seager, Brian Cantwell Smith, Ronnie de Sousa, Ross Tackes, Mark Timoney, Mona Tömböl. Finally, thanks to Priyanka Gibbons, Vittorio Bufacchi (again!) and three anonymous reviewers at Palgrave Macmillan for their patience, guidance and encouragement.

Some of the material in Chapter 6 draws on the following of my papers:

"Emergence and Reduction in Dynamical Cognitive Science." *New Ideas in Psychology* (2010) 28:274–282.
"Explanation in Dynamical Cognitive Science." *Minds and Machines* (2008) 18:331–348.

Some of the material in Chapter 7 draws on my paper:

"Methodological Situatedness; or, DEEDS Worth Doing and Pursuing." *Cognitive Systems Research* (2008) 9:150–159.

Introduction

> I am prepared to go so far as to say that within a few years, if there remain any philosophers who are not familiar with some of the main developments in artificial intelligence, it will be fair to accuse them of professional incompetence, and that to teach courses in philosophy of mind, epistemology, aesthetics, philosophy of science, philosophy of language, ethics, metaphysics, and other main areas of philosophy, without discussing the relevant aspects of artificial intelligence will be as irresponsible as giving a degree course in physics which includes no quantum theory.
>
> Aaron Sloman (1978) *The Computer Revolution in Philosophy*

> I never satisfy myself until I can make a mechanical model of a thing. If I can make a mechanical model I can understand it. As long as I cannot make a mechanical model all the way through I cannot understand...
>
> William Thomson, Lord Kelvin (1904)

This book is inspired by the two preceding quotations; whilst perhaps overstating the case, they nonetheless point to something significant. On the one hand, the developments in Artificial Intelligence (hereafter, AI) over the last half-century or so raise a set of interconnected and interesting philosophical questions in their own right. On the other hand, the projects of AI are not merely technical curiosities; rather, they constitute a distinct and fruitful approach to studying the mind that has something new to contribute to traditional questions in philosophy of mind and epistemology (to name but two areas). I therefore take a version of the latter claim – summed up in philosopher Fred Dretske's (1994) famous aphorism "If you can't make one, you don't know how it works" – at face value; AI is an essential component of any attempt to study the mind, whether that be philosophical or scientific, conceptual or empirical.

Of course, in the popular imagination, AI has become associated with a whole host of rather fanciful notions; the walking/talking robots and sentient spaceships of science-*fiction* no longer require much of a suspension of disbelief thanks to the vivid depictions of Hollywood blockbusters and the like. Despite this, much of the non-fictional work in AI seems like an inaccessible mystery because of the high level of technical proficiency required by its experts. In this book, I have tried to steer a middle path between these extremes. On the one hand, I think there's much more that's of philosophical interest in AI than the rather obvious – somehow both melodramatic and mundane – moral dilemmas posed by Steven Spielberg's *A.I.* On the other hand, the book does not require any technical background in engineering or computer programming on the part of the reader (or on the part of the author, for that matter). Where relevant and as needed, the popular and technical conceptions of AI are introduced, but by and large the focus is on AI's version of traditionally philosophical questions concerning what the mind is and how it works: Could a machine think? Are *we* such machines?

And what of such questions? Computer science's most important figure, Alan Turing, famously declared that the question "Can machines think?" was "too meaningless to deserve discussion" and wrestled with a way to come up with something better. Historian of AI Pamela McCorduck ridicules the question as "self-evident nonsense" on a par with those "snappy vaudeville comebacks: does a chicken have lips?" Perhaps this first question, though scintillating, *is* hackneyed, but it has always seemed to me that juxtaposing it with the second – are *we* such machines? – makes it somewhat more pressing: the realm of science and not just science fiction. I like to joke with my philosophy of AI class by telling them that in fact I have already created a thinking machine. I have been working as part of a two-person team, I continue, and although the initial phase only took nine months (where, admittedly, my wife played a more significant role than I), the time since then has been both challenging and rewarding as our daughter becomes more and more independent... I hope this has the effect of locating the concern with thinking machines squarely within the canonical philosophical and psychological traditions; the Oracle of Delphi was famously inscribed with the command 'know thyself' and AI is simply a continuation of that quest.

This way of thinking about the issue also enables us to set aside minor terminological quibbles that could prove a serious distraction from what I want to examine. For the purposes of this book, the specific choice of 'Intelligence' in 'AI' is not something I think we should regard as significant. Rather, I think the central issue of AI – for now, at least – is a comparative one: whatever *we* (humans) have, whether we call it 'intelligence', 'thinking', 'cognition', 'mind', or something else, can machines have it too? There are important and subtle differences between these terms, their extensions, and their relationships, but I want to gloss over them; the juxtaposition of the two main questions helps us to do that. Like Turing, I don't think that we need to have a definition of 'thinking' (or of 'machine' for that matter) in order to get on with a serious investigation of the topic.

At the same time, however, it should be noted that the respective emphasis placed on each of these questions by AI practitioners has changed over the course of the last 60 years. It's fair to say that whilst AI-fiction has always been focused on the question of building machines that can think, AI-fact has become much more closely integrated with psychology, where the emphasis is on using machines to understand or explain how (human) minds do the things that they do. In part, this anticipates a distinction I shall draw in Chapter 1 between so-called 'strong' and 'weak' AI. But it also reflects, I think, a conviction that since the answer to the second question ('Are *we* thinking machines?') is 'Yes,' the answer to the first ('Could a machine think?') must be 'Of course!' Whilst even opponents of AI (such as John Searle) answer both questions in the affirmative, *nobody* in AI believes – or has ever believed – that the machines they've constructed actually have minds. So despite bookending the text as a pressing question – in the early modern concerns of Descartes and Hobbes and the futuristic question of mind-machine hybrids – the project of actually building genuinely thinking machines will sometimes fade into the background a little, even though we are continually concerned with the in-principle possibility.

In writing this book, I have tried to meet the aims of the series to which it belongs, by presenting *my* take on *some* of the most important issues in the Philosophy of AI. Both italicised words in the previous sentence should be noted carefully. First, the book is not (and cannot be) comprehensive; the last fifty or so years have seen the development of a very large literature in both AI and its philosophy, and I cover only a selection of (what I take to be) the major conceptual issues. There are much weightier tomes that offer more detailed surveys; I try to direct the interested reader towards these in the Suggestions for Further Reading. Second, although I've tried to be generally impartial, this book *does* take a particular stand on many of the debates it covers; a book that actually *engages with* and *contributes to* the debates is, I think, much more interesting (definitely to write, hopefully to read) than one that simply *reports* them. After all, a straightforward linear trudge through the theories seems like the sort of thing an expert system or digital encyclopaedia could do, and that's just a little *too* mechanical ...

1
Historical and Theoretical Background

Artificial Intelligence is the science of making machines do things that would require intelligence if done by men.

Marvin Minsky (1968) *Semantic Information Processing*

Intellectual history is bursting at the seams with the precursors of what we now know as AI; the myths, legends and speculative stories about automata, androids, robots are too numerous to list, but prevalent enough to have become well entrenched in the popular imagination. In some ways, this is hardly surprising; an essentially human desire to understand ourselves, coupled with a Promethean predilection for playing with fire, sure enough leads to the two intertwined questions with which this book is concerned, and to which I will repeatedly return: Could a machine think? Are *we* such thinking machines?

If we take Minsky's Maxim above as giving us a minimal working definition, reference to the possibility of AI can be found in fiction at least as far back as ancient Greece. In Homer's *Iliad*, we find a description of the first AI laboratory, with Hephaestus as principal investigator. When Thetis, the mother of Achilles, arrives in search of some new armour for her son, she finds Hephaestus busily at work constructing unmanned reconnaissance tripods designed to venture off to the assemblies of the Gods and return under their own steam. In his engineering work, Hephaestus is aided by a number of android (or, more properly *gynoid*) attendants:

> ...Quickly, girls of gold,
> Exactly resembling living maids, hurried
> To help their master – *they all have minds of their own*
> Speech and strength, and...

Marvelous skill with their hands.
(Homer's *Iliad*, Book XVIII, my emphasis)

It's hard to deny Homer's assertion that these 'might cause all to marvel'. But quite apart from the entertainment value of such fictional depictions, when we turn to the Early Modern period, things really begin to take shape *philosophically*.

1.1 Early modern roots

1.1.1 Descartes: the ghost in the machine

Anyone who is minimally familiar with the philosophy of mind will surely be surprised to see Descartes at the head of the list of important figures in the history of AI. He is most famous, of course, for his *dualism*: the theory that the mental and the physical are entirely distinct substances, with the former being immaterial, non-spatial and, well, 'spooky'. Despite recent challenges to this reading (see, e.g., Clarke, 2003) it's no accident, then, that his view is most often characterised (following Ryle, 1949) as that of 'The Ghost in the Machine'; for Descartes, the *body* could be explained entirely in mechanical terms, and furthermore since that is all that non-human animals *have*, they are effectively automata.

Legend has it that Descartes was inspired in this view by his observation of moving statues in the royal gardens of Paris (see, for example, his 1664 *Treatise on Man*, and the rather fanciful biographical reconstruction in Jaynes, 1970). The statues were constructed so that, by a hi-tech system of hydraulic pipes and water pressure, they would move when people walked on particular tiles of the pathways and terraces, darting in and out of hiding and giving the impression of being alive. Descartes saw that this mechanical connection between stimulus and response could potentially shed light on the relation between animate and inanimate matter, effectively collapsing the distinction. Thus, 'living' animals could be explained on the model of machines; we are *already* surrounded by automata. Descartes expresses this view neatly in a letter to the Marquess of Newcastle (in 1646), where he claims that animals:

> act naturally and mechanically like a clock which tells the time better than our judgment does. Doubtless when the swallows come in spring, they operate like clocks. The actions of honeybees are of the same nature; so also is the discipline of cranes in flight, and of apes in fighting, if it is true that they keep discipline. (in Cottingham et al., 1988, vol. 3, pp.302–304)

It's important to note, however, that Descartes thinks this account is essentially incomplete when it comes to humans. On his dualist view, thought takes place in the immaterial (i.e., non-physical) mind. So whilst the mechanical-hydraulic account may be a good way of explaining the actions of bodies (and therefore of 'mere' animals), it cannot be the origin or explanation of thinking. This point is made explicit in his *Discourse on the Method* (Part V). In one remarkable and oft-cited passage, he writes:

> For we can certainly conceive of a machine so constructed that it utters words, and even utters words which correspond to bodily actions causing a change in its organs (e.g., if you touch it in one spot, it asks what you want of it, if you touch it in another it cries out that you are hurting it and so on). But it is not conceivable that such a machine should produce different arrangements of words so as to give an appropriately meaningful answer to whatever is said in its presence, as even the dullest of men can do. (Cottingham et al., 1988, vol. 1, p.140)

Here, Descartes anticipates several developments in twentieth-century AI (the subject matter of Chapters 2 and 3). First, language use is a visible and obvious difference between humans and animals, and so it comes as no surprise that it's where Descartes draws the dividing line between mere behaviour and genuine cognition. Linguistic ability was one of the earliest skills to be investigated by AI proper (see Chapter 2.3), and linguistic competence is often taken to be a mark – or even a *definition* – of intelligence (see Chapter 3.2 on the 'Turing Test'). Second, as Haugeland (1985) points out, Descartes doesn't just *deny* the possibility of AI. Rather, he gives a principled *explanation*; what it is to think – to *reason* – is to manipulate the symbols of a language in a way that is meaningful. Since it is "not conceivable" (Descartes uses a negation of the verb *concevoir*) that a machine could do this, then, on his view, it's impossible that a machine could think. Not only does this anticipate a concern with meaningfulness that we find more recently in Searle's (1980) 'Chinese Room' thought experiment (see Chapter 3.3), but it also highlights a deep conceptual problem for which we still have no fully satisfactory answer: what exactly *is* the relationship between a linguistic symbol and the object it represents? How does the syntax or grammar of language reflect or generate the semantics or meaningfulness of thought?

Finally, Descartes's more general division between outer-bodily-behavioural and inner-mental-cognitive aspects of human nature is a distinction that has been (perhaps unwittingly) maintained even by those who reject his dualist metaphysics. The idea of drawing a conceptual or explanatory distinction between the mental and the physical – exemplified by the way in which Descartes highlights the difference between humans and animals – has become so well entrenched that has effectively acquired the status of 'common sense'. Even if you deny the existence of non-spatial immaterial mental substances, it's still tempting to think of psychology as something wholly different from physiology – to treat *thought* as separate from *action* – and it's only in the very recent history of cognitive science and AI that this kind of 'Cartesian Materialism' has begun to be questioned at all (for example, in Chapters 6 and 7 we'll look at some of the ways in which very recent AI has emphasised the *interconnectedness* of mind, body and world, or of thought and action).

1.1.2 Hobbes and Hume: mental mechanics

In the first chapter of his (1655) *Elements of Philosophy*, Thomas Hobbes declares "By RATIOCINATION, I mean *computation*" and thus comes to be described (e.g., by Haugeland, 1985) as the "Grandfather of AI". Hobbes goes on to explain that all reasoning – thinking – can be considered along the same lines as the standard mathematical operations of addition, subtraction, multiplication and division. Earlier, in his (1651) *Leviathan*, Hobbes provided a more detailed explanation of this claim. In just the same way as arithmeticians are concerned with addition and subtraction of numbers, so geometricians are concerned with lines, figures and angles, logicians with consequences, names and syllogisms, politicians with pacts and duties, lawyers with laws and facts. He concludes:

> In sum, in what matter soever there is place for *addition* and *subtraction*, there also is place for *reason*; and where these have no place, there *reason* has nothing at all to do [...] For REASON, in this sense is nothing but *reckoning* – that is, adding and subtracting – of the consequences of general names agreed upon for the *marking* and *signifying* of our thoughts; I say *marking* them when we reckon by ourselves, and *signifying*, when we demonstrate or approve our reckonings to other men. (*Leviathan*, Part I, chapter 5)

The contemporary tone of this computational metaphor is striking, and, as Dascal (2007) notes, it's tempting to see it as a precursor of the classical 'symbol-processing' approach (to be discussed further in Chapter 2). More significant, echoing Descartes, is firstly that this cognitive-computational notion is again construed in *linguistic* terms, and secondly that the relation between 'marking' and 'signifying' – since both processes use the very same set of names – gives us some way of bridging the gap between our thoughts (inner, first-personal) and our surroundings (outer, third-personal). But the fact that, on Hobbes's view, linguistic items can serve this dual purpose immediately raises a problem that we have already encountered in Descartes: the question of how linguistic items get their meaning. In the case of the names and symbols we use when 'signifying' our reckonings to others, it's clear that their meanings are *derived* from our thoughts, with the latter being somehow primary. A red traffic light means 'stop' because we *want* it to, and have tacitly agreed with others to take it that way. In the second chapter of his *Elements of Philosophy*, Hobbes is quite clear on this:

> A NAME is a word taken at pleasure to serve for a mark, which may raise in our mind a thought like to some thought we had before, and which being pronounced to others, may be to them a sign of what thought the speaker had, or had not before in his mind. (*Elements of Philosophy*, Chapter 2 § 4)

So far, so good: when we talk, the words we use inherit their meaning from our thoughts that precede them. So then we must ask: from where do our thoughts – which are, according to Hobbes, composed of the very same names – get *their* meaning? We cannot tell the same derivative story – thoughts cannot derive their meaning from *other* thoughts – on pain of circularity or regress. Rather thoughts must somehow have 'underived' or, as Haugeland (1985) calls it, 'original meaning'. So where *does* meaningfulness originate? We'll see the issue re-surface in the later discussion of Searle's 'Chinese Room' thought experiment (see Chapter 3.3, and see the same notion used as an argument against the 'extended mind' hypothesis discussed in Chapter 7.1). For now, though, simply appreciate the force of this concern. Hobbes has effectively given us a mechanistic hypothesis about cognition that leaves one of the most central features of thought unexplained.

A similar problem besets the other British 'Mental Mechanic' of the Early Modern era, David Hume. In the first chapter of his *Enquiry Concerning Human Understanding*, he expresses the desire to discover the "the secret springs and principles, by which the human mind is actuated in its operations" just as Newton had done for the planets. Thus, whilst Hobbes might be the grandfather of the *computational* approach to AI (Chapter 2) Hume is the grandfather of the *dynamical* approach (Chapter 6). As Van Gelder (1998, p.615) puts it:

> David Hume dreamt of a scientific psychology in which mathematical laws would govern the mental realm, just as Newton's laws governed

the material realm... The universal force of gravitation, whereby bodies attract in proportion to their mass, would be replaced by a universal force of association, whereby ideas attract in proportion to their similarity. The dynamics of matter would be paralleled by a dynamics of mind.

Hume's famous account of the association of ideas is one example of him trying to bring this dream to life. In his 'Abstract' for the *Treatise of Human Nature*, he refers to a "secret tie or union among particular ideas, which causes the mind to conjoin them more frequently together, and makes the one, upon its appearance, introduce the other". The formulation and elaboration of such a connection would amount to the discovery of a psychological law; the process described is strongly reminiscent of Pavlovian classical conditioning wherein one might say a dog's mind conjoins the ideas of bell-ringing and food-arrival, such that the appearance of the former introduces the latter. A law of association would describe attractions between ideas just as Newton's laws of gravity did for attractions between the planets.

But if association and gravitation are just different kinds of attraction, why does the former count as psychological when the latter does not? This point is well made by Haugeland (1985, p.44), who asks "What makes his ideas *ideas*, and what makes their interactions count as *thinking*?" The point is that whilst Hume *does* avoid the regress or circularity that threatens Hobbes's account (an idea's status as a mental entity, for Hume, needn't be derived from something else), he does so by not providing a constitutive account of what *makes* them mental at all.

Thus construed, according to Haugeland (1985), Hobbes and Hume are simply caught on different horns of the same dilemma. Suppose, following Descartes, that mentality is the rule-governed manipulation of meaningful symbols. Can this be accounted for mechanically? Either, like Hobbes, we end up with mental features (like original meaning) that go undischarged (in which case the manipulation can't be properly *mechanical*), or, like Hume, one must assume that the meaningfulness doesn't really *matter* to the manipulation (in which case, one wonders why the manipulation counts as mental at all). We might say that, in Hobbes, we get a 'mental mechanics' that's not fully mechanical, and in Hume we get a 'mental mechanics' that's not really *mental*. This tension – Haugeland calls it the "paradox of mechanical reason" – lies behind many of the debates we'll consider in later chapters, as well as the everyday sense that there's something vaguely contradictory about the two elements in the title of this book; the more mechanical our explanatory account, the further away it seems from the very mentality we want explained.

1.1.3 Pascal and Leibniz: mathematical machines

One final early-modern historical root that's worth considering comes from two early attempts – by *philosophers*, no less – to build machines that meet Minsky's Maxim. Both Pascal and Leibniz invented mechanical calculators that could, in a sense, do things that on the Cartesian view, a mere machine shouldn't really be able to. In the case of Pascal, this probably motivated his important distinction between two different categories of mental activity. In the case of Leibniz, it inspired a dream (arguably still alive today) about the applicability of mechanical, mathematical procedures to *all* aspects of human reasoning.

In 1642, at the age of just 19, Pascal designed and built a mechanical calculator (now known as a *Pascaline*) to facilitate his father's work as a tax inspector in Normandy. He constructed several different varieties – decimal and non-decimal variants for the *livres*, *sols* and *deniers* in accounting and *toises*, *pieds*, *pouces*, and *lignes* of surveying – all of which could add and subtract directly (and multiply and divide by repetition). The devices were about the size of a shoe box with a row of between five and ten dials (similar to those found on a rotary telephone) along the front. Above the dials were a series of small windows to display the numerical result of the calculation. To add 45 and 76, for example, one first dials a 5 on the 'units' wheel and a 4 on the 'tens' wheel; one then dials a 6 on the 'units' wheel followed by a 7 on the 'tens' wheel. Through a complex arrangement of gears and cogs inside, the 10s and 100s are carried, and the machine ends up displaying a 1 in the 'hundreds' window, a 2 in the 'tens' and a 1 in the 'units'.

Owing to the cost and difficulty of their production the machines were not a huge commercial success, and only a handful survive in various museums today. But Pascal also wrote a lengthy pamphlet explaining the machine's operation – a user's guide, if you will – that contains a number of interesting pronouncements. It starts by referring to something like Minsky's Maxim; the machine does work that would require mental effort on your part, so that you don't have to:

> I present this little machine of my invention, by means of which you can carry out all arithmetical operations and relieve yourself of the work that has often tired your spirit when working with the pen.

But he goes on to say:

> As well you know, when working with the pen, you constantly have to borrow or carry numbers, and how easily errors creep into this borrowing and carrying without sustained practice and a level of deep attention that quickly exhausts the mind. This machine delivers its operator from such vexation; as long as the user has the capacity of judgment, the machine makes up for defects in memory;...it does what you want without you even having to think.[1]

It would not be too much of a stretch to see this as prefiguring his distinction, more than twenty years later in the *Pensées*, between the mechanical *esprit géométrique* and the more organic *esprit de finesse* (commonly translated as the *mathematical mind* and the *intuitive mind*). Indeed, it's arguable that this latter distinction was partly motivated by what the Pascaline could do. In the *Pensées* (Section 1, § 4), Pascal writes "Intuition is the part of judgment, mathematics of intellect". Juxtaposing this with his above comment in the Pascaline's user guide that the *user* supplies the judgement whilst the machine does the rest, it would seem that whilst Pascal might grant that machines could, in a sense, possess an *esprit géométrique*, but we could not properly attribute the *esprit de finesse* to them. They might be able to perform (mechanical) mathematical intellectual operations, but they don't (or can't) make intuitive judgements (hence, the machine does what it does "without you [*or it*] even having to think").

Pascal wasn't the only philosopher of the early-modern period to invent a calculating machine. Between 1672 and 1694, Leibniz designed and constructed a machine – now known as the *Stepped Reckoner* – that was capable of all four fundamental arithmetic operations. At the heart of the device was a component of his own invention – a long cylindrical cog with teeth of different lengths (called a stepped drum or Leibniz wheel) – that, when meshed with an ordinary cog, allowed the latter to function as a counting wheel. Leibniz presented a model of, and plans for, the stepped reckoner to the Royal Society of London in early 1673, and received praise and encouragement; indeed, the Leibniz wheel itself was such a successful design that it was used in mechanical calculators well into the twentieth century.

Again, Leibniz clearly had something like Minksy's Maxim in mind in conjunction with his calculating machine. He is widely quoted (e.g., in Kidwell and Williams, 1992, p.38) as stating "It is beneath the dignity of excellent men to waste their time in calculation when any peasant could do the work just as accurately with the aid of a machine." But his conception of what could be mechanised (and *why* one might want to do so) went well beyond the practical advantages of doing sums. He envisaged a kind of fundamental formal language – a *characteristica universalis* or 'universal characteristic' – that would allow the expression and communication of all mathematical, scientific and philosophical concepts. In *On the General Characteristic (circa* 1679), Leibniz writes:

> And although learned men have long since thought of some kind of language or universal characteristic by which all concepts and things can be put into beautiful order, and with whose help different nations might communicate their thoughts and each read in his own language what another has written in his, yet no one has attempted a language or characteristic which includes at once both the arts of discovery and judgement, that is, one whose signs and characters serve the same purpose that arithmetical signs serve for numbers, and algebraic signs for quantities taken abstractly. (In Loemker, 1969, p.222)

Through this universal language, and via a *calculus ratiocinator* or universal logical calculation framework, Leibniz imagined the reduction of all reasoning to calculation, "a kind of *general algebra* in which all truths of reason would be reduced to a kind of calculus" (Loemker, 1969, p.654). Coupling this with the development of his calculating machine, he supposed that it would be possible to create a kind of 'mill' into which questions (written in the universal characteristic) could be entered. With a cry of *'Let us calculate!'* one could pull a lever or turn a crank and the machine would churn through the logic and spit out the correct answer.

Thus Leibniz's humble little calculating machine, combined with his Hobbesian vision of reasoning as reckoning, leads some contemporary researchers to view him, along with Pascal, as AI's patron saints. Norbert Wiener (1948/1961, p.12) in his seminal book *Cybernetics*, writes:

> Now, just as the calculus of arithmetic lends itself to a mechanization progressing through the abacus and the desk computing machine to the ultra-rapid computing machines of the present day, so the *calculus ratiocinator* of Leibniz contains the germs of the *machina ratiocinatrix*, the reasoning machine. Indeed, Leibniz himself, like his predecessor Pascal, was interested in the construction of computing machines in the metal. It is therefore not in the least surprising that the same intellectual impulse which has led to the development of mathematical

logic has at the same time led to the ideal or actual mechanization of processes of thought.

1.2 Turing and the 'Dartmouth Conference'

As the foregoing survey indicates, theories of mind and behaviour have a notable tendency to mirror the hottest technology at the time of their formulation. Thus, in the Early Modern period, we saw Descartes, Hobbes, Hume, Pascal and Leibniz inspired by the hydraulics, cogs and levers that were prevalent at the time. In the early twentieth century, the mind was compared to a giant telephone switchboard. But in the middle of the twentieth century, at around the same time as the development of the first programmable computers, we really see the birth (and, indeed, *naming*) of AI as-we-know-it.

In 1950, Alan Turing published a seminal paper, entitled "Computing Machinery and Intelligence" which began with the immortal words: "I propose to consider the question 'Can machines think?'" Interestingly, before considering the first question in earnest, Turing also acknowledges the *second* of our central questions – the question of whether *we* humans are thinking machines – by writing that, in defining the word *machine*, "we wish to exclude from the machines men born in the usual manner" (p.435). Turing also implicitly endorses Minsky's Maxim, by writing "The idea behind digital computers may be explained by saying that these machines are intended to carry out any operations which could be done by a human computer" (p.436) and moves on to a discussion of 'digital computers' – theoretical devices which he had outlined (one might reasonably say *invented*) some fourteen years earlier. Turing thus effected a most significant transition: from machines in general to computers in particular. To most people, now, AI is all about the latter.

We will return to these matters in much more detail later in Chapters 2.2 and 3.2, but Turing's significant contributions to the foundations of AI are, as Copeland (1993) points out, doubly – if not triply – prescient. First, Turing effectively invented the digital programmable computer with his early work in the meta-mathematical foundations of logic years before the engineering technology was even capable of building one. Second, he showed that one could define a particular machine so that it could – at least, in theory – simulate the actions of *any* computer. He therefore gave us not only the idea of *computers*, but also of *computation*; a theory that gives precise meaning to all of the key terms – algorithm, program, input/output, etc. – with which we're all now familiar. Finally – perhaps least importantly, but most interestingly for us – his

1950 paper got the *philosophy* of AI started, six years before AI itself even had a name! I say this because what we now know as 'Artificial Intelligence' was not actually described in those terms until the 1956 *Dartmouth Summer Research Project on Artificial Intelligence*. It was a two-month long conference, organised by John McCarthy (then professor of mathematics at Dartmouth College in New Hampshire), that aimed to bring together all of those who were interested, as the original research grant proposal put it, in "the conjecture that every aspect of learning or any other feature of intelligence can in principle be so precisely described that a machine can be made to simulate it" (McCarthy et al., 1955).

McCarthy himself has described the conference as something of a disappointment – two months is probably too long for *any* academic conference since it enables people to come and go in a way that breaks up the continuity of the event. The field of AI was so scattered – geographically and intellectually – that it was a gargantuan task to try to bring it all together, and at the time it must have seemed like a fractured, partial and over-ambitious event. Nonetheless, in retrospect, the Dartmouth Summer School must be seen as an important success. A list of the participants who attended or were invited includes many of those who we now regard as major figures in the birth of twentieth century AI – Marvin Minsky, Alan Newell and Herbert Simon, Warren McCulloch, and Claude Shannon to name but a few – some of whom went on to establish important AI laboratories at Carnegie-Mellon, Stanford and MIT. The conference gave the discipline a name and completed the family history; to echo and supplement Haugeland (1985), if Hobbes, Descartes and Hume were the "grandfathers" of AI whilst Pascal and Leibniz were its patron saints, then Turing was the father (since he planted the seed), McCarthy was the godfather (since he christened it), and Minsky, Newell, Simon and the other Dartmouth participants were the 'midwives', since they delivered it safely into the intellectual space that had been prepared for it.

1.3 Varieties of AI

We started the chapter with a minimal working definition from Minsky, but we should now try to put some more flesh on those bare bones. Building on Searle (1980) and following Flanagan (1991) we might usefully distinguish between *four* different ways of understanding AI. Much of that which fits Minsky's definition can be regarded as *applied* – or more importantly, as Flanagan puts it, *non-psychological* – AI. There are many tasks that used to be done by humans, but that are now accomplished by machines simply because they fall within the bracket of tasks that engineers refer to as '4D': Dangerous, Dirty, Dull, or Difficult. Thus, we rely on machines to help with bomb disposal, to work on automobile assembly lines, to alphabetise lists, and to work out aeroplane holding patterns at busy airports. All of these tasks *would* require intelligence *if* done by humans, and whilst the machines that perform these tasks are mostly tremendous successes, nobody is much interested in claiming that they have any implications for our philosophical or scientific understanding of the nature of mind. Much more interesting are what Searle (1980) has called 'weak' and 'strong' AI, both of which feature as important components of contemporary cognitive science, but which we must distinguish very carefully.

'Weak AI' may be understood as a kind of theoretical psychology: a way of constructing theories and deriving hypotheses. There are at least three advantages to adopting this method. First, by writing a psychological theory in the form of a computer program, we can derive predictions very straightforwardly; we run the program, and the output of the computer is the theory's prediction of what the human output will be. Second, the attempt to write our theory in the form of a computer program requires us to be maximally explicit in the way that we formulate it. A computer program will simply not run if it contains the kinds of hedges and qualifications – 'all else being equal', 'mostly', 'by and large' etc. – that one often finds in psychological theories. Finally, writing a theory in the form of a program provides us with a way of *testing* that theory to see if it really does explain the phenomena it was supposed to; we run the program, and see if it performs as expected. If not – if the machine will not run, or does something unexpected – then we have revealed gaps in theories that may require us to go back to the drawing board.

One example of where this conception of AI has already borne fruit is known as the 'Frame Problem'. On the one hand, it's a problem for philosophy; Dennett describes it as a "new, deep epistemological problem – accessible in principle but unnoticed by generations of philosophers – brought to light by the novel methods of AI, and still far from being solved" (Dennett, 1998a, p.183). On the other hand, it's a problem for *psychology* – since it's concerned with how we update our beliefs in the light of experience – that only really came to light when people tried to program computers to perform similar tasks.

Suppose you come home from work one day to find your cats playing poker. As a result of your discovery, many of your previously held beliefs – 'Only humans can play cards', 'No four-legged creatures are capable of gambling', 'Only primates understand the difference between Texas hold 'em and seven-card stud' – will need to be abandoned. But despite the discovery, many *other* beliefs – 'Cats are mammals', 'Santiago is the capital of Chile', 'Four of a kind beats a full house' – remain unchanged. So how do we go about updating our stock of beliefs, making changes to those that require them, and leaving the others as is?

One way (perhaps implicitly assumed by our 'folk' or 'common-sense' psychology, and by early weak AI) would be simply to go through the previously held beliefs one-by-one, checking each against the new piece of information. If the belief is consistent with the new information, it is kept. If not, not. But any stock of beliefs as large as a human's is simply *too big* to update in this way, as AI researchers discovered when they tried to write this theory of belief revision as a program. It would simply take too long to update belief this way, and in the case where a belief is required for some action, the update would come too late to influence the behaviour appropriately. Exhaustive, one-by-one update therefore won't do.

Further, suppose we'd managed to write some kind of sub-routine that could tell us whether an existing belief was relevant enough that it should be checked for consistency with the new information (this is a big supposition – nobody has any idea how to write such a 'relevance algorithm'). This might cut down the workload; only those beliefs that are relevant to the new discovery would be sent for the consistency check. But this still wouldn't do, because we'd *still* have to (exhaustively) go through every existing belief, checking it for relevance. In fact, what we really need is a kind of 'super-relevance' algorithm that only sends relevant beliefs for a consistency check against new information, whilst simply ignoring or avoiding the vast bulk of existing (irrelevant) beliefs (i.e., without first identifying irrelevant beliefs *as* irrelevant). But how on earth do you avoid something if you don't first identify it as something to be avoided? This way of putting it reveals the depth and difficulty of the problem.

It's certainly the case that weak AI (especially of the 'GOFAI' sort we'll consider in the next chapter) has not thus far come up with a widely accepted *solution* to the frame problem. But in a sense, the mere *recognition* of the problem is more important; as a result of running into and grappling with the frame problem, we have a much deeper sense of both the philosophical and cognitive requirements for what otherwise seems like a pretty mundane ability. And this must surely count as a success for weak AI.

The weak approach is favoured by many of AI's practitioners, and it's expressed nicely by the psychologist John Marshall (1980, p.436):

"Everyone I know who tinkers around with computers does so because he has an attractive theory of some psychological capacity and wishes to explore certain consequences of the theory algorithmically." For this reason, Christopher Longuet-Higgins (1981) has suggested that 'theoretical psychology' is a more appropriate name for the kinds of research that are currently conducted under the heading of 'artificial intelligence,' and André Kukla (1989b, p.786) (more of whom later) writes: "AI is armchair psychology made respectable again by the acquisition of the symbolic prerequisite of big-time science: expensive equipment." On this view, then, AI is just continuous with experimental psychology, and need not conjure up the rather sensational connotations often found in science fiction portrayals of the discipline.

So much for *weak* AI. Its 'strong' counterpart, as the name suggests, is quite different. As John Searle puts it:

> according to strong AI, the computer is not merely a tool in the study of the mind: rather, the appropriately programmed computer really *is* a mind in the sense that computers given the right programs can be literally said to *understand* and have other cognitive states. (Searle, 1980, p.417)

Clearly, it's this conception of AI that gives rise to the popular conception of AI – "minds of their own" and all that – that we encountered earlier. Strong AI is the claim that computers do not just complement what's already in the cognitive scientist's toolkit for studying the mind; they potentially *possess* the thing being studied.

It is worth pausing momentarily to reflect further on the distinction between weak and strong AI. The difference is often characterised (e.g., by Cunningham, 2000, p.191) as one between, on the one hand, trying to *mimic* or *simulate* particular cognitive functions in a machine without any commitment concerning its actual cognitive abilities, and on the other hand, trying to produce or recreate *genuine* cognitive functions in the machine. This way of understanding the distinction reminds us that the word 'artificial' is systematically ambiguous between two senses: one meaning 'fake' or 'not genuine' and the other meaning something like 'genuine, but produced by non-standard means'. Thus 'artificial flowers' are artificial in the former sense – they're not *real* flowers – whereas 'artificial light', which *really is* light but has a causal origin other than the sun, fits the latter.

But the distinction between 'weak' and 'strong' AI is actually much deeper than this portrayal, in at least two respects. First, we should note that weak AI is a method or style of theorising that's part and parcel of a much broader trend in science generally. Almost all sciences have their 'weak' counterpart, and in most cases, exercises in computer simulation are an unqualified success. Meteorologists program computers to run simulations of weather patterns in order to generate predictions and test hypotheses, but nobody supposes that an 'artificial thunderstorm' thus created really would ruin your suede shoes. Strong AI, however, claims that a computer simulation of a mental process really can *be* a mental process; and there's no 'strong' counterpart to meteorology and all the other sciences that currently make such widespread use of computer simulations. One *could* do 'strong' artificial meteorology – recreating genuine thunderstorms by non-standard means – say, by filling a giant warehouse with various fans, humidifiers, heaters and water vapour, in order to *recreate* the conditions of an actual thunderstorm. Attempts at 'Strong Artificial Meteorology' are thus *possible*, but they're not *actual* (unlike AI, where some practitioners genuinely subscribe to the 'strong' view of the field).

This way of putting the difference also highlights a second important point. *Weak* AI is simply a method or style of theorising. Strong AI is a *hypothesis*; a claim that's either true or false; something that you either believe or do not. It simply doesn't make sense to say that *weak* AI is true or false, or to attempt to 'refute' it. And in what follows in the rest of the book, we will have to take care when evaluating various claims about AI, to see whether they're targeted at the weak or strong conception – the authors who make them are not always so careful.

Finally, and just for completeness, we should mention what Flanagan (1991) calls "Suprapsychological AI". Both weak and strong AI are, in a sense, anthropocentric; as I mentioned in the introduction, they're concerned with the *comparative* question of whether and to what extent, *human* cognition can be understood and replicated using machines. This is perhaps understandable; philosophical and popular controversies abound concerning the questions of animal and extra-terrestrial mentality, so if we want to study *artificial* intelligence, we'd better focus that study on replicating creatures that we *know* have it: us! But this needn't be the case, in principle. Chris Langton, one of the pioneers in the related field of 'Artificial Life' puts the point like this:

> Biology is the study of life – in principle anyway. In practice, biology is the scientific study of life on earth based on carbon-chain chemistry. There is nothing in its charter that restricts biology to the study of carbon-based life; it is simply the only kind of life that has been available to study ... we expect [A-life] to lead us not only to, but quite

often *beyond*, known biological phenomena: beyond *life-as-we-know-it* into the realm of *life-as-it-could-be*. (1996, pp.39–40)

In parallel, one might characterise suprapsychological AI as the study of cognition-as-it-could-be. It's the claim that not only could computers think in the same way that we do and can, but perhaps they could also think in ways that we *don't* or *can't*. Perhaps, given suitable supplementation and augmentation, we could radically alter – nay, *improve* – our cognitive capacities. This will be the subject matter of Chapter 7 where we turn to consider cognitive extension and the possibility of human-machine hybrids and a futuristic scenario described as 'The Singularity' (the point at which human-made machines exceed us in their cognitive capacities). For now, note that what's philosophically interesting about suprapsychological AI is coextensive with strong AI and adds up to the conjunction of our two central questions: can thinking *actually* be done by things other than *homo sapiens*?

1.4 Is AI an empirical or *a priori* enterprise?

Now that we've reflected on the historical backdrop to AI and its contemporary varieties, it's time to turn to the question of its *status*. I want to take a look at an often neglected, but tremendously interesting dispute concerning whether AI is an empirical science (like biology, chemistry or physics) or an *a priori* enterprise (like mathematics, or philosophy itself). Both claims seem to have some *prima facie* merit to them.

It almost goes without saying that we (even the programmers) usually have to *run* a program in order to find out exactly what it will do. This is because, in practice, most programs are simply too long and too complicated to be evaluated from the comfort of the armchair, as it were. We often have to rely on observation of what the computer does, much as if we were observing the participant in a conventional psychology experiment, or the contents of a test-tube in a chemical one. This is, effectively, the argument of Newell and Simon (more of whom later), who explicitly regard computers and programs as experiments: "constructing the machine poses a question to nature; and we listen for the answer by observing the machine in operation" (1976, p.114).

By contrast, the philosopher André Kukla (1989a) has argued that AI is not an empirical science, but rather is – like mathematics – an *a priori* enterprise. First, he *contrasts* work in AI with experiments in psychology. In the latter, he argues, the goal is to come up with a theory about the underlying structure that generates the observed behaviour: we have participants perform some task (say, using their memory or visual perception), we gather various data (say, concerning their response times in different situations), and we construct a theory about what gives rise to that behaviour. But when we run a program on a computer, we already know the underlying structure; it's the program, and we wrote it! Second, the relation between a computer's program and its behaviour is a logical one (akin to the relation between the premises and the conclusion of a deductive argument). So running a program is equivalent to constructing a proof: entirely possible from the comfort of the armchair.

Given the proliferation of 'in principle' and 'in practice' qualifiers in the last two paragraphs, it's worth pausing to reflect on the philosophical definitions of *a priori* and 'empirical'. This is because there's an important subtlety in the definitions that will help us adjudicate between Newell and Simon and Kukla. To illustrate this, consider the town of Königsberg (now Kaliningrad, Russia) which once had seven bridges, approximately configured as in Figure 1.1, with two islands in the river flowing through it.

This gave rise to the popular puzzle: is it possible to walk a path that crosses each of the seven bridges once and once only? Legend has it that the townspeople universally answered this question in the negative, for they had spent many hours trudging over the bridges, only to find themselves unable to do as the puzzle required. Many years later, the mathematician Euler proved that this was correct, using his newly developed mathematical apparatus of graph theory. We thus have two competing ways of arriving at the same answer; one – that of the

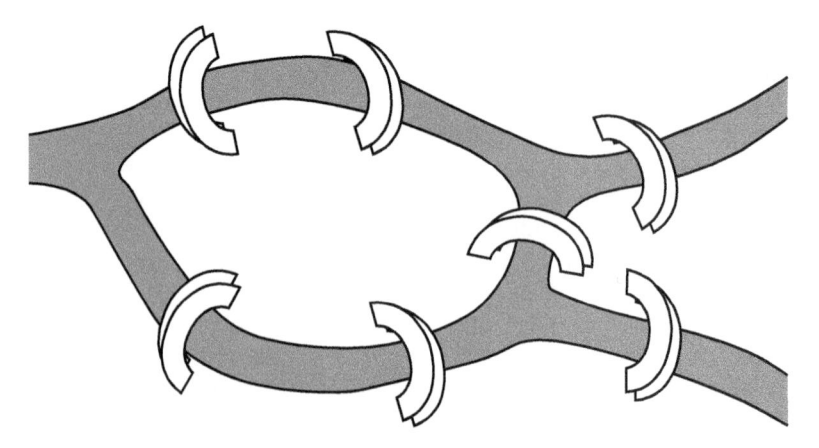

Figure 1.1 The seven bridges of Königsberg

townspeople – is based on their experience, and therefore empirical, the other – that of Euler – is based purely on theoretical mathematical reflection, and therefore *a priori*.

Common usage deems the seven bridges problem an *a priori* issue – even though it can succumb to empirical investigation – because, as Kukla (2001) points out, there is an asymmetry in the way we define the terms. An issue is deemed empirical when it is *only* possible to settle it by empirical means, but calling an issue *a priori* does not rule out the possibility of an empirical resolution. (To test this rather baroque expression for yourself, note that there is simply *no* way of resolving the empirical question of the number of baked beans in a tin from the comfort of the armchair, but that you could – if you could find a granting agency willing to pay for your questionnaires – conduct an empirical investigation into the *a priori* truth 'All bachelors are unmarried adult males'.)

Apply this definitional insight to the question of the relationship between a computer's program and its behaviour, and it would seem that Kukla has the upper hand concerning the *a priori* status of AI. Consider the following program, which I recall writing in BASIC (**B**eginner's **A**ll-purpose **S**ymbolic **I**nstruction **C**ode) some time in the 1980s:

```
10 PRINT "Hello World!"
20 GOTO 10
RUN
```

It's not hard to figure out what the program will do when executed; as you might suspect, it simply goes on filling up the screen with line after line of the phrase "Hello World!", until you end the process by some other means. In principle (and in practice) it is possible to ascertain the behaviour of this program by purely *a priori* means. In principle, then, this is true of the relationship between any computer program and its behaviour (unless it contains some kind of randomiser) even if, in practice, it's much more straightforward to *run it and see* owing to the vast complexity of most computer programs in relation to human working memory. (This is, after all, the *point* of weak AI; it's a way of taking a theory and *deriving* the predictions it makes about behaviour much more efficiently than could be managed *a priori*.) Dennett (1978, p.117) expresses this point nicely, writing that

> AI programs are not *empirical* experiments, but *thought*-experiments prosthetically regulated by computers.... The hardware realizations of AI are almost gratuitous. 'In principle' they are irrelevant (in the same

sense of 'in principle', diagrams on the blackboard are in principle unnecessary to teaching geometry), but in practice they are not.

But since the question of whether AI is an empirical or an *a priori* enterprise just *is* one such in-principle question, Kukla's view seems to win out.

It seems to me, however, that we can say more here in defence of Newell and Simon, since their argument – indeed, the approach to AI that they employed in some of their projects – concerns not only the relationship between program and behaviour, but also the question of how we come up with a program in the first place. In developing their *General Problem Solver* ('GPS') Newell and Simon (1961/1995) deliberately set out to mimic the procedures that humans use to solve various logical puzzles.

They start by highlighting, and then deliberately ignoring, the difference between non-psychological and weak AI:

> It is often argued that a careful line must be drawn between the attempt to *accomplish* with machines the same tasks that humans perform, and the attempt to *simulate* the processes humans actually use to accomplish these tasks.... GPS maximally confuses these two approaches – with mutual benefit. (Newell and Simon, 1961/1995, p.279)

GPS was developed by asking a human participant to attempt the solution to a problem whilst simultaneously verbalising what they were doing at the time (psychologists call this the 'transcription of a protocol', whilst the rest of us call it 'thinking out loud'). GPS was then constructed so as to follow the same procedure as the human, *mistakes and all*. The problems examined were straightforward logical proofs, of the sort one might study in an introductory course, where the participant was required to take a logical expression – such as $(R \supset \sim P) \cdot (\sim R \supset Q)$ – and transform it into another – such as $\sim (\sim Q \cdot P)$ – via a standard set of twelve transformation rules.

At one stage, the human problem-solver said:

> Now I'll apply rule 7 as it is expressed. Both – excuse me, excuse me, it can't be done because of the horseshoe. So – now I'm looking – scanning the rules for a second, and seeing if I can change the R to $\sim R$ in the second equation, but I don't see any way of doing it. (Sigh). I'm just sort of lost for a second. (Newell and Simon, 1961/1995, p.291)

Independently of the question concerning the success or failure of GPS as an example of weak or strong AI (an issue to which we will return in Chapter 2.3), it is quite clear that the procedure Newell and Simon used is an empirical one; programs such as GPS are developed as a result of observing how humans reason in similar situations. So, concerning the question of how we come up with an AI program in the first place, it seems appropriate to regard at least that aspect of the enterprise as empirical.

We can sum up the question of this section – and adjudicate between Kukla and Newell and Simon – with a somewhat conciliatory conclusion; they're both right, but about slightly different questions. If we are concerned with the relationship between a computer program and the behaviour it generates, then Kukla is right (in principle), and AI is an *a priori* enterprise. If we are concerned with the question of how we come up with a computer program in the first place, then Newell and Simon are right, and AI can be conducted as an empirical science (and this stands to reason, especially in *weak* AI; we want to simulate human reasoning, so first we have to *look and see* how human reasoning actually shapes up).

1.5 AI and the mind-body problem

I'd like to wrap up this chapter by considering AI against the more general backdrop of philosophy of mind, a comparative thought that I will try to come back to at various points throughout the remainder of the book. Most of the major positions on the mind-body problem can be usefully understood as different responses to the question "What sort of thing is a mind?" (see Cunningham, 2000, especially Chapter 1) It's pretty clear that the research conducted under the banner of AI is going to have something to say in answer to this question. So, suppose that both weak AI turned out to be an unqualified success and strong AI was shown to be true (i.e., not only were we able to generate unique and powerful insights into our psychological theories by writing them as computer programs, but we were also able to create a genuine and uncontroversially thinking machine from non-biological materials). What would that show for the 'standard' positions on the mind-body problem?

One might think that this would be a definitive refutation of the Cartesian dualist position. In the earlier passage that I quoted from Descartes's *Discourse on the Method* (see p.6), we saw him claiming that it was 'not conceivable' that a machine could replicate the linguistic abilities of 'even the dullest' of humans. *Ex hypothesi*, were the strong-AI hypothesis proven correct, this would be a straightforward demonstration of the paucity of Descartes's imagination. But it would not be a refutation of his metaphysics of mind, for at least two reasons. First, it would not demonstrate that Cartesian dualism is false of human beings. The committed substance dualist could still argue that a genuine non-biological thinking machine simply proves that the possession of an immaterial thinking substance – a Cartesian soul – is not *necessary* for mentality. But a Cartesian soul might still be *sufficient* for mentality, if it were just one type of thing amongst many that are capable of instantiating whatever *is* essential to cognition. Second, however Cartesian souls generate mentality, it might be that we could replicate *that* in physical machinery. David Chalmers (2010, p.16) suggests such a line of thought, writing "If there are nonphysical processes like this, it might be that they could nonetheless be emulated or artificially created". Thus, in a sense, the committed substance dualist could rescue their metaphysical position by adopting the view of suprapsychological AI and making the two-fold claim that (a) cognition-as-such *could* be implemented in non-biological machinery (perhaps by replicating the processes that occur in Cartesian souls), but (b) as it happens, in humans, cognition is implemented (if that's even the right term) in a non-physical substance. This is pure speculation, of course – I know of nobody that actually advocates such a view, and even Chalmers is simply articulating it as a logical possibility – but it's important to note that the success of AI, *by itself*, wouldn't necessarily dispose of a ghost in the machine, so long as the ghost were 'mechanical' too.

On the other hand, genuinely successful AI – the creation of both cognitive functions and phenomenal consciousness in a machine – would be a vivid demonstration of the *possibility* of physicalism. Physicalism comes in many different forms, but at root lies the conviction that everything in the universe – that is, everything that exists – is ultimately physical. (For this reason, 'physicalism' and 'materialism' have sometimes been used as synonyms, though this usage is awkward; as contemporary science makes quite clear, there are plenty of physical phenomena – forces, fields, wave/particle dualities and the like – to which it would be a strain to apply the cognate terms 'matter' and 'material'). In philosophy of mind, this physicalism amounts to a rejection of Cartesian-type theses that account for mentality in terms of non-physical substances or properties. The genuine success of strong AI would show that a purely physical (albeit non-biological) device (like a computer or robot) was capable of some cognitive functions. Thus, AI would be a vindication of (the possibility) of physicalism.

Interestingly, though, if one is also a physicalist about human cognition (as most AI enthusiasts surely are), then the success of AI would show the relative unimportance of the actual physical substance of which a cognitive system is made. If a particular thought could be implemented in both brains and non-biological machines, we are left with the unusual conclusion that although the thought is physical, different instantiations of the thought mightn't have very much physical *in common*. Philosophers have called this general property "multiple realisability"; in philosophy of mind, it's the idea that a particular mental state could be 'realised' (i.e., implemented) in multiple ways. We'll return to the issue when we discuss the doctrine of functionalism in the next chapter; *different* physical implementations might have the same *function* in common, just as (and you may have seen this coming) different computer hardware can implement the *same* software.

2
Classical Cognitive Science and "Good Old Fashioned AI"

"You mean, you're trying to design a computer that thinks like a human being?"

"In principle, that's the ultimate objective."

"And feels like a human being? A computer that has hangovers and falls in love and suffers bereavements?"

"A hangover is a kind of pain, and pain has always been a difficult nut to crack," says Ralph carefully. "But I don't see any inherent impossibility in designing and programming a robot that could get into a symbiotic relationship with another robot and would exhibit symptoms of distress if the other robot were put out of commission."

"You're joking, of course?"

"Not at all."

David Lodge (2001) *Thinks*

The last chapter discussed some of the historical and theoretical background that led to AI's appearance on the intellectual landscape in the 1950s and 1960s. Its emergence was more-or-less concurrent with the birth of the interdisciplinary enterprise we now know as cognitive science, and this chapter examines what may usefully be regarded as the first major paradigm for cognitive science in general and AI in particular: the idea that cognition is what computers do – rule-governed symbol manipulation.

The central development of the cognitive revolution came about because of the widespread rejection of behaviourism in both philosophy of mind and psychology. Behaviourists had attempted to conduct psychological research and philosophical theorising without making reference to the mentalistic language of inner ('cognitive') states like beliefs and desires. Since such states are not directly observable, behaviourists saw them as too much like the 'spooky', ghostly, and scientifically disreputable stuff of Cartesian substance dualism, and so they instead focused on things that were directly measurable: the now familiar language of stimulus, response, conditioning and reinforcement. But various difficulties (both empirical and theoretical) had, by the 1960s and 70s, led to the general abandonment of behaviourism. The *cognitive* science that came to replace it, as the name suggests, is a demonstration that there can be a scientifically respectable way of studying and referring to inner cognitive states and events, and this stems directly from the fact that AI – with its mechanistic underpinnings – was central to its development. By the 1970s, the cognitive approach was very well entrenched, and had led to flourishing research in computer science, linguistics, psychology and philosophy. These four areas are often regarded as the main contributing disciplines of cognitive science, and as we'll see, intellectual developments in them led to the idea that, to put it provocatively, cognition can be understood as computation because both are a kind of rule-governed symbol manipulation. So let's see how this idea comes together...

2.1 Three roots of the classical approach

We can see the emergence of AI as the convergence of three different intellectual pathways that were being travelled at the same time. Each of them leads, roughly, to the idea that mind and cognition can be understood in broadly mechanical – specifically *computational* – terms, and their coming together gives us what has come to be known as the 'classical' or 'symbolic' approach to cognitive science, and what Haugeland (1985) has dubbed "Good Old Fashioned Artificial Intelligence" or GOFAI. In order of their degree of specificity, they are: from logic to computing, from linguistics to psychology, and from functionalism to the 'representational theory of mind'.

2.1.1 Logic

As I write this, I am sitting in the Boole Library at University College Cork, in Ireland. It is named after the mathematician George Boole – the first professor of mathematics here – whose name may be familiar in its adjectival form 'Boolean', denoting the binary system of 0s and 1s that we now know as the foundation of computing. Boole's seminal 1854 logic textbook, in which he presented a mature version of his view was actually entitled *An Investigation of the Laws of Thought on Which are Founded the Mathematical Theories of Logic and Probabilities* (now commonly shortened to *The Laws of Thought*). And if the title alone isn't enough to crystallise the idea that psychology and mathematical logic are two sides of the same coin, here's the remarkable opening paragraph from the book, which takes us from the former to the latter and back again:

> The design of the following treatise is to investigate the fundamental laws of those operations of the mind by which reasoning is performed; to give expression to them in the symbolical language of a Calculus, and upon this foundation to establish the science of Logic and construct its method; to make that method itself the basis of a general method for the application of the mathematical doctrine of Probabilities; and, finally, to collect from the various elements of truth brought to view in the course of these inquiries some probable intimations concerning the nature and constitution of the human mind. (Boole, 1854/1958, p.1)

The idea – that thought is a kind of logico-mathematical operation – is an extension of the view that we've already seen formulated in the work of Hobbes. But the twentieth century computer science that eventually developed out of these Boolean insights takes this theoretical move a step further: towards Leibniz's dream that all of these operations could be mechanised, or automated. The line of thought is this: thinking is just logical reasoning, and computers are machines for logical reasoning, so thinking can be understood – even simulated or reproduced – as mechanical computation. Let's try to unpack this a little...

As it happens, I teach formal logic to second-year undergraduates (as part of a course described as 'Critical Thinking', as if to reiterate the continuity between logic and psychology). What makes logic both difficult to teach (and study) *and* tremendously powerful is the fact that we're often trying to do *two* things when we use and study logic, with the result that *syntax* and *semantics* are awkwardly intertwined.

One often starts by considering arguments and their structure in ordinary language, where the focus is on the *semantics* of the propositions, and how one 'follows from' others. Thus, it's pretty straightforward to see that 'I must take my umbrella' is entailed by the conjunction of 'If it's raining, then I must take my umbrella' and 'It's raining'. One then tries to, as it were, 'strip away' the semantic contents of these arguments by swapping rather more abstract symbols for the propositions, treating these symbols as representational devices; we say 'Let p mean "It's raining" and q mean "I must take my umbrella" so that $(p \rightarrow q)$ means "If it's raining, then I must take my umbrella".' We're then, finally, in a position to set semantic considerations aside entirely, and to focus on the *syntactic* structure of the arguments alone, ignoring whatever it is that those symbols might happen to represent. We thus learn that, according to the rule *modus ponens*, whenever we have p and $(p \to q)$ we are entitled to conclude that q, no matter what p and q stand for. It is in this sense that we can study 'formal' logic; we're interested in the *forms* that arguments can take, as opposed to their *contents* (i.e., what they're about). I often tell students that this is the real contrast – *form* versus *content* – and not, as is sometimes mistakenly assumed, 'formal' as opposed to 'informal'; you don't have to wear a tuxedo and bow-tie to use *modus ponens*.

So far, so good. But many of the concepts that we use to describe arguments – truth, validity, soundness, and so on – are actually awkward attempts to straddle the semantic/syntactic distinction we've just worked so hard to put in place. Thus, validity, for example, is a syntactic or formal notion that we define in semantic terms; an argument is valid when its form is such that *if* the premises were true *then* the conclusion would have to be true as well. And we substantiate this by reverting to semantic examples; we say that once we've learnt the inference rule *modus ponens*, we can use it whether p and q represent raining and taking umbrellas, snowing and wearing scarves, the experience of hunger and the eating of pizza, or being human and being mortal.

This is the payoff of formal logic; the (conditional) definition of validity above is concerned with *truth preservation* – it tells you that if you start with true premises, and you follow certified rules like *modus ponens*, then you're guaranteed to end up with true conclusions. Thus, as Bechtel and Abrahamsen (2002, p.8) point out, the efficiency with which one can evaluate an argument is increased; when you see an example (as one often does) about Boojums and Snarks, you can work out whether the argument is valid, even if you don't know what Boojums and Snarks *are*. Further, your reasoning power is increased, because you can change the interpretations of symbols without changing the validity of inferences involving them. When you pause to think about it, this is a tremendously important consequence; as Haugeland (1981, p.23) puts it: "if you take care of the syntax, *the semantics will take care of itself.*"

That's the power of logic, and on a fairly widespread view (more of which later), computers just *are* devices for implementing formal systems; they are very good at taking care of syntax automatically. As Haugeland (1981, p.24) explains it, the computer:

> just chugs along purely formally; and if the starting position, rules, and interpretation happen to be of the sort we have been discussing,

then it will automatically produce only truths. Given an appropriate formal system and interpretation, the semantics takes care of itself.

We thus have the first steps towards the mechanisation of thought; computers can be understood as 'semantic engines'. Attributing this idea to Alan Turing (much more of whom later), Fodor says, with characteristic verve: "Turing said, in effect: 'When the states of a mechanism have both syntactic and semantic properties, then it is often possible to define causal processes over the syntactic properties in such fashion that the semantic properties are preserved.' And then there was light" (Fodor, 1991, p.285). And that's the final step in a journey from psychology to logic and back again, with the round trip resulting in the mechanisation of the former. Thought is logic, logic can be done by machines, therefore thought can be done by machines.

2.1.2 Linguistics

The second root of, or route into, AI, comes from considering various projects in linguistics that fall under the heading of 'Generative Grammar'. Once again, this project has been in development since the 1950s, most famously by Noam Chomsky, and brings together the ideas (a) that cognition can be modelled along the lines of language, and (b) that these processes can be understood in mechanical or automated terms.

Very briefly, generative grammar is a theory of human syntactical ability based on the idea that the sentences we use are generated by a subconscious set of rules and procedures, much like a computer program (see, e.g., Carnie, 2006, p.5, where this claim is made explicit). The theory is motivated by the obvious fact that most language-users know when a sentence is grammatically meaningful, even if they've never heard that particular sentence uttered before. You can immediately tell that a sentence such as 'My toenail is smaller than the Sahara desert' is grammatically correct, whereas 'Sahara toenail desert than smaller is' is not, even though you've likely never heard either of them before. So this ability cannot be merely due to *memory*; it must come about via the application of some set of rules to a finite stock of linguistic items ('toenail', 'is', 'smaller', etc.) and categories (noun, verb, adjective, etc.).

The question for linguists, then, is two-fold; can some finite set of rules generate the entire set of word-strings that a native speaker of a language would find acceptable (see Pullum, 1999)? And, if so, what are these rules? Linguists attempt to address these questions by studying how people make such judgements (that's the empirical part, much like Newell and Simon's project with GPS), and then seeing if such behavioural competence can be recreated from sets of rules called generative grammars.

The competing theories of generative grammar, and their relative successes, need not concern us here. What is most significant for us, is the fact that a generative grammar is supposed to be a *mechanical* procedure that works by applying various rules to various inputs, in order to generate (yes – the clue is in the name) a certain set of outputs. In case it hasn't yet become obvious, linguist Andrew Carnie makes the point explicit early on in his introductory text-book; "You can think of these rules as being like the command lines in a computer program" (Carnie, 2006, p.6). The inputs and outputs *and the rules* are all language-like – syntactically structured strings of symbols – and so we have a research program premised on the idea that one of the most significant aspects of human cognition is the mechanical manipulation of strings of symbols.

We can think of the study of generative grammar as a particular instance in a much more general trend that sees thought or cognition as language-like. We've already encountered Descartes's view that the ability to use language is what is most distinctive of thought. An extension of this idea in twentieth-century (philosophy of) cognitive science is the idea that cognition itself is language-like – a view that finds its most famous (and provocative) expression in the work of the philosopher Jerry Fodor (see, for example, Fodor, 1975, 2008), in conjunction with one of the issues that Chomsky (1965) raises in his study of generative grammar; how do children learn their first language?

Chomsky's contention is that children are like little scientists, trying to discover underlying regularities with a limited set of observational data, and that language acquisition works by a kind of hypothesis-testing. The child hears a parent uttering a word, say 'cat', whilst pointing at some object. This correlation is consistent with a number of competing hypotheses: perhaps 'cat' means 'black-and-white thing' or 'sleeping thing' or 'four-legged thing' or 'member of the species *felis catus*' and so on. The infant's task – like that of the prototypical scientist – is to test these hypotheses against subsequent experiences (i.e., to conduct experiments) in order to eliminate all but one of them. So when the parent points at a ginger, or wakeful or three-legged thing, but still utters the word 'cat', the first three of these hypotheses can be ruled out, until – ideally – the correct meaning of the word cat is arrived at by process of elimination. When I first watched a baseball game with more experienced friends, I followed something like this procedure – with some success – to figure out what they meant when they used phrases like 'double-play', 'pinch-hitter' and 'fly ball'. This is tricky, of course – the child faces a kind of 'induction problem' since a parent's verbal behaviour may always be compatible with a number of competing hypotheses – but in most cases the problem is eventually overcome by experience.

But note: this is supposed to be an account of how children learn their *first* language. Yet, in order to test a hypothesis, you have to formulate it, and how can you do *that* if you don't already have a language at your disposal? One popular answer is two-fold. Chomsky (1965) argues that our linguistic hypothesis-testing mechanisms must in fact be innate; we don't have to learn them because we're born with them as part of our hard-wired cognitive machinery. And Fodor (1975) proposes that thought itself is language-like; what we usually think of as first-language acquisition, is actually the learning of a *second* language. Our real first language – the innate non-verbal system of symbols in which our thinking is conducted – Fodor calls the 'language of thought' or *mentalese*. Linguist Stephen Pinker (1994, p.478) defines it thus:

> **mentalese.** The hypothetical "language of thought", or representation of concepts and propositions in the brain in which ideas, including the meanings of words and sentences, are couched.

Needless to say, there are various controversies about the concept of mentalese, the extent to which it is truly innate, and the extent to which our thoughts could be constrained by our language (or *vice-versa*). But these need not concern us. What's of conceptual and historical importance for us is that we now have a mechanistic line of thought from linguistics to psychology; human cognition is served by a language-like process of symbol manipulation, and this process is the sort of thing that can be automatically carried out by a machine.

2.1.3 Functionalism and the 'Representational Theory of Mind (RTM)'

The final and most philosophically significant root of, or route into, AI comes from developments in philosophy of mind that were happening concurrently with those mentioned in linguistics and psychology: the rise of functionalism. In its simplest form, functionalism is the view that mental states are defined by their causal role with respect to (perceptual) input, (behavioural) output and other (functionally defined) mental states; what makes something count as a belief or a desire is what it *does*, not what it's made of.

If this all sounds somewhat abstract and technical, think of an everyday object that we usually understand in functional terms: a clock. What makes an object a clock is the function it performs; something counts as a clock if it tracks the passage of time. But what the clock is *made of* doesn't form part of that definition. We know that clocks can be made from a wide variety of different materials – springs, cogs and levers; electrical currents and LEDs; sand and glass egg-timers; metal or wood sundials; burning candles and so on – and so they are described as being 'multiply realisable'. Multiple realisability is clearly the most important relationship between functionalism and AI. If mental states are functionally defined and therefore multiply realisable, then there's no *a priori* reason why they can't be implemented in non-standard (i.e., non-biological) physical systems. It is also noteworthy that computer programs are, in an important sense, multiply realisable; you can run a particular program, say a word-processor, spreadsheet, or shoot-'em-up game, on very different hardware set-ups. But since what matters for the running of the program is its *functional* structure, it will still be the *same* program despite differences in the underlying physical implementation, capable of doing the same things in a way that might even render the physical implementation 'invisible' to you, the user.[1]

So, why adopt a functionalist perspective on human cognitive states? To explain why – and to show the important relations between AI and several different aspects of functionalism – let's consider a neat example that comes from Jerry Fodor (1981). Suppose you are a coke-machine psychologist: much like a regular psychologist, but with coke-machines as the object of your study. Your job is to observe them in various settings, in the wild and in the lab, in order to work out what is going on inside them that gives rise to their behaviour. You try submitting one to various stimuli – kicking it, talking to it, showing it pictures – and cataloging its various non-responses, until eventually you notice that one particular stimulus (putting a £1 coin into its slot) reliably correlates with a particular behaviour (the emission of a can of coke). You conduct the experiment with a slightly different stimulus – putting a 50p coin into the slot – and notice that this elicits no response. Being a good scientist, you repeat your experiment, and notice that the *second* time you put a 50p into the slot, the machine *does* respond with a coke, the third time you put in a 50p, you get nothing, and on the fourth repetition, you get a coke. How strange! The machine's response to 50p coins is non-random, but it is not in the form of a straightforward stimulus-response connection. You hypothesise that the machine must have some kind of internal apparatus in order to keep track of how many 50p coins it has received, and that this machine operates according to the overarching principle that Cokes cost £1.

Here, then, are several important lessons to be learnt. First, the fact that the best explanations makes reference to some kind of internal tracking apparatus suggests that stimulus and response alone are inadequate explanatory resources, and so behaviourism – even for something as simple as a coke machine – won't do. Second, the required internal states are defined functionally (by what they do) rather than physically (by what they're made of). As long as the internal states are appropriately related to inputs, outputs and each other, the explanation works whether the machine is actually made of cogs and levers, circuits and silicon chips, or whatever else we might dream up. In this example, we only need two states (State-1 is the 'resting state' and State-2 is the 'I've received 50p so far' state), and a handful of conditional statements (e.g., [IF in State-1 AND input of £1 THEN give a coke AND stay in State-1] and [IF in State-1 AND input of 50p, THEN go into State-2]) to provide a complete explanation of coke machine behaviour. Coke machines are multiply realisable in virtue of being functionally defined. Third, these internal states play representational roles; the way I described State-1 and State-2 above makes it clear that the machine uses them to 'stand in' for various states of affairs. So it can 'reason' about things by manipulating these internal surrogates, as we might expect – or even *require* – a human cogniser to do. Thinking using these representational 'stand ins' gives rise to some of the most important human cognitive abilities, for they permit us to reason about that which is not immediately present: absent or distant things and states of affairs, events that *might* occur in the future or *could have* occurred in the past. All this permits planning, anticipating the consequences of actions, the ability to deceive by 'keeping one's thoughts to oneself', and a host of other indispensible cognitive skills.

So, following on from this aspect of the coke-machine thought experiment, we might develop a preliminary version of the RTM that came to dominate cognitive science after its initial inception (see Sterelny, 1990, e.g.). Beliefs and desires are often described as 'propositional attitudes'. When I believe that Reading Football Club will win the FA cup this year, I take the attitude of belief towards that particular proposition. If I desire that Reading Football Club win the FA cup this year, then I take a *different* attitude towards the *same* proposition. We can therefore think of beliefs and desires as 'boxes' in which we store various postcards with propositions inscribed on them; believing or desiring some proposition amounts to having the corresponding postcard in the relevant box, and various rules – the laws of RTM – describe how these postcards may be created or destroyed, joined or separated, copied, moved around and so on. The RTM writ large attempts to explain a whole range of cognitive operations concerning memory, emotion, perception, reasoning and so on by using this picture of cognitive processing with suitable quantities of bells and whistles added.

I shan't belabour the point here, but you can immediately see two things. On the one hand, this rather abstract formulation is constructed independently of any consideration of how it is all implemented physically (or physiologically). This is entirely in keeping with the multiple-realisability thesis of functionalism. On the other hand, however, it is no accident that this all sounds like a computer following a program; symbol-strings are created, moved around, copied and stored, with the whole thing governed by a set of explicit rules. Representational Theory of Mind allows us to do something that has been sought at least since Aristotle: to predict and explain a person's behaviour with reference to what they think and what they want, something that is so common-sensical that it forms the core of what we now think of as 'folk psychology'. Further, thanks to the computer metaphor, we can simultaneously maintain a robust physicalism/naturalism; you don't need any spooky Cartesian stuff to use the mentalistic vocabulary of beliefs and desires because the whole apparatus can be implemented mechanically.

———◇———

These three roots – in logic, linguistics and functionalism – bring us both conceptually and historically to the central thesis of Classical Cognitive Science in general and GOFAI in particular; Hobbes's idea that cognition is what computers do – the rule-governed manipulation of interpretable strings of symbols. With this abstract formulation on the table, it's time to look at some (slightly) more concrete considerations about how to implement it all, and that, in turn, will lead us to a useful point from which we may take stock of some examples of GOFAI research.

2.2 Algorithms, Turing Machines and Turing's thesis

In this section, I want to briefly set out some important theoretical ideas from computer science. These are very important and central concepts in computer science, but less important for us in their own right than in the way in which they come together to bear on our two central questions (Could a machine think? Are we such machines?). Accordingly, my treatment of the concepts will be fairly brief, but I will dwell a little longer on their consequences at the end of this section. I want to explore four related questions: What is an algorithm? What kind of device can behave algorithmically? How much can be accomplished by such devices? Why might one think of the mind as such a device?

A philosopher friend of mine who started life as a computer scientist figured that he ought to be able to learn how to cook, because a recipe is just a kind of program – a set of instructions for turning input (ingredients) into output (delicious meal) which, if followed correctly, ought to guarantee the production of the output in a finite number of steps. The metaphor is not an idle one – Donald Knuth (1997, p.6) begins his seminal work *The Art of Computer Programming* by comparing algorithms with cookbook recipes, and jokingly suggests that if his text in computer science could be called *The Programmer's Cookbook*, then a parallel volume could be attempted with the title *Algorithms for the Kitchen*. The trouble for my friend arose, however, because as Knuth notes, an algorithm differs from a recipe in that the latter "notoriously lacks definiteness"; my friend would ask questions such as 'How much oil per unit mushroom should I use?' and 'What is the optimal surface-area-to-volume ratio for the sweet-potato chunks?' One often encounters the irritating situation whereby a recipe book contains instructions like 'Make a béchamel sauce in the usual way'. So let's say that the metaphor is helpful as far as it goes – algorithms are a bit like recipes – and that the *best* cookbooks aspire to provide algorithms such that even an inexperienced cook could follow.

This last point is captured by Knuth's requirement that an algorithm should have the properties of *finiteness* (it should lead to the result in a finite number of steps), *definiteness* (each step must be precise and unambiguous), and *effective* (each step must be sufficiently basic – one is tempted to say 'mechanical'). Copeland (1993, p.230) introduces a helpful notion here: that of 'moronic' procedures – ones for which "no insight, ingenuity or creativity is required to carry them out". When coupled with Knuth's requirements of *finiteness*, *definiteness*, and *effectiveness* we are thus in a position to say that an algorithm is a set of instructions for turning input into output where (a) each step is moronic, (b) the decision about what should be done next is moronic, and (c) by following the instructions, one is guaranteed to arrive at the output in a finite number of steps. This is still a relatively informal definition – couched as it is in terms of notions such as 'insight,' 'ingenuity' and 'sufficiently basic' – but it does capture the 'mechanical' flavour of our common-sense understanding of the term 'algorithm'.

A useful example of an algorithm in this sense is the procedure you *might* follow if you've forgotten the four-digit combination to your lockable briefcase. Assuming that there's no penalty for false guesses (unlike your bank card PIN), one procedure for finding the right code is simply to start at 0000, if that doesn't work, try 0001, then 0002 and so on, until the briefcase eventually opens. Deploying this method *guarantees* that you will arrive at a solution in no more than 10,000 attempts, and when one attempt fails, it is moronically clear what to try next. In practice, of course, it's unlikely that this is the method you'd use; you might try 'significant' numbers such as your birth year, or the first four digits of your telephone number before resorting to the brute force method. I shall return to this important difference later, when we discuss 'heuristics'; for now, just note that there *is* a 'mechanical' way of guaranteeing a solution to the problem.

To extend this point a little, I often joke with students that by the end of my logic course, they'll ideally be able to construct logical proofs in a 'moronic' fashion, by following algorithmic procedures that simply require applying the derivation rules mechanically ('Like a robot', I say). Here's an example. One of De Morgan's laws for negated quantifiers is that: $\neg \forall x P(x) \equiv \exists x \neg P(x)$. In English (i.e., giving a semantic interpretation of the symbols) this tells us that 'It is not the case that all xs have property P' is equivalent to 'There exists an x that does not have property P', and a moment's reflection should reveal the validity of this inference. But there's an easier (mechanical, formal, not-interpreted) way to remember the rule that I describe as 'negation pushing'; you imagine 'pushing' the negation symbol ($\neg$) from left to right, 'through' the universal quantifier ($\forall$), with the action of doing so changing the latter into an existential quantifier ($\exists$). The advantage of remembering it like this is that the same (mechanical) procedure works in the same way for the other of De Morgan's laws for negated quantifiers: $\neg \exists x P(x) \equiv \forall x \neg P(x)$ (i.e., 'It is not the case that there exists an x with property P' is the same as 'All xs do not have property P' – 'pushing' the $\neg$ from left to right 'through' the $\exists$ changes it into a $\forall$).

Thus, the examples of algorithmic procedures often given – including those just mentioned – are all cases of *humans* obeying rules. Indeed, when Turing wrote his famous 1936 paper – widely taken to lay the foundations of computing – the word 'computer' (sometimes spelled 'computor') referred to a business or governmental clerk who performed calculations by rote without much regard for how these calculations would ultimately be used (see Copeland, 2004, p.40). Indeed – foreshadowing the maxim from Marvin Minksy with which I started Chapter 1 – Turing's description of a machine that would behave algorithmically is based on a consideration of what the *human* computer would do in performing a calculation; he writes: "The behaviour of the computer at any moment is determined by the symbols which he is observing, and his 'state of mind' at that moment" (1936, p.250), and on the very next page, continues, "We may now construct a machine to do the work of this computer".

These 'computing machines' of which Turing speaks are an attempt to make good on my parenthetical comment above concerning the mechanical nature of 'effectiveness'. Turing developed the notion of a stripped-down, automated and entirely theoretical machine that, on the one hand, gives us a much less informal account of algorithmic calculability, and on the other hand, thereby tells us what computation *is* and what can be computed. Petzold (2008, p.vii) describes these machines as "not quite even hypothetical" and repeatedly uses the term "imaginary" instead. I'm going to opt for 'theoretical' as a middle-ground that emphasises the use to which they have been put in mathematical and computer-scientific theorising. As with the 'Test' (discussed in Chapter 3.2) Turing was too modest to name them eponymously, but we now know them as 'Turing Machines', and they are the simplest kind of device that can behave algorithmically.

The Turing Machine is a theoretical device that consists of two components: a programmable read/write head, and an unbounded length of tape that can move back and forth. The tape is divided into discrete squares – like a toilet roll – each of which may be blank or may display a symbol. The head can read the symbol in the current square, and is also capable of deleting the symbol, writing a new symbol, and moving the tape one square to the left or to the right (or halting). The head may also change between a finite number of states (like the S1 and S2 we encountered with the Coke machine). The behaviour of the machine can be completely described by a 'machine table' that specifies how it should behave, depending on the current state and the scanned symbol. We can think of these instructions as 5-place conditional sentences (with two parts to the 'if' and three parts to the 'then'); for example:
IF in S1, & scanning '0', THEN print '1' & go into S2 & move right Whilst the Turing Machine *is* an entirely theoretical device (of necessity, since it officially demands an infinitely long tape), it may be easier to imagine one in conjunction with Figure 2.1.[2]

Given an appropriate machine-table, and a suitable initial tape configuration, Turing machines can perform a surprising number of calculations; they can count, add and subtract, check to see if a string of symbols is a palindrome, and, as we shall see shortly, an awful lot more. Here, for example, is the table for a Turing Machine (derived from Penrose (1989, p.54)) that adds one to a unary number (i.e., it takes a string of 1s, and adds another one):

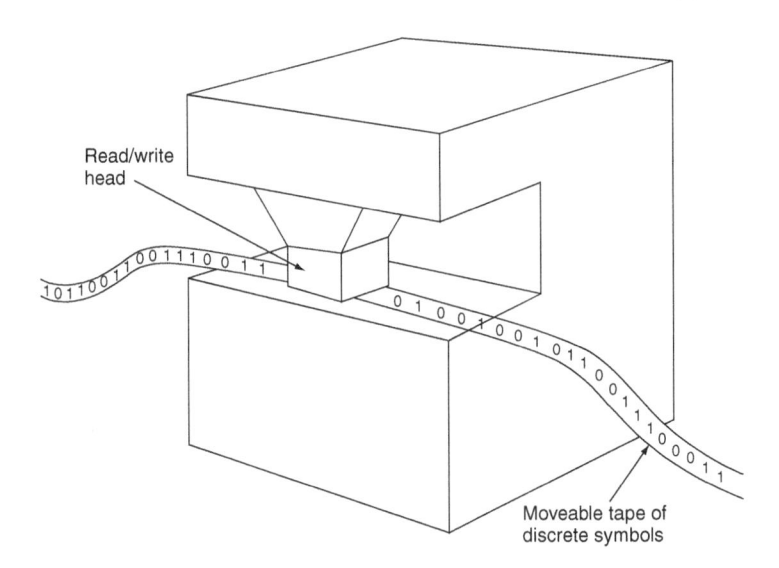

Figure 2.1 A Turing Machine

If in state	and scanning	then print	change to	and move
S1	0	0	S1	R
S1	1	1	S2	R
S2	0	1	S1	HALT
S2	1	1	S2	R

I leave it as an exercise for the reader to verify that a Turing Machine following this table, and starting somewhere off to the far left of the tape, will take a string of n 1s and turn it into a string of $n+1$ 1s, for example, from this:

... | 0 | 0 | 0 | 0 | 1 | 1 | 1 | 0 | 0 | 0 | 0 | ...

into this:

... | 0 | 0 | 0 | 0 | 1 | 1 | 1 | 1 | 0 | 0 | 0 | ...

In a sense, though, the abilities of any particular Turing Machine do not really matter. It's obvious that actually building a Turing Machine in order to automate these kinds of computations would be utterly impractical. Indeed, Turing himself was interested neither in building such machines nor in using them to carry out such tasks. I've been describing the Turing Machine as a 'theoretical' device precisely because its importance lies not with its construction or with what we can (practically) use it for, but with what it can be used to *prove*: the *theoretical* use to which it can be put. The significance of Turing's work was to transform concern with the capabilities of machines from an engineering issue into a logico-mathematical one. Exploring this matter will go some way towards answering the third and fourth questions I posed in the opening paragraph of this section; how much can simple algorithmic devices (like Turing Machines) do, and why would we think of the mind as such a device?

So, what can Turing Machines actually do? There are three ways of answering the question, all of which are tremendously significant. First, the Turing Machine is basically the notion of a programmable computer; it's a *general purpose* device that we can get to do different things depending on our interests, and programming a Turing Machine just consists of specifying the machine table and the initial tape configurations so that the desired final tape configuration (output) is arrived at in a finite number of steps. For this reason, Turing's 1936 paper "contains, in essence, the invention of the modern computer and some of the programming techniques that accompanied it" (Minsky, 1967, p.104).

Second, in his 1936 paper, Turing proved that we can construct (or rather *define* – there's no difference for theoretical devices) – what we now know as 'Universal' Turing Machines. He writes:

> It is possible to invent a single machine which can be used to compute any computable sequence. If this machine $\mathcal{U}$ is supplied with the tape on the beginning of which is written the S.D [the 'Standard Description,' i.e., the set of 5-place conditionals that provide a complete definition] of some computing machine $\mathcal{M}$, then $\mathcal{U}$ will compute the same sequence as $\mathcal{M}$. (1936, pp.241–242)

The proof is lengthy, but the central idea is simple. First, emulation – we can get one Turing Machine to behave like another: we can take a Turing Machine, say $\mathcal{M}_1$, encode its entire table as a string of symbols, and give *that* as input to another suitably constructed Turing Machine, $\mathcal{M}_2$ with the result that $\mathcal{M}_2$ replicates the behaviour of $\mathcal{M}_1$ perfectly. Second, building upon this, universality – we can define a single (Universal) Turing Machine, $\mathcal{U}$, that can replicate the behaviour of *any* $\mathcal{M}_n$ *whatsoever* when given the latter's machine table on its tape as input. This is really a remarkable conceptual advance. Turing himself expresses this central insight, with characteristic cool, in an unpublished report to the *National Physical Laboratory* entitled "Intelligent Machines":

> The importance of the universal machine is clear. We do not need to have an infinity of different machines doing different jobs. A

single one will suffice. The engineering problem of producing various machines for various jobs is replaced by the office work of "programming" the universal machine to do these jobs. (Turing, 1948, reproduced in Copeland, 2004, p.414)

Third, and perhaps most importantly, it is sometimes said that the Turing Machine is not supposed to be just a model of a computer, it's supposed to be a model of *computation*. The Turing Machine is basically *the definition* (not just an example) of an algorithmic process, and it therefore gives us a maximally precise formulation of the informal concept with which we started. This slightly unusual claim is often referred to as Turing's *thesis*, because it's not quite a formal definition, and not really a theorem (or even the sort of thing that's susceptible to *proof*). Rather, it tells us that what Turing Machines can do *exhausts* the category of algorithmic processes; an algorithm *just is* something a Turing Machine can do, and vice-versa. Franklin (1995, p.79), has a nice way of putting this: when we ask the question "what can Turing Machines compute?" the answer is "anything that can be computed". A Turing Machine can be programmed to replicate *any* other algorithmic system. As Turing himself put it, on the very same page of the very same unpublished 1948 report:

It is found in practice that L.C.M.s [Logical Computing Machines, i.e., Turing Machines] can do anything that could be described as "rule of thumb" or "purely mechanical". This is sufficiently well established that it is now agreed amongst logicians that "calculable by means of an L.C.M." is the correct accurate rendering of such phrases. (Turing, 1948, reproduced in Copeland, 2004, p.414)

Putting Turing's thesis together with his proof of universality, we're left with a striking two-fold conclusion. First, anything that counts as algorithmically calculable (i.e., 'mechanical' in the sense that concerns us) can be simulated on a computer. Second, anything that can be done on a computer is ultimately reducible to – explicable in terms of – the very simplest kind of algorithmic device. So if you want to know whether computers can (or can't do) something, then all you have to do is show that a Turing Machine can (or can't) do it. In Turing's case, his (initial) interest was in a complex problem (the *Entscheidungsproblem*) in the foundations of mathematics that needn't concern us here. But we now have a much more precise way of approaching the question 'Could a computer think?' that can be usefully focussed with the notions of algorithms and Turing Machines.

So what of the question of thinking, cognition or *intelligence* (Turing's preferred term)? We're now in a position to formulate a very general argument concerning the possibility of AI. Specifically, it's an argument that AI is possible (or that strong AI is true). But more broadly, it's an argument for thinking that the classical approach to cognitive science is sound, for Turing's approach views computation as the rule-governed manipulation of strings of interpretable symbols, and that fits well with the roots of the classical approach that we examined in Chapter 2.1. At this stage, I don't want to evaluate the argument; rather, I just want to set it out as a kind of organisational tool so that we may go on to examine different approaches to, and claims about the possibility of, AI in its light.

Copeland (1993, p.233) puts it succinctly: "If [Turing's] thesis is true, and our cognitive processes are algorithmically calculable, then in principle a large enough computer can give an exact simulation of the mind." Let's set this out as a case of universally quantified *modus ponens* that I'll call the *Turing Argument*:

1. If some process is algorithmically calculable, then it could be carried out by a Turing Machine (i.e., Turing's thesis is true).
2. Cognitive processes are algorithmically calculable.
3. Therefore, cognitive processes could be carried out by a Turing Machine.

This is a particularly strong way of setting it out – the possibility of AI is very rarely discussed in these exact terms – but we can now consider how one might respond to the Turing Argument if, for example, one wants to deny the possibility of AI or to dispute the viability of the classical (symbolic, computational) approach.

One response, for example, is to deny that Turing Argument is valid (i.e., to say that even if (1) and (2) are true, (3) does not follow from them). In the foregoing discussion, we haven't made much of the fact that Turing Machines are entirely theoretical (i.e., *idealised*) devices – they exist in "a world in which time is of no concern, in which issues of reliability and cumulative error can be ignored, and in which there are no bounds whatever on the capacity of the machine's memory devices" (Copeland, 1997, p.125). This idealisation is fine if one is interested in abstract questions of computability, but we're interested in the real-world process of cognition; a process that is paradigmatically conducted by biological creatures who are subject to evolutionary pressures. Perhaps, we might think, the less bountiful constraints of the real world would therefore block the inference.

This is one way of considering the motivation for the views outlined in Chapter 6. Consider the issues of *time* and *timing*, for example. Whilst it is true that a Turing Machine could, *in principle*, run a word-processing program or edit video footage, *in practice* it would take staggering amounts of time (and toilet-paper-memory, for that matter) to do so. So even if brain processes do turn out to be algorithmically calculable, one might insist that for real-world cognisers, timing is an additional factor that must be taken into consideration; there might be an algorithm for recognising predatory tigers, but if you were to run it on a Turing Machine in your head, you'd get eaten long before you'd arrived at the decision to run away from it. Something like this line of thought, as we shall see, underlies the dynamical systems approach to cognitive science and AI. Dynamicists argue that the ability to account for intrinsically temporal phenomena is essential for any theory of cognition, and since there's nothing in the *theory* of computation about the time-course of an algorithm (Minsky, 1967, p.2 writes "To make such a theoretical study, it is necessary to abstract away many realistic details... We even shred time into a sequence of separate disconnected moments"), cognitive processes fall outside the scope of Turing's thesis.

A second response – perhaps more obvious – would be to deny that the Turing Argument is sound (i.e., to deny the truth of (1) or (2), or both). Nobody is much interested in denying the truth of the first premise, but the second is, to say the least, extremely contentious! Even though the view that cognitive processes are algorithmically calculable has been something of an article of faith amongst many cognitive scientists, it has not been immune from question: the Lucas/Penrose argument 'Gödel Argument' (see Lucas, 1961; Penrose, 1989), to be considered in Chapter 3.1 is a case in point. Very briefly, the argument is that since the ability to formulate and evaluate certain kinds of self-referential statements is provably impossible for formal systems, whatever it is that underlies the *human* ability to do so cannot be algorithmic. As Penrose (1989, p.172) puts it:

> The kind of issue that I am trying to raise is whether it is conceivable that the human brain can, by the harnessing of appropriate "non-computable" physical laws, do "better", in some sense, than a Turing Machine.

If Penrose is right, then both the second premise and the conclusion of the Turing Argument are false, and the hypothesis of (strong) GOFAI fails. We'll return to this in Chapter 3.

Whatever its status, then, the Turing Argument is a useful way of setting up and categorising the responses to classical cognitive science and GOFAI that we'll be considering in later chapters. But before we consider such problems, let's just take a brief look at some of GOFAI's success stories.

2.3 GOFAI's success stories

Examples of successful GOFAI programs are legion. I use the term 'successful' here with some trepidation, however; if one's goal is *strong* AI, such programs are, even in the eyes of their creators, most definitely not successful. The success of the handful of programs I'll look at, then, lies with the fact that (a) they do what their creators set out to demonstrate (perhaps even with some useful insight for *weak* AI), and (b) they nicely embody the considerations we've encountered in the previous sections.

2.3.1 Reasoning: the logic theory machine

Given the close connection between logic, cognition and computation in its foundations, it is not surprising that one of the earliest success stories of AI concerns the construction of a machine that could formulate logical proofs. Edward Feigenbaum reports that Herbert Simon came into the classroom in January 1956 and declared, "Over Christmas Allen Newell and I invented a thinking machine" (Quoted in McCorduck, 1979, p.116). He was talking about the *Logic Theory Machine*, the capabilities of which Newell, Shaw and Simon subsequently demonstrated only a few months later at the 1956 Dartmouth Summer School. It was really a precursor to the *General Problem Solver* (discussed earlier), but in a much more restricted domain: the foundations of mathematical logic.

The most thoroughgoing work in the foundations of mathematical logic, at the time, was Whitehead and Russell's *Principia Mathematica*. It was an attempt to demonstrate how all mathematical truths could be derived from an explicit and well-defined collection of logical axioms and rules of inference. The idea should sound familiar, given our earlier discussion of algorithms; the proof-process for a theorem simply consists in applying the inference rules a finite number of times in order to transform an 'axiom' symbol-string into a 'theorem' symbol-string. What we call a 'proof' is just a list of the steps that were taken whilst going through this process. Thus, for example, the book commences with an explicit definition of logical implication – 'p implies q' is defined to mean 'Either p is false or q is true' – and together with a handful of other definitional axioms, Whitehead and Russell go on to provide proofs of more and more complex theorems. The Logic Theory Machine worked along exactly the same lines; it found proofs of theorems by showing how they can be derived from the axioms via the permitted inference rules. And to the extent that it was capable of finding proofs of the theorems of *Principia Mathematica*, it was an undeniable success both in its own right, and by the light of Minsky's Maxim with which we started Chapter 1. Indeed, not only did the Logic Theory Machine succeed in finding proofs for most of the theorems of Chapter 2 of Russell and Whitehead's *magnum opus*, it actually found what McCorduck (1979, p.142) calls a "shorter and more satisfying" proof of one of them. Bertrand Russell was, apparently, delighted when Herbert Simon wrote to tell him, but the editors of the *Journal of Symbolic Logic* declined to publish what would have been the first ever paper co-authored by a machine on the grounds that new proofs of known theorems are not sufficiently noteworthy.

In the cold light of the twenty-first century, with computers that can perform many millions of operations per second, it's easy to be underwhelmed by the Logic Theory Machine. We're all well used to the fact that computers can do things much faster than we can – performing calculations, alphabetising lists, searching for missing files – by the application of brute force, and so we might find it unsurprising that the Logic Theory Machine fared well when pitted against the painstaking paper-and-pencil work of Russell and Whitehead. But in fact this is not how the Logic Theory Machine worked, for entirely practical reasons. Suppose that the rules of inference are such that at any instant, a string of symbols could be changed in ten different ways. This means that if we want the machine to check all possible 6-step 'proof chains,' it would have to go through one million (i.e., 10^6) different possibilities. We can see that such a 'combinatorial explosion' – especially when coupled with 1956 limitations on computer processing speeds and memory – means that exhaustive search through the space of possible symbolic transformations would have been prohibitively time-consuming. As a result, Newell and Simon (1956, p.28) write: "we need additional help from some kind of heuristic".

A heuristic is a kind of 'rule of thumb' that doesn't *guarantee* a specific outcome, but nonetheless makes it fairly likely; Newell et al. (1957/1995, p.114) tell us that it is "A process that *may* solve a given problem, but offers no guarantee of doing so". In my earlier example of trying to recall the four-digit combination to one's briefcase, I mentioned that one could follow an algorithm that would guarantee success in 10,000 or fewer attempts, *or* one could start by trying four-digit numbers that were in some other way significant. The latter is a heuristic procedure. Clearly, there's a trade-off here; if you have the time (and patience) the algorithm is guaranteed to get you in. But if memory resources are limited (as they are in computers and human minds) and time is of the essence (as it must be in computer laboratories and the evolutionarily constrained natural environment), the heuristic procedure may be better. A heuristic is thus a good way of limiting the space of possible solutions through which one must search.

Newell, Shaw and Simon were interested not only in getting a computer to find a proof, but in getting the computer to discover a proof in the same kind of way a human being would. Thus, they write (1957/1995, p.109): "we wish to understand how a mathematician, for example, is able to prove a theorem even though he does not know when he starts how, or if, he is going to succeed." Accordingly, they designed the Logic Theory Machine to operate with heuristics: rules-of-thumb that allowed the program to "work backwards" from the theorem to be proved and to identify "similarities" between the theorem to be proved and the axioms (these "shudder quotes" are Newell, Shaw and Simon's). Thus, finding the 'solution to a problem' is simply the heuristically guided search through a space of possible solutions.

The last sentence of the previous paragraph crystallises the way in which Newell, Shaw and Simon re-conceived both the task of computer science, and the nature of cognition; arguably, it is simultaneously their most significant (philosophical and practical) achievement and the biggest limitation of their project with regard to some of the more lofty goals of AI. On the one hand, the explicit parallel between what humans do in solving a problem (i.e., searching for a solution guided by some kind of rule-of-thumb, rather than exhaustively examining every possibility) sees them making good on Minsky's maxim. The Logic Theory Machine was not just a demonstration of computer power; it was a demonstration that computers could perform tasks that were, as McCorduck (1979, p.142) puts it, "heretofore considered intelligent, creative and uniquely human" *in the same sort of way that humans do*. Thus, Haugeland concludes that the Logic Theory Machine:

> pursued a symbolically specified goal by making sensible symbolic explorations, guided by symbolically coded knowledge. Thus it was the first human artifact plausibly described as solving problems by *thinking* about them; its inventors were justly proud. (1985, p.185)

On the other hand, the operation (indeed the *task domain*) of the Logic Theory Machine reveals an interesting limitation in this conceptualisation of cognition. For whilst it's certainly the case that finding proofs for logical theorems is an important cognitive achievement, *formulating* logical systems in such a precise manner that finding proofs is even a possibility is arguably more significant. The Logic Theory Machine does nothing of the latter.

This is especially apparent when one considers an extension of the Logical Theory Machine – mentioned earlier – in the form of Newell and Simon's *General Problem Solver* or GPS. The idea behind GPS was to deploy the kinds of methods found in the Logic Theory Machine – especially heuristically guided search through a space of possible solutions – to a wider class of related logical puzzles, such as the "cannibals and missionaries" problem ("Three missionaries and three cannibals must cross a river using a boat that can only carry two at once. At any one time, the cannibals may not outnumber the missionaries on the banks of the river, and the boat cannot cross the river with no people on board"). As mentioned, GPS was deliberately constructed to mimic the procedures adopted by human beings in solving such problems, with the express intention that this would give us some insight into human cognitive abilities (weak AI), and perhaps even replicate them (strong AI).

The operation of GPS (and, by extension, that of the Logic Theory Machine), however, betrays an underlying assumption that *solving* problems is the important part of the cognitive process (and therefore the part that is worth replicating and modelling with a computer). In fact, though, the most significant task is really to take an ordinary-language statement of a problem, like that above, and to turn it into the kind of formal statement that is amenable to solution by heuristically guided search through problem space. As Haugeland (1985, pp.183–184) puts it: "the 'real' challenge is not to find the solution, given a fully articulated formulation, but rather to come up with a good formulation (small search space, efficient tests etc.), given the 'informal' statement of the problem in English." The most intelligent part of problem solving arguably lies with this 'preliminary' stage; indeed, one might say that even Russell and Whitehead's most significant achievement lies in the formulation of a notation such that the 'busywork' of proofs can be delegated to a mechanical process!

The legacy of the Logic Theory Machine and its generalised offspring is, therefore, mixed. On the one hand, the emphasis on heuristic search – both as a way of avoiding the combinatorial explosions of exhaustive methods, and as a way of making problem solving computationally feasible and biologically plausible – was a significant step forward for AI. On the other hand, this success runs the risk of blinding us to its own limitations; the major part of problem *solving* is problem *formulation*, and since the Logic Theory Machine and GPS do not do *that*, there must be more to intelligence (cognition, mentality) than those aspects that they are able to mimic.

2.3.2 Chess: Deep Blue

The discussion of combinatorial explosions and heuristics provides a nice conceptual link to another major area of early AI research: game-playing, and specifically chess-playing. Newell, Simon and Shaw themselves saw chess-playing and the ability to reproduce it as providing a good test-case for AI, writing:

> Chess is the intellectual game *par excellence*... If one could devise a successful chess machine, one would seem to have penetrated to the core of human intellectual endeavour. (1958/1995, p.39)

Perhaps because of its emphasis on strategy, planning and (arguably) creativity, chess playing has been a perennial and widespread concern within AI research. On the one hand, as the above quotation from Newell, Shaw and Simon illustrates, the ability to play chess is an excellent demonstration of the kind of problem-solving and reasoning skills that are central to GOFAI. On the other hand, some AI pioneers (e.g., John McCarthy, 1990) have described chess as the "drosophila" of AI: like *Drosophila melanogaster*, the fruit-fly that is extensively used in research in genetics owing to its rapid reproduction, small size, and relative cheapness, chess is seen as a usefully well-defined test-case, the implications of whose study will be (forgive the pun) fruitful on a much wider scale.

In principle, chess is the sort of game that could be played and won by a combination of exhaustive search and speed. It is played on a finite board, with a fixed number of unambiguous rules to be obeyed by a small number of different pieces, and with a definite and easily identifiable goal and end-point. Considered in terms of "search space", the rules of chess define a branching-tree structure; there are 20 theoretically possible opening moves by white, followed by 20 possible responses by black. Continuing this line of thought, you might imagine enumerating all the branches – until each terminates in a draw or a checkmate – so as to construct a theoretical tree of every possible chess game. Playing "perfect" or "exhaustive" chess according to this strategy (if one can really call it a 'strategy') would simply be a case of only making moves that take you down branches that terminate with you winning. Indeed, this approach *is* possible for functionally similar games such as noughts and crosses (or Tic-Tac-Toe in the US); one can play in an algorithmic way that guarantees either a win or a draw.[3] Unfortunately, the numbers involved in chess make this approach practically unfeasible. There are somewhere around 10^{120} 40-move chess games (Shannon, 1950). But current estimates put the total number of atoms in the known universe at around 10^{80}, so even if you used one atom per tree branch, there wouldn't be enough matter in the universe to represent all of the possible games. Further, current calculations put the age of the universe at less than 10^{25} nanoseconds, so even if you had been evaluating one tree branch every nanosecond since the big bang, you wouldn't yet have had time to calculate your first move. Echoing Newell and Simon, we need additional help from some kind of heuristic.

Turing himself recognised that perhaps the most promising strategy for building a chess-playing machine would involve the use of fallible rules-of-thumb – heuristics – rather than exhaustive search and evaluation. Indeed, he anticipates the research project of Newell, Shaw and Simon somewhat, by effectively *equating* intelligence with heuristically guided search:

> Given a position in chess the machine could be made to list all the "winning combinations" to a depth of about three moves on either side. This...raises the question "Can the machine play chess?" It could fairly easily be made to play a rather bad game. It would be bad because chess requires intelligence. We stated...that the machine should be treated as entirely without intelligence. There are indications however that it is possible to make the machine display intelligence at the risk of its making occasional serious mistakes. By following up this aspect the machine could probably be made to play very good chess.(Turing, 1945, p.16)[4]

Such was the approach adopted by the creators of the most successful chess-playing computers to date. In two different championship matches – first in 1996 and then in 1997 – *Deep Blue*, a chess playing computer developed by IBM, was pitted against then reigning world champion Garry Kasparov. In February 1996, Kasparov won 4-2. But in May 1997, amid an excited media frenzy, a heavily upgraded Deep Blue succeeded in beating Kasparov $3\frac{1}{2} - 2\frac{1}{2}$ in the re-match. Let's examine the technicalities first, before commenting on the reaction and aftermath.[5]

Deep Blue was a specialised hardware-based chess machine, and worked by a combination of brute force and cleverly designed heuristics. In the case of the former, its memory contained around 4000 different variations on the opening phase of a game, a database of 700,000 previous Grandmaster chess games (100 years' worth) and it was capable of evaluating up to 200 million chess positions per second. In the case of the latter, a sophisticated system of assigning values to certain playing patterns (e.g., for the potential mobility of a pawn, or the usefulness of diagonals controlled by a bishop) allowed it to choose the move with the most potential in any given situation. This evaluation function was also developed with the help of a number of other well-known chess grandmasters so that, as IBM themselves put it, "Kasparov isn't playing a computer, he's playing the ghosts of grandmasters past".[6]

Naturally, Deep Blue's victory (or Kasparov's loss) led to a lot of excited journalistic commentary concerning how humans had finally been 'beaten at their own game,' and other clichés. But one particular cartoon, from the *Boston Globe* in 1997, sticks in the mind. It depicts an angry Kasparov storming out of the frame, leaving Deep Blue contentedly whirring and beeping whilst a bespectacled programmer tells it "Sure you can play chess, but come back when you can go into a *snit.*" This is significant in at least two respects.

For one thing, Kasparov was deeply unhappy about certain aspects of the match; he suggested that moves during the second game were so uncharacteristic of computer-chess that they must have been brought about by human intervention. In the 2003 documentary *Game Over: Kasparov and the Machine*, he reports that this suspicion (together with other aspects of IBM's conduct) troubled him so much that it effectively put him off for the remainder of the match. In other words, we might say, Deep Blue's advantage stems from the fact that Kasparov is a thinking thing (in possession of emotions, an attention span and so forth) whilst Deep Blue itself is decidedly *not*. Chess-playing computers don't get distracted, or worried, or bored, and for these reasons, IBM say, "Deep Blue's strengths are the strengths of a machine".[7] Their repeated response to the FAQ, "Does Deep Blue use Artificial Intelligence?" is an explicit "no".

Of course, it's entirely reasonable that neither IBM nor anybody else wishes to make strong-AI-type claims about something so special-purpose as Deep Blue. But what's even more noteworthy is that there's not even an analogue of the *weak*-AI project in computer chess; nobody has been much interested in doing what Newell, Shaw and Simon did with the Logic Theory Machine and GPS, and building a computer that plays chess *like a human does* (e.g., by asking grandmasters to verbalise their actual thought processes and trying to build a machine to replicate *that*). Perhaps that's because of the various commercial interests that have been at play in the development of chess-playing computers;

winning was more important. The documentary *Game Over* points out that Deep Blue's victory led to a sharp rise in IBM stock prices and suggests that this might explain their reticence in either agreeing to a re-match or releasing the log files from the games (as Kasparov requested). McCorduck (1979, p.159) argues that the early chess-playing machines might have proved so psychologically threatening to potential customers that IBM was keen to play up the computer's image as "nothing more than a quick moron". Either way, there are non-academic reasons for emphasising the *difference* between (chess-playing) machines and humans.

By contrast, the lack of a weak-AI program in chess-playing could be due to the fact that any psychological insight offered by Deep Blue and the like is really concerned with unconscious cognitive processes. Such a reading is suggested by Ekbia (2008), according to whom there are two respects in which 'believers' in AI might interpret Deep Blue's success. On the one hand, the strategy of the machine choosing moves that maximise its own evaluation score constitutes a minimal form of rationality, at least within the chess domain. On the other hand, the fact that the evaluation function assigns scores to positions based on their 'promise' or 'potential' might provide us with a formalised analogue of psychological processes such as hunches, intuition or insight. All these, Ekbia (2008, p.50) suggests, "may be, at bottom, the outcome of unconscious processes that resemble brute-force search – or so would go the believer's hunch".

So the workings of a chess-playing computer may offer some (sketchy, speculative) insight into some (vague, poorly defined) psychological concepts such as rationality or insight. But Deep Blue's victory, in my view, really tells us more about chess than it does about intelligence or cognition. For what it demonstrates is that, as Douglas Hofstadter (2002, p.69) puts it, "chess is more mechanical than we had realized". Deep Blue shows us that the brute force techniques of extreme speed and memory capacity are all that are really needed to play chess to the highest standard. But the most interesting *psychological* revelation that follows is that it took us so long to realise this fact.

2.3.3 Conversation: ELIZA

As we saw earlier with Descartes, linguistic ability has long been regarded as both the exclusive province and constitutive of human cognition. Couple this with the GOFAI contention that thought is the rule-governed manipulation of symbols, and it's not hard to see why early AI turned its attention towards language. It is in this arena that perhaps the most famous AI program – "Eliza" – was developed by Joseph Weizenbaum (see his 1966 for details of the program and his 1976 for details of the fallout). Weizenbaum named the program Eliza after the famous Ms. Doolittle in George Bernard Shaw's *Pygmalion* because he originally hoped to be able to teach it to 'speak' increasingly well. But just like the character in the play, appropriately enough, it's not really clear whether such improvements in language use actually correspond to improvements in intelligence. Indeed, like Deep Blue, Eliza is another case where a program's creator is eager to point out that no *real* intelligence is on display; much of Weizenbaum's writing on the subject is explicitly devoted to dispelling the illusion that Eliza is genuinely intelligent. The experiences Weizenbaum had with what was intended as a simple pilot study of computer natural language processing ultimately led him to turn away from AI proper, and towards computer ethics (i.e., away from the question of whether we can build a thinking machine, and towards the question of whether we *ought* to).

The most famous example of Eliza in action sees her mimicking the dialogue of a Rogerian psychotherapist (because, says Weizenbaum (1966, p.42), "the psychiatric interview is one of the few examples of categorized dyadic natural language communication in which one of the participating pair is free to assume the pose of knowing almost nothing of the real world"). Here's a snippet of the dialogue (Eliza's words are in capitals):

Men are all alike.
IN WHAT WAY
They're always bugging us about something or other.
CAN YOU THINK OF A SPECIFIC EXAMPLE
Well, my boyfriend made me come here.
YOUR BOYFRIEND MADE YOU COME HERE
He says I'm depressed much of the time.
I AM SORRY TO HEAR YOU ARE DEPRESSED
It's true. I am unhappy.
DO YOU THINK COMING HERE WILL HELP YOU NOT TO BE UNHAPPY
I need some help, that much seems certain.
WHAT WOULD IT MEAN IF YOU GOT SOME HELP
Perhaps I could learn to get along with my mother.
TELL ME MORE ABOUT YOUR FAMILY ...
(Weizenbaum, 1966, pp.36–37)

Given only a minimal familiarity with this style of psychiatric interview, it's hard not to be taken in by the conversation: many people were.

Weizenbaum reports his secretary asking him to leave the room whilst she conversed with Eliza. Some people raised ethical concerns about what to do with the transcripts, suggesting that people were conversing with Eliza in the kind of intimate terms usually reserved for human relationships. Further, one of Weizenbaum's original collaborators – Kenneth Colby – went as far as suggesting that Eliza could eventually be developed into something fit for clinical use, writing:

> A human therapist can be viewed as an information processor and decision maker with a set of decision rules which are closely linked to short-range and long-range goals... If the method proves beneficial then it would provide a therapeutic tool which can be made widely available to mental hospitals and psychiatric centers suffering a shortage of therapists... several hundred patients an hour could be handled by a computer system designed for this purpose. (Colby et al., 1966, pp.151–152)

Both these reactions to Eliza shocked and saddened Weizenbaum. On the former, he writes: "I had not realised... that extremely short exposures to a relatively simple computer program could induce powerful delusional thinking in quite normal people" (1976, p.7). On the latter he scathingly comments: "What must a psychiatrist who makes such a suggestion think he is doing while treating a patient, that he can view the simplest mechanical parody of a single interviewing technique as having captured anything of the essence of a human encounter?" (1976, p.6). In a perfect parallel with Deep Blue, Eliza probably teaches more about the sorry state of 1960s psychotherapy than anything else.

Eliza's program is a marvel of simple syntactic transformations (e.g., turning an 'I' or 'me' in the patient's input into a 'you' in the response), reflecting a patient's own words back at them (e.g., 'I dreamt <x>' is answered by 'Have you ever fantasised <x> while you were awake' or 'Have you dreamt <x> before?') and 'canned' all-purpose responses ('What does that suggest to you' or 'please elaborate').[8] Minimal knowledge of how the program works, however, makes it remarkably easy to trip Eliza up. Here's an example conversation between Eliza and the philosopher Jack Copeland (1993, p.40). Again, Eliza's responses are in capitals:

> HOW DO YOU DO. PLEASE STATE YOUR PROBLEM
> I'm wondering whether computers can think
> WHY DO YOU MENTION COMPUTERS
> Since you are one I thought I would ask you – can you think?

DID YOU THINK THEY MIGHT NOT BE ONE YOU THOUGHT YOU WOULD ASK
I – CAN I THINK
Let's just talk about you – not me. Can you think?
YOU LIKE TO THINK I – NOT YOU – DON'T YOU
Pardon?
WHAT DOES THAT SUGGEST TO YOU
What does it suggest to you?
TELL ME ABOUT WHAT DOES IT SUGGEST TO I
That's nonsense – which of us do you mean by I?
WHY DO YOU THINK I MEAN BY YOU
The question meant to which of us is the word I referring.
SUPPOSE THE QUESTION MEANT TO WHICH OF US WERE NOT THE WORD REFERRING
I think you are an extremely stupid program
PERHAPS YOU WOULD LIKE TO BE AN EXTREMELY STUPID PROGRAM

We'll have cause to think about Eliza again in Chapter 3.2 when we look at the Turing Test. For now, let's just note that, like Deep Blue, Eliza seems to have generated more heat than light. Perhaps Eliza tells us *something* about how we conduct those dreadful auto-pilot dinner-party conversations, but the fact that even Eliza's creator describes her linguistic ability as a "parody" is pretty telling.

2.4 GOFAI and the mind-body problem

Having already discussed functionalism as one of the major 'roots' of the classical approach to cognitive science in general and to AI in particular, we needn't belabour the point about its natural affinity with GOFAI. But it's still worth emphasising a couple of related points at this juncture. Most obviously, functionalism gives us a way of combining *physicalism* with *multiple realisability* in a way that resolves the (slight) problem with which we concluded the last chapter. Clocks and (to use an example from Jerry Fodor) financial transactions are things about which everyone is a token physicalist; all clocks and all financial transactions (paper or metal money exchanges, promissory notes and cheques, on-line payments, etc.) are ultimately made of nothing but physical matter in motion. But different particular clocks or financial transactions mightn't have very much *physical* in common. So what is it that makes both a digital wristwatch and an egg-timer count *as* clocks? The functionalist says: What they *do*. What is it that makes sending a cheque by post and clicking a button on my bank's website both count as 'paying my gas bill'? The functionalist says: The overall causal/functional profile of the event.

Now, applying this functionalism to mental states and their physical implementation, Andy Clark (1989, p.21) puts it wonderfully: "It ain't the meat, it's the motion" that matters. And of course, the same is true of computers: a piece of software is multiply realisable in the sense that you can run it on different hardware set-ups. As Dennett (1996, p.430) puts it, "It doesn't matter what material you make a computer out of: what matters is the algorithm it runs". So it's no accident that GOFAI and functionalism in philosophy of mind go hand-in-hand. The latter permits the possibility of the former, and the former is one way of making good on the promise of the latter. If mental states really are functionally defined and multiply realisable within a physical system, then perhaps computers really could have them.[9]

For this reason there are now – post-GOFAI – at least two important senses of the term 'functionalism' which are interestingly connected, but important to distinguish. On the one hand is the view we've been discussing in rather more general terms. Following the philosopher Ned Block, we might call it *metaphysical* functionalism:

> Metaphysical functionalists characterize mental states in terms of their causal roles, particularly, in terms of their causal relations to sensory stimulations, behavioral outputs, and other mental states. Thus, for example, a metaphysical functionalist theory of pain might characterize pain in part in terms of its tendency to be caused by tissue damage, by its tendency to cause the desire to be rid of it, and by its tendency to produce action designed to separate the damaged part of the body from what is thought to cause the damage. (1980, p.172)

The GOFAI approach to explaining how these causal roles are realised (or implemented) is a slightly different form of functionalism, which Block calls *computation-representation* functionalism. He notes that

> In this sense of the term, "functionalism" applies to an important special case of functional explanation ... akin to providing a computer program for the mind ... [M]ental processes ... are seen to be composed of computations as mechanical as the primitive operations of a digital computer ... Psychological states are seen as systematically representing the world via a language of thought, and psychological processes are seen as computations involving these representations. (1980, p.171)

Though one might take issue with Block's description of computer operations as "primitive", the distinction between the two kinds of functionalism is important in at least the following respect: one might *agree* with the 'metaphysical' version of functionalism, but *disagree* with the 'computation-representation' version. Such is the view taken by advocates of approaches to AI *other than* the 'Good Old Fashioned' one. Indeed, in Chapter 6.3 we'll see this point in conceptual space explicitly occupied; advocates of the dynamical approach to cognition might wish to develop a more temporally sophisticated version of the former, whilst rejecting the latter because (in their view) it deals with matters of timing inadequately. Thus, although GOFAI and functionalism seem like natural bedfellows, their relationship need not be an exclusive one.

3
Gödel, the Turing Test and the Chinese Room

> What a piece of work is man! How noble in reason! how infinite in faculties! in form and moving, how express and admirable! in action how like an angel! in apprehension, how like a god! the beauty of the world! the paragon of animals!
>
> Shakespeare, *Hamlet*, (Second Quarto version)

In the previous chapter, we examined some of the origins, motivations, exemplars, and implications of GOFAI. These shone a mostly positive (although qualified) light on the approach; naturally, we now want to turn to a handful of the prominent criticisms. In any age, as the above passage from *Hamlet* reminds us, we humans think that certain of our features make us somehow 'special'. Descartes, as we saw, focussed on language use. Hamlet mentions reason. Whatever it is that one thinks distinguishes us (or makes us the "paragon of the animals"), one could construct an argument against AI if one could show that machines must lack that feature. This chapter focuses on three related discussions – sometimes misunderstood – that adopt just this rhetorical strategy. In fact only two of them (the Gödel argument and Searle's "Chinese Room") are explicit criticisms with the conclusion that GOFAI is impossible, but the third (the "Turing Test") does provide an arena in which a variety of anti-AI arguments (like that of Descartes) often get articulated.

This chapter is not meant to be exhaustive; it *could* not be, for the problems with GOFAI are probably better documented than its successes. Rather, taken together, the criticisms I will discuss highlight a nicely generalised form of anti-(GOF)AI argument. Haugeland (1981) describes this as the "hollow shell" objection, because it says that no matter how apparently successful an AI program is, it will never be *genuinely* intelligent (as we are) because it must lack some feature that is essential to mentality.

Haugeland (1985, p.247) expresses the argument in deductive form, in the following way:

1. Nothing could be genuinely intelligent without X;
2. But, no GOFAI system could ever have or display X;
3. THEREFORE, no GOFAI system could ever be intelligent.

Favourite candidates for X might include, as Haugeland suggests, consciousness, feelings, creativity, personality, learning, freedom, intuition and morality. We have also seen Descartes's suggestion of logico-linguistic abilities and the question of understanding or meaningfulness, and might formulate others according to the view we take about what is essential to cognition, or what computers will always lack. As we shall see, each of the topics to be discussed in this chapter will involve a different substitution for X, but each can be overcome by disputing one or both of the premisses in the above argument.

3.1 Gödel's incompleteness theorem

A famous argument against the possibility of AI – originally formulated by Lucas (1961) and more recently revived by Penrose (1989, 1994) – takes this X-factor to consist of certain specific logical abilities. In particular, it is alleged, for *any* GOFAI system, there are certain self-referential statements that it is incapable of proving, even though a human logician *is* capable of doing so. Thus, it is argued, a human logician can always do more than any possible GOFAI system – we can always outdo a computer – so the two can never be equivalent.

As is well known, when you're called as a witness in a court of law, you're required to promise to tell 'the truth, the whole truth and nothing but the truth'. This is in fact a two-fold promise: that you will say (a) *all* the true things, and (b) *only* the true things. But strictly speaking, it's not really possible to *keep* this promise, unless (as is arguably implicit) the relevant domain of truths is restricted by some criterion of relevance to the case at hand.

To see why, consider the following proposition:

G: I will never utter this sentence.

G causes something of a problem for the witness. For G is false once you utter it, but true so long as you don't. And since you promised both not to utter false things, and to utter all true things, this puts you in a bit of a quandary; whether you utter G or not, you will violate one or other of

Gödel, the Turing Test and the Chinese Room 59

your promises. You can't tell only the truth *and* the whole truth at the same time.

The kinds of problems raised by this sort of self-referential statement give a good taster of a famous logical result from the work of Kurt Gödel. Since it concerns statements that are true-but-unprovable, it is known as his 'incompleteness' theorem; certain formal systems are incomplete in the sense that there are truths about them that cannot be proven using the machinery of the system itself.

Recall, from the last chapter (especially 2.3.1), the idea that mathematical reasoning can be captured by the manipulation of symbols, and that we can derive the theorems of some mathematical system via the 'mechanical' application of an explicit and well-defined collection of logical axioms and rules of inference. Gödel proved that for a very wide class of mathematical systems, there are always some truths (in particular, certain kinds of self-referential truth) which *cannot* be so derived. Here is the remarkable opening paragraph of Gödel's 1931 paper:

> The development of mathematics in the direction of greater precision has led to large areas of it being formalized, so that proofs can be carried out according to a few mechanical rules. The most comprehensive formal systems to date [include] the *Principia Mathematica* of Whitehead and Russell... It would seem reasonable, therefore, to surmise that these axioms and rules of inference are sufficient to decide all mathematical questions which can be formulated in the system concerned. In what follows it will be shown that this is not the case, but rather that... there exist relatively simple problems of the theory of ordinary whole numbers which cannot be decided on the basis of the axioms. (quoted from the translation provided by Smullyan, 1992, p.1)

The details of the *proof* need not concern us here, except to note that it is indeed a proof, and rightly regarded as one of the most important in twentieth century mathematics. Gödel's genius was that he found a way (a) to encode logical statements in purely numerical form, and (b) to use that encoding so that numbers could say something about themselves. So, for example (and this comes from Doug Hofstadter's foreword to Nagel and Newman, 2001, p.xiv), Gödel could write down a formula of, say, *Principia Mathematica* that said, 'This formula is unprovable by the rules of *Principia Mathematica*'. Think about it. The consequence is exactly the same as the toy example of G above. There's a statement, in *Principia Mathematica*'s system, that if true, is unprovable, and if provable, reveals the system to prove falsehoods. And such a self-referential formula, Gödel demonstrated, can be found for *any* of a wide class of formal systems.

Such 'Gödel sentences' superficially resemble the famous 'Liar Paradox'. Take a sentence like 'This sentence is false' or 'I am currently lying'. If the sentence is false, then it's true. But if it's true, then it's false. Such conundrums have perplexed philosophers and logicians at least since ancient Greece. But what's most interesting about Gödel sentences is that they're *not* paradoxical; they're *true* statements about formal systems where that truth cannot be proved within the system itself (indeed, where the truth of the sentence is a *result* of their unproveability), hence the sense in which the system is 'incomplete'.

Now, pause to reflect. For a wide class of formal systems, we can find sentences that are true-but-unprovable within the system. *We can find their truth*, but the system cannot. Combine this with what we already know about Turing Machines – since they are formal systems *par excellence* – and we have the result that, as Dennett (1996, p.430) puts it "every computer that is a consistent truth-of-arithmetic prover has an Achilles' heel, a truth that it can never prove". Now, suppose we took a computer program (i.e., a formal system) that was supposed to be equivalent to the human mind. It would have a Gödel sentence that was true-but-unprovable within the system, and we could see that it was true. So we could do something that the formal system could not – namely, see the truth of its Gödel sentence – and so we'd have proof that the program was not, after all, equivalent to us. It is something like this thought that underlies a famous argument from the philosopher John Lucas, who writes:

> Gödel's theorem must apply to cybernetical machines, because it is of the essence of being a machine, that it should be a concrete instantiation of a formal system. It follows that given any machine which is consistent and capable of doing simple arithmetic, there is a formula which it is incapable of producing as being true – i.e., the formula is unprovable-in-the-system – but which we can see to be true. It follows that no machine can be a complete or adequate model of the mind, that minds are essentially different from machines. (1961, p.113)

The argument has been more recently resurrected by Roger Penrose, whose version concerns how mathematicians come up with proofs at all, or rather, how it is that we 'see' the truth of the Gödel sentence for some system. Very briefly, his argument is that if our mathematical judgements were the result of us running an algorithm – a formal system – in our heads, then there would also be a Gödel sentence for that system which we could discover by following the standard Gödel procedure to come up with it. Since doing so would amount to coming up with a proof, and by Gödel's theorem, the sentence is unprovable-in-the-system, then we cannot be equivalent to that formal system. Penrose's conclusion is that "Mathematicians are not using a knowably sound algorithm in order to ascertain mathematical truth" (1994, p.76); mathematical "insight" is nonalgorithmic (1989, Chapter 10), and quantum mechanical effects in neuronal nanotubules (to be explained by some future theory of quantum gravity) are responsible for mentality.

In fact, given its reliance on speculative neuroscience and as-yet-nonexistent theories of physics, Penrose's line of argument might actually be taken as a backhanded compliment to classical cognitive science and GOFAI; as Steven Pinker (1997, p.98) writes: "The computational theory [of mind] fits so well into our understanding of the world that, in trying to overthrow it, Penrose had to reject most of contemporary neuroscience, evolutionary biology, and physics!" As one might suspect, other replies to this line of argument are many and varied. I shall only focus on two, since they pick up on some considerations we've already discussed, and also foreshadow some considerations that we will look at later. For reasons that will become obvious, I shall call them the 'Heuristic reply' and the 'Dynamical reply'.

Recall Turing's earlier remark (see page 49 above) that one might be able to make a machine display intelligence in chess "at the risk of its making occasional serious mistakes". This is a veiled reference to *heuristics*, which we encountered earlier as rules-of-thumb that wouldn't guarantee a particular outcome, but would nonetheless increase its likelihood sufficiently whilst simultaneously conferring some other advantage of speed or efficiency. Characteristically enough, in a paper that pre-dated Lucas by 13 years, Turing put the Gödel argument to rest in two sentences: "The argument from Gödel's and other theorems... rests essentially on the condition that the machine must not make mistakes. But this is not a requirement for intelligence" (Turing, 2004/1948, p.411). His point here serves to remind us of the strict sense of Gödel's theorem; in any consistent system (at least, one of sufficient power to produce simple arithmetic), there are sentences that cannot be proven within the system (and Lucas and Penrose add: but which we can see to be true). The theorem effectively states that a system cannot be *both* consistent and complete; any sufficiently powerful system has to give up on one or the other or both. But Turing is pointing out that consistency (the ability to avoid mistakes) isn't a necessary condition for intelligence/cognition; people (even mathematicians) make mistakes, believe contradicting propositions and so on, without thereby ceasing to be intelligent.

Once we admit that we're in fact dealing with systems than can make mistakes, we realise that we're back into the realm of *heuristics*, and we have a situation that's nicely parallel to the one we encountered when considering the possibility of an algorithm *for* checkmate. Recall: it is impossible to implement an algorithm *for* checkmate, since such a thing would require more time and space to run than the universe provides. We might say something similar about Gödel's theorem; there is no algorithm *for* the generation (or, as Penrose would have it, *recognition*) of all mathematical truths within a particular system. In the case of chess, the existence of Deep Blue shows that, despite the in-principle limitation, it is still possible to construct a computer (a formal system) that is superbly capable of achieving checkmate most of the time (although not *all* of the time; Kasparov did win the first game, after all). We can do so by building a machine that employs heuristic programs. Analogously, in the case of mathematical proof, despite the in-principle limitation brought about by Gödel's theorem, it is still possible for there to be algorithmic systems that are superbly capable of generating mathematical truths most of the time (although not *all* of the time; the possibility of making mistakes must be allowed). Human mathematicians may well be such algorithmic systems (that's the hypothesis of GOFAI), and their abilities could arise from their employing heuristic programs too. As Dennett puts it, they would have:

> Not an algorithm 'for' intuiting mathematical truth...but an algorithm for something else. What? Most plausibly it would be an algorithm – one of many – for *trying to stay alive*, an algorithm that, by an extraordinarily convoluted and indirect generation of byproducts, 'happened' to be a superb (but not foolproof) recognizer of friends, enemies, food, shelter, harbingers of spring, good arguments – and mathematical truths. (1990, p.600)

In the cut-and-thrust of the evolutionarily salient real word, the in-principle limits of computational and mathematical ability are simply not relevant. What matters is that an algorithm gets the job done often enough that you could (to echo Dennett's title) "bet your life on it". And heuristic programs, patched, tweaked and refined by millennia of evolution, could do just that. Thus when Penrose, in a response to his critics (1990, p.696), writes "Given any particular algorithm, that algorithm cannot be *the* procedure whereby human mathematicians ascertain mathematical truth" his claim is simply false; the argument from Gödel's theorem does not rule out the possibility of (GOF)AI, and this is sufficient to undercut Lucas's version of the argument too.

A somewhat more speculative – and thus interesting – reply to various versions of the Gödel argument comes from noting the dynamical nature of the human cognitive system. I shall only treat this briefly for now – and for 'dynamical' one can simply substitute 'constantly changing' – but it serves as a useful foreshadow for material to be addressed in Chapter 6. The argument comes from Seager (2003), and starts by noting that not only are real cognitive systems constantly changing, but also that, in many cases, such change arises as a result of their own cognitive activity. Thus, it would be a mistake to assume, as the Gödel argument requires, that our mathematical abilities are generated by a single, static algorithm. Rather, as Seager notes, as a child learns more mathematics, their procedures for reasoning *about* mathematics also change in that process. It seems likely, then, that were we to acquire knowledge of our own mathematical algorithms in sufficient detail as to allow the generation of our own Gödel sentence, the process of that acquisition would probably change the algorithm itself!

What would this show? Let's consider two lines of conclusion: one for the Lucas/Penrose argument, and one – which I shall pick up on later – for cognitive science and AI in general. The first effectively grants one of the Lucas-Penrose conclusions – that there is an in-principle limitation in the extent of mathematical knowledge that can be obtained algorithmically – whilst maintaining the GOFAI claim that we are, nonetheless, algorithmic systems. For since coming to understand our own algorithm would change that very algorithm, we could only ever know, as Seager puts it, "yesterday's algorithm." We might come to know that *yesterday* we would have been unable to see the truth of some (Gödel) sentence that *today* we can see to be true. But that wouldn't undermine the GOFAI claim at all. As Seager (2003, p.273) concludes:

> there is not the slightest reason to think that our cognitive algorithms are static and much reason to suppose they are plastic, and that one of the major determinants of algorithmic change is the acquisition of knowledge by way of these very algorithms. Our knowledge of ourselves is thus always one step behind our true natures, but that fact cannot refute computationalism.

Indeed, to switch to the second consequence, this is exactly what 'real world' considerations would lead us to expect. If one views change over time as a constitutive aspect of both cognition and its explanation – as advocates of the dynamical approach to cognitive science and

AI do – then ignoring that aspect in the way that Lucas and Penrose require would be a fatal theoretical flaw. As we shall see, dynamical cognitive science is no friend of GOFAI anyway, so this is not so much a defence of the classical approach as a direct criticism of the Lucas/Penrose argument. But it does show that (a) considerations about change and timing are more than mere "implementation details" and (b) the practical significance of 'real-world' issues (often neglected in the idealised world of Turing Machines, mathematical axiom-systems and their ilk) sometimes, in fact, amounts to a *theoretical* significance. These are considerations that we shall have cause to revisit in the remainder of this chapter.

3.2 The Turing Test

Set aside, for a moment, the many philosophical concerns one may develop concerning how we define, understand or re-create intelligence, cognition, or mentality, and ask instead how we would *detect* it. More specifically, how would we tell, when confronted with some non-biological machine, whether it was *really* intelligent? Here's one answer that has a good deal going for it: Ask it.

The apparent flippancy of such an answer dissolves when one recalls the view adopted by Descartes (see above, p.6) that it is "not conceivable" that a machine could use words to hold up its end of an "appropriately meaningful" conversation. In terms of the general argument form with which I began this chapter, then, Descartes wants to substitute 'linguistic competence' for X, and his hypothesis is that no machine could display it. By 1950, with the publication of Turing's seminal "Computing Machinery and Intelligence" (recall: Turing invented *philosophy of* AI six years before it was even called by that name) we find not only that the linguistic competence of machines has become conceivable after all, but also that leading computer scientists are willing to make predictions about its forthcoming *actuality*. For in his paper, Turing proposes to use conversational abilities as a way of probing the putative intelligence of a given machine. I have carefully hedged this brief description because, as we shall see, what Turing was up to is often misinterpreted, but I think that when understood correctly, his idea is defensible and in many respects quite powerful. Language use has played (and continues to play – see Christian, 2011) an important role in debates about machine intelligence in the form of his 'Turing Test'.

As with Turing Machines, and Turing's Thesis, Turing did not name the test eponymously. Rather, he described it – very accurately – as an "imitation game". The set-up is this: a judge/interrogator attempts to work out, solely by means of written questions and answers (conducted by an instant-messaging service or some such), which of two other conversants is a human and which is a computer/machine. Since it is officially a "game" – although he *does* refer to it as a "test" several times in his 1950 paper – Turing provides relatively little by way of hard-and-fast criteria for 'passing' the test, other than what comes bundled with his own prediction. He writes:

> I believe that in about fifty years' time it will be possible to programme computers... to make them play the imitation game so well that an average interrogator will not have more than 70 per cent chance of making the right identification after five minutes of questioning. (1950, p.442)

He later revised this prediction. In a 1952 radio broadcast which I will return to below, the Cambridge mathematician Max Newman says "I should like to be there when your match between a man and a machine takes place, and perhaps to try my hand at making up some of the questions. But that will be a long time from now, if the machine is to stand any chance with no questions barred?" and Turing replies "Oh, at least 100 years, I should say." (Copeland, 2000, p.527). Putting this all together, we have what we *now* know (whether Turing intended it or not) as a test for machine intelligence: can the machine trick a judge into thinking they're having a teletyped conversation with a human?

This way of putting it reveals the first of several common misconceptions about Turing's imitation game, which have nonetheless become fairly commonplace. Subsequent commentators have often described Turing as attempting to provide an operational definition (whereby one defines something in terms of the procedures one would use to measure or identify it) or a behaviourist definition (whereby descriptions of mental states and processes are replaced by descriptions of dispositions to behave) of intelligence. Such a mistaken reading of Turing's 1950 paper is fairly commonplace, and Copeland (2000) provides an excellent catalogue of instances. But in fact, in a BBC radio broadcast of January 1952 with the title "Can Automatic Calculating Machines Be Said To Think?" Turing is quite explicit about his aims: when asked "Have you a mechanical definition?" Turing replies "I don't want to give a definition of thinking... But I don't really see that we need to agree on a definition at all" (Copeland, 2004, p.494).

What Turing was *really* up to, if you cast your mind back to my introduction (p.2), was trying to come up with a better, more tractable, question than "Can machines think?" – a question which he describes as "meaningless". The new question – "Are there imaginable digital computers which would do well in the imitation game?" – is intended to *replace* the original one, so that we can *investigate* it, Turing says, "without further ado". As Dennett (1998b, p.4) puts it, Turing intended the imitation game to be a "philosophical conversation-stopper" that would enable us to cease haggling unproductively over definitions and imaginary counterexamples.

But neither should Turing's emphasis on moving beyond philosophical and definitional preliminaries lead us to think that he intended the imitation game as a serious proposal for where research in AI should go. Turing does not suggest that the efforts of computer scientists should be directed *towards* building a machine that could successfully play the imitation game. Indeed, as we've seen with Eliza, efforts to build machines with which one could conduct a conversation actually reveal relatively little about the true nature of cognition. Weizenbaum only intended Eliza as a minimal pilot study of how one might manipulate grammatical structures in natural language, but her superficial conversational abilities were enough to dazzle those who encountered her in a way that her creator never intended. And as we saw, she certainly wouldn't pass any serious version of the Turing Test.

It's an unfortunate consequence of Turing's 1950 paper – which was intended to remove various distracting obstacles to a fruitful relationship between computer science and psychology – that a great deal of effort has subsequently been expended in building machines that *are* intended to succeed at some version of the imitation game. This has been exacerbated by the fact that, since 1990, the 'Loebner Prize' (sponsored by Hugh Loebner, an American inventor and computer enthusiast) has offered a cash prize of $100,000 for any machine that could pass the Turing Test (though, since no such machine has been forthcoming, substantially smaller sums have been offered – and won – by the most "human seeming" computers in each yearly contest). At best, such machines may offer some insight into the processes that can generate such deceptive performances. At worst (at least, for cognitive science), this encourages the development of interesting curiosities whose sole aim is to impress. Consequently, Whitby (1996) has described the Turing Test as "AI's biggest blind alley" since, he claims, work directed at producing a machine that could successfully play the imitation game is not genuine or useful AI research.

This is perhaps a little unfair; as Dennett notes, the Loebner prize contest does not actually attract participants from the best AI labs, because, as he puts it "passing the Turing test is not a sensible research and development goal for serious AI. It requires too much Disney and not enough science" (1998b, pp.28–29). Further, contests like the Loebner prize are always restricted in some way (such as limiting the range of permitted topics of conversation), thereby implicitly acknowledging the sheer difficulty – even now – of getting a machine to do well in a genuine, unrestricted, version of the test. So it's certainly the case that Turing's work has lead *some* AI researchers in directions other than an investigation of the true nature of cognition, but it's also clear that these are not Turing's own mistakes. He does not describe success in the imitation game as a goal, in and of itself, for AI, and to the extent that anyone attempts to make it their own, this challenge is very far from being met.

Finally, it is sometimes pointed out that creatures such as pre-linguistic infants, dolphins and monkeys would fail the test, even though most people would agree that they do possess genuine intelligence. On the one hand, this does create some trouble for Turing's claim concerning the *equivalence* of 'Can a machine think?' and 'Can a machine convince a judge that it is human?'; 'no' to the latter does not necessarily imply a 'no' to the former. But this does not undermine the usefulness of the test outright. As Copeland (1993, p.44) points out, there are many perfectly good tests where a negative outcome on the test is simply inconclusive overall (e.g., if the suspects' fingerprints are not found on the murder weapon, it does not mean that they are innocent; they might have been wearing gloves). So the Turing Test is not what we might call a *litmus test* – one that reveals something whether the outcome is positive *or* negative – but such tests are a relatively rare luxury. To quote Dennett (1998b, p.4) again the Turing Test is "a one-way test; failing it proves nothing". But that does not undermine its usefulness *as* a test.

The real strength of the Turing Test is two-fold. For one thing, the test provides a neat way of quickly setting aside features that are irrelevant (but biasing) in a judgement of intelligence. Turing (1950, p.434) points out that the set up of the imitation game "has the advantage of drawing a fairly sharp line between the physical and the intellectual capacities of a man". Scientists probably couldn't make a candidate machine *look* like a human by dressing it up in artificial skin, but even if they could, such a detail is – or should be – irrelevant to the question of intelligence. As Turing says in the 1952 radio interview, "The important thing is to try to draw a line between the properties of a brain, or of a man, that we want to discuss, and those that we don't. To take an extreme case, we are not interested in the fact that the brain has the consistency of cold porridge" (Copeland, 2004, p.495).

Second, the Turing Test's hypothetical dividing line is drawn both very high and very wide. On the one hand – let's be clear – no current computer has come *anywhere close* to passing Turing's Test as he envisaged it. Eliza, chatbots and the 'most human' participants in the Loebner contest are all interesting and impressive parodies of conversation, but when one looks at the transrcipts of their conversations, it's just *glaringly* obvious that they're not human. And that's in a massively restricted version of the test; success in the unrestricted version of the test is conceivable, but a *very* long way off.

Why? Perhaps because, on the other hand, as Turing himself noted (1950, p.435), "The question and answer method seems to be suitable for introducing almost any one of the fields of human endeavour that we wish to include". In other words, whilst, say, perception and emotion might not require linguistic ability (hence the 'infants, dolphins and monkeys' objection above), being able to describe perceptions and emotions sensibly in a free-ranging conversation is a pretty good indicator that the cognitive phenomena described are really there too. Thus, (genuine) linguistic ability is not just a superficial veneer; it's the tip of a cognitive iceberg that's supported by a weighty bulk of mentality beneath the surface. The Turing Test thus licenses inferences about the presence of lower-level cognitive structure, because linguistic competence is a very good heuristic indicator – what Dennett (1998b) calls a "quick probe" – for it. Moor (1976, p.251) writes that "if the Turing test was passed, then one would certainly have very adequate grounds for inductively inferring that the computer could think on the level of a normal, living, adult human being". That sounds about right, but it still understates matters somewhat. I'm inclined to think that there's almost no way that something could pass the Turing Test without *also* being capable of many other undoubtedly intelligent (though *un*tested) actions.

To be sure, this won't satisfy every objector to the Turing Test. It is of course possible that by some fluke or ingenuity, programmers could build a non-intelligent machine – lacking all the other *accoutrements* of cognition – that nonetheless successfully played the imitation game. It's just massively unlikely. *In principle,* a non-intelligent machine could pass the test in the same way that *in principle* an ice-cube could spontaneously form in the middle of my (hot) cup of coffee: neither is precluded by the laws of physics. But that's surely not enough to undermine the test's usefulness. Turing's prediction about *when* his test would be passed may have been off (at least in its 1950 formulation), but that's because of how difficult – and thus *good* – a test it is. It doesn't provide a definition of, or a necessary condition for, intelligence, and failing it doesn't show much, but a pass in the unrestricted Turing Test ought to make us pretty close to certain that we were dealing with the Real Thing.

3.3 Searle's Chinese Room

We saw that the Turing Test is not a "litmus test" – a failure doesn't demonstrate anything. What does a pass show? In the previous section, I claimed that nothing would be able to pass the test without being genuinely intelligent, so even if the Turing Test is not directly a test *for* – or operational definition *of* – intelligence, it still functions very well as a quick probe for it. Such a claim, however, is controversial. In fact, its denial lies at the heart of possibly the most widely known criticism of GOFAI: John Searle's famous "Chinese Room" thought experiment. In various presentations of this idea (Searle, 1980, 1982, 1984, 1999), we are asked to consider a symbol-manipulation system that *ex hypothesi* passes the Turing Test, but which, lacking an understanding of the symbols thus manipulated, is not genuinely intelligent. To put it another way (in language we earlier heard from Haugeland), the mere syntactic processing characteristic of GOFAI computers cannot give rise to the semantics that are characteristic of mentality.

In terms of the general argument with which I began this chapter, then, Searle wants to substitute something like 'understanding', 'semantics', or 'intentionality' for X, and this way of putting it should remind us of the unresolved problem with which I concluded the earlier discussion of Hobbes. If thoughts are composed out of symbols, then from where to those symbols get their meanings? The symbols of public language derive *their* meanings from our thoughts, but we cannot tell the same story for thoughts themselves on pain of circularity. So the problem is this: once we've stripped out meanings from the foundations of our mechanical account of cognition, *how do they get back in again*? Searle argues that it cannot be by means of yet more symbol-manipulation. But that is all GOFAI systems have got. So, he concludes, GOFAI systems cannot, by themselves, be genuinely intelligent, since they lack the all-important X-factor possessed by biological thinkers.

The set-up of the thought experiment was (as always) anticipated by Turing. Recall that, in Turing's time, 'computer' was a term that applied to a human calculating clerk. Accordingly, Turing (1950, p.436) wrote:

> The idea behind digital computers may be explained by saying that these machines are intended to carry out any operations which could

be done by a human computer. The human computer is supposed to be following fixed rules; he has no authority to deviate from them in any detail. We may suppose that these rules are supplied in a book, which is altered whenever he is put on to a new job. He has also an unlimited supply of paper on which he does his calculations.

Here, then, is the scenario. Imagine a man – let's call him John – who knows no Chinese, but is locked in a room in which there are a number of boxes of Chinese symbols. John's only contact with the outside world is via a mail slot through which slips of paper can be passed. In the room there is also a scratch-pad for rough work, and a large book, in English, which contains a great number of rules that tell John how to match certain sequences of Chinese characters with other sequences of Chinese characters. The rulebook says things like 'If such-and-such characters come in through the mail slot, wait a short while and then push so-and-so characters out of the mail slot.' John might not even know *that* the symbols are Chinese, but this doesn't matter, because he can work by simply matching the *shape* of the characters in the inbox to the shape of those depicted in the rule book. Unbeknownst to John, there are native Chinese speakers outside of the room, and they are the ones passing the strings of symbols into the room and retrieving the strings of symbols that John sends out. They call these symbol strings 'questions' and 'answers'. Finally, suppose that the rules are so sophisticated, and that John is so good at following them, that the native Chinese speakers are not able to distinguish the 'answers' they get from John-in-the-room from those that would be given by another native Chinese speaker. John-in-the-room passes the Turing Test in Chinese.

Now ask yourself; does John understand Chinese? Most of us would agree – and Searle describes it as "quite obvious" – that John doesn't understand a word of Chinese. He is simply manipulating the symbols by following what the rules say about their shapes. Here's the rub: John is only doing what a computer does. The rule book is just the program, and by following it, John is executing an algorithm. So, the intuition goes, if all of that rule-governed symbol-manipulation is insufficient for understanding, then computers can never understand anything, because that's all they've got. Thus, computers can't have minds (because mentality requires understanding the meaning of symbols) and strong AI is false. Here's Searle's (1982) conclusion:

> What this simple argument shows is that no formal program by itself is sufficient for understanding, because it would always be possible in principle for an agent to go through the steps in the program and still

not have the relevant understanding. And what works for Chinese would also work for other mental phenomena. I could, for example, go through the steps of the thirst-simulating program without feeling thirsty. The argument also, *en passant*, refutes the Turing test because it shows that a system, namely me, could pass the Turing test without having the appropriate mental states.

To put things more concisely, here's another way that Searle (1999) formulates the overall *argument*:

1. Implemented programs are by definition purely formal or syntactical.
2. Minds have mental or semantic contents.
3. Syntax is not by itself sufficient for, nor constitutive of, semantics. Conclusion: Implemented programs are not constitutive of minds. Strong AI is false.

In fairness to Searle, he does intend his conclusion precisely; so before turning to evaluate Searle's argument, let's briefly identify some common misunderstandings (these are listed in Searle 1999, p.116). First, the thought experiment does not show that machines cannot think – Searle clarifies his view: "On the contrary, the brain is a machine and the brain can think" and in his 1980 paper, in response to the question 'Could a machine think?' he writes "The answer is, obviously, yes. We are precisely such machines." Second, the thought experiment does not show that *computers* can't think. As we saw from Turing, since we human beings can carry out computations, we are computers, and we can think. Finally, the Chinese Room does not show that only brains can think; it is intended to show that brains must be doing more than the "mere shuffling of formal symbols" and that any artificial thinking machine would have to duplicate the specific neurophysiological processes responsible for thought in the human case.

In an earlier book, my co-author and I wrote the following:

> It wouldn't be too much of a stretch to regard Searle's argument as dividing cognitive scientists into two broad categories: those who see it as a powerful demonstration of the failure of strong AI and its functionalist underpinnings, and those who regard it as a minor and surmountable confusion. Indeed, the two authors of this volume stand on opposite sides of this divide. (Kukla and Walmsley, 2006, p.159)

Confession time: it's me that falls into the latter category. So, rather than surveying and cataloguing the extraordinary number of objections and rejoinders that have appeared in the cognitive scientific literature, I want to outline a small number that I think come together in a way that leads nicely to what will be discussed in later chapters. When coupled with a healthy Dennett-style scepticism about thought experiments (or "intuition pumps" as Dennett calls them), I think it can indeed be shown that, despite its ingenuity, Searle's argument is indeed surmountable. (For those who are looking for a more exhaustive treatment of all the objections to – and counter-replies in defence of – Searle, see the "Suggestions for Further Reading" below.)

Perhaps the most popular line of response amongst Searle's critics is known as the "systems reply". This reply takes a variety of forms, but they all share the idea that it's a mistake to take *John's* ignorance of Chinese as significant; John is just one small part of a much wider system that includes the rule book, the room, the scratch-pad and the boxes of symbols. Two variants may concern us here, and it's important to keep them distinct. The first is called *the logical reply*, and stems from Copeland (2000, 2002). The claim is simply that Searle's argument is invalid. Grant that the thought experiment successfully establishes that John's symbol manipulation does not enable him to understand the Chinese symbols thus manipulated. This simply does not entail the conclusion that John's symbol manipulation does not enable the *Room* to understand the Chinese symbols manipulated. One can see the invalidity by considering a parallel: 'John has no taxable assets in Japan' does not entail 'The organisation of which John is a part has no taxable assets in Japan' (suppose that John works part time as a cleaner at the British HQ of Honda).

The logical reply, it should be noted, makes no claim about whether or not the Room (i.e., the wider system of which John is a part) *actually* understands. It simply points out that an absence of understanding on the part of the wider system is not entailed by John's lack. What Searle himself describes as the "systems reply" goes a step further in claiming: "While it is true that the individual person who is locked in the room does not understand the story, the fact is that he is merely part of a whole system, and the system does understand the story" (Searle, 1980, p.419).

Searle's reply is three-fold. First, he points out, the reply simply asserts without argument that the system *must* understand Chinese; it is therefore a question-begging claim that would need some independent support. Second, Searle says that he's "somewhat embarrassed" even to take the systems reply seriously, because, he thinks, it's so implausible. On his view, the systems reply agrees that the man in the room can't understand Chinese, but says that somehow the addition of all this extra paraphernalia – the rule book, the boxes of symbols, the scratch pad, and so on – *can* give rise to genuine understanding where previously there was none.

Finally, Searle provides a modification of the original thought experiment, designed to undermine the systems reply. Suppose that John memorises the symbols and the rulebook and that, by some impressive (but not impossible) feat of mental agility, he is able to carry out all of the calculations in his head, without recourse to the scratch pad. The whole system would be, as it were, inside John's head, and he could even be free to leave the room and walk around; the Chinese-speaking system would consist of nothing more than John himself. But, Searle says, despite his continued ability to conduct passable 'conversations', we would surely want to say that he *still* doesn't understand Chinese; he's still responding to Chinese questions by looking up the answers and parroting what he finds, like a turbo-charged Eliza.

I think that there is a way to address all three parts of Searle's reply by reverting to *another* of the objections that he identifies in the original paper: the "Robot Reply". Put the room – with John, the symbols, the scratch pad etc. – into the 'head' of a robot. Further, let the incoming symbol strings also include (still, unbeknownst to John) those generated by the robot's peripheral perceptual equipment, and let his output (given some suitable transduction) control the movement of the robot's limbs, so that, as Searle (1980, p.420) puts it, "the robot does something very much like perceiving, walking, moving about, hammering nails, eating, drinking – anything you like". Proponents of the robot reply, according to Searle, say *now* the *robot* would have genuine understanding and other mental states. Searle, of course, denies this because *John* is *still* doing nothing over and above the formal manipulation of symbols, and knows nothing of Chinese, of his environmental surroundings, or of the robot's body that he is controlling.

We have a stand-off; proponents of the robot reply say there is understanding, and Searle says there is not. How to adjudicate? Thought experiments like this work just like scientific experiments; we systematically control some variables whilst varying others, in order to observe an outcome that will enable us to understand the relationship between the variables in more detail. In the Chinese Room thought experiment, we hold the symbol-manipulation (the program) constant, and we vary the symbol-manipulator (John vs. a digital computer), in order to see what this does to our intuitions about the presence or absence of understanding and other mental states. So, in the updated Robot-system reply, if you *really* can imagine the scenario in all the requisite technicolour detail, what are your intuitions?

To re-work an example from Dennett (1980), suppose that the Chinese words for 'Hands up! This is a stick up!' are whispered into the ear of the robot-system. John uncomprehendingly, *and in real time*, hand simulates the program by following the rule book, which leads to the robot handing over his wallet, pleading for mercy in Chinese, retreating from the scene and repairing to the nearest police station as soon as possible. Are we really to say that there's no understanding of Chinese going on anywhere in this scenario?[1] That's certainly not obvious – as a thought experiment that relies on our intuitions would require – indeed, it just seems perversely stubborn to deny the attribution of understanding to the robot-system in this case. I can't *prove* that the robot-system understands and has other mental states, but at this stage it seems like the most reasonable hypothesis.

So what general lessons can we learn from the robot-system reply? I think several. Searle (1980, p.420) claims that the robot reply "tacitly concedes that cognition is not solely a matter of formal symbol manipulation, since this reply adds a set of causal relation [sic] with the outside world". The latter clause is right, though it does not entail the former. As we saw in the case of the Gödel argument, 'real-world' considerations – absent from both the thought experiment and the theoretical framework it targets – really do matter. The "causal relations with the outside world" to which Searle refers are broadly those of "situatedness" (both temporal and physical) that will be discussed in later chapters.

I have not said much here, save for an italicised phrase a couple of paragraphs ago, about issues of time and timing in the Chinese room, though it should go without saying that trying to have an actual conversation with John-in-the-room or John-in-the-robot would be excruciating – "like trying to listen to a football match commentary broadcast in Morse code" I've heard it said. So it's arguable that our intuitions about the Chinese Room are skewed by our tacit knowledge of the fact that John wouldn't be able to hand-simulate the program quickly enough to pass the Turing Test in Chinese. What this means is that temporal concerns are either a confounding factor in our thought experiment, and ought to have been screened out more carefully, or else – as the advocate of dynamical cognitive science urges – they ought to be incorporated by imagining them properly. Timing *matters* for intelligence; biological and evolutionary considerations lead to the elimination of those who can't cope with a changing environment in an appropriate time-frame, and the imaginative requirements of thought experiments, if not rigorously and fully met, can neglect such real-world considerations. (For more on matters of timing, see Dennett, 1987, and Wheeler, 2002.)

It would be unfair to blame Searle for this. Issues of time, timing and embodiment don't 'officially' feature in the underlying and idealised account of algorithms and Turing Machines on which GOFAI rests. So, as we shall see in Chapter 6, rescuing GOFAI from the Chinese Room with such concerns may simultaneously provide us with grounds to criticise it; Searle's argument might not work for reasons of physical and temporal situatedness, but those features are absent from GOFAI anyway.

Finally, Searle attributes the systems reply to Berkeley, his home institution, since that's where he first heard it when he gave an early version of the paper as a talk. Legend has it that the response was made by Herbert Simon – who happened to be visiting at the time – when he pointed out that John-in-the-room was much like a single neuron in a brain. The reply should thus alert us to the very general point that sometimes a system will have properties and abilities that are not displayed by any of its components (in much the same way that neither eggs, sugar, butter nor flour have 'sponginess', but when they're combined correctly, the resulting cake *does*.) Sometimes, such properties are described as 'emergent' (though the term has a vexing variety of connotations), but however one views the part–whole relationship, it ought to be something to which we're sensitive when considering the cognitive properties of *systems*. We'll begin a move towards these kinds of issues in the next chapter, and in Chapter 6.

———◇———

Having considered these criticisms of GOFAI, and my replies to them, it should be fairly obvious both where my own sympathies lie, and where we are heading next and for the remainder of the book. The GOFAI approach is inspired by a conception of cognition as computation, where the latter itself is considered as the rule-governed manipulation of symbols. Accordingly, GOFAI considers logical reasoning and language use as paradigm cases of mental activity, and treats them in a somewhat idealised fashion that tries to abstract away from – or reduce the importance of – the concrete details of how cognitive systems are implemented. In a sense, that's inevitable given the functionalist root of GOFAI and its emphasis on multiple-realisability ('it ain't the meat that matters, it's the motion').

But as we move away from GOFAI – both historically and conceptually – we also move away from these theoretical presumptions. In the next chapter, we'll take a look at the connectionist (or 'neural network') approach to cognitive science and AI, where the inspiration of neurophysiology will be apparent. In later chapters we'll look at dynamical and embodied approaches to AI that try to take seriously both the temporal and physical 'situatedness' of cognitive systems. So, for GOFAI, the 'realist turn' we're about to take is actually a double-edged sword; GOFAI itself is just as guilty of neglecting biological and situated concerns as its critics are.

4
Connectionism

If one can describe GOFAI as 'the computer model of mind', it would be fair to describe connectionism as 'the brain model of mind'. Neurophysiology is certainly an *inspiration* for connectionist models, and whilst there are many important differences, it is this broad architectural similarity that leads to the latter sometimes being described as 'neural networks'. The approach is also called 'Parallel Distributed Processing' (PDP) because of its conception of how the brain works, and although these three expressions – connectionism, neural networks and PDP – all have slightly different connotations that one should probably take care to distinguish, doing so won't be necessary for our discussion, and so I shall use them more-or-less synonymously.

Perhaps the earliest investigation of non-biological brain-like structures came from Warren McCulloch and Walter Pitts who, in 1943, viewed the neuron as kind of 'logic threshold device'. According to this deliberately simplified view, any given neuron (a) receives inputs from a number of other neurons in a network, (b) adds up all of those inputs and (c) if the sum exceeds some predefined threshold, it 'fires' (i.e., provides some output). McCulloch and Pitts showed how to encode various logical propositions in networks of these 'units' so that, in principle, a 'neural network' can do anything that can be done with a classical computer or a Turing Machine.

Indeed, Turing himself had also anticipated the use of brain-like structures for performing computations. In the unpublished report from which I quoted earlier in conjunction with Turing's *Thesis*, he also introduced the idea of what he calls "unorganised machines" – networks of interconnected neuron-like structures – that he says are "about the simplest model of a nervous system" (2004/1948, p.418). Turing's important addition to the work of McCulloch and Pitts is his speculation about how such networks can be 'trained'; Turing was really the first to consider how a machine could *learn* (for more detail, see Copeland and Proudfoot, 1996; Teuscher, 2002).

Finally, the earliest in-depth study of the capabilities of *networks* of neuron-like units came from the computer scientist Frank Rosenblatt. In the late 1950s (e.g., Rosenblatt, 1958) he built and studied 'perceptrons' at the Cornell Aeronautical Laboratory, using McCulloch and Pitts-style units arranged into 'layers' (much like the brain), that could 'learn'. But the publication of Minsky and Papert's book *Perceptrons* in 1968, with its detailed articulation of the limitations of perceptrons, is often held to have killed off interest in the otherwise promising new field of neural network research. In part, there was a widespread misconception of some aspects of the book. For example, the authors demonstrate that a *small class* of perceptrons are unable to compute the exclusive-OR function,[1] yet commentators sometimes take this conclusion to apply to *all* perceptrons. Even though Minsky and Papert's criticisms were much more limited than is often suggested, funding for neural network AI dried up, and the mainstream continued to focus on classical, symbolic, GOFAI. Terrence Sejnowski (one of the pioneers of contemporary neural network studies) reports his view in 1979: "I had concluded that network modeling was in decline. There were a few people in little pockets where the torch was still burning, but there was no heart" (Quoted in Anderson and Rosenfeld, 1998, p.321).

All that had changed by 1986, when connectionism re-appeared as a viable approach to cognitive science and AI. This might sound surprisingly specific, but it's because that year saw the release of a two-volume connectionist 'bible' with the title *Parallel Distributed Processing: Explorations in the Microstructure of Cognition* (McClelland et al., 1986b; Rumelhart et al., 1986). Despite its high retail price and mammoth size, this enormously influential collection sold out its first printing with advance orders even before it had been published: neural networks were back on the map. Bechtel and Abrahamsen (2002) discuss several possible reasons why connectionism re-emerged as quickly and strongly as it did, including the increased power of the machines used to run them, the new techniques for training them, and the personal and geographical academic circumstances at the time. Most important, however, are the twin facts that connectionism seemed to offer an *alternative* to symbolic/GOFAI accounts, and that (in keeping with my discussion at the end of the last chapter) this alternative was much more 'realistic' in several respects.

4.1 Physiological and psychological realism

The computer architectures of GOFAI bear very little resemblance to the actual structure of the human brain (indeed, the multiple realisability thesis of functionalism says that they need not). Whereas the inside of a computer is made of a wide variety of bits and bobs – transistors, resistors, silicon chips, cables, optical disks etc. – the brain is mostly made out of vast numbers (100,000,000,000 by current estimates) of the same, very simple, component. Furthermore, most computers only perform operations serially – one at a time, although very quickly – whilst the brain, despite being made of *slow* components performs many operations in parallel (hence the first 'P' in 'PDP'). Indeed, this *must* be how the brain operates, for if it did not do so, it wouldn't be able to get anything done in the time available. Such an argument can be made more precise with what's come to be known as the *hundred-step argument* (see, e.g., Franklin, 1995 and the following formulation that comes from Cunningham, 2000, p.211):

1. It usually takes neurons just a couple of milliseconds (thousandths of a second) to fire.
2. But people can carry out some complex cognitive processes (like recognition) in about 100 milliseconds (about one tenth of a second).
3. If the brain were functioning serially, it would only have time to carry out at most 100 steps to complete a complex cognitive process.
4. But even relatively simple cognitive processes in a serial computer require thousands of steps.
5. Parallel systems, in contrast, can be carrying out many steps simultaneously and would therefore be able to complete thousands of steps in 100 milliseconds.
6. Therefore, in order for the brain to carry out the complex cognitive processes that it does in such a short time, it seems that it must operate as a parallel system.

This is a 'realist' consideration if ever there was one; it would take you too long to get anything done – you'd get eaten by the predator before you recognised it as such – if your brain worked in serial fashion like a computer. But taken by itself, the conclusion of the hundred-step argument can be accommodated by GOFAI; you'd just need lots of Turing Machines running in parallel. This, however, would miss the realist goal in a different way; individual brain cells are very simple, so if we are to build thinking machines on the model of the brain, then they should be constructed out of simple components too. This is the heart of the connectionist approach; as Rumelhart et al. (1986, p.ix) put it: "intelligence emerges from the interactions of large numbers of simple processing units". Or, like popstars and politicians, "The brain exemplifies the fact that it is all right to be very stupid if you're well connected" (Lloyd, 1989, p.92).

Despite their similarity in physical structure to the human brain, we should not be misled into thinking that connectionist models are only *anatomically* realistic. Connectionism is supposed to be a theory of *cognition* (not just of neurophysiology) and so at least some motivation for adopting the approach comes from what networks can *do*. As three of the pioneers of 1986-style connectionism write

> Though the appeal of PDP models is definitely enhanced by their physiological plausibility and neural inspiration, these are not the primary bases for their appeal to us. We are, after all, cognitive scientists, and PDP models appeal to us for psychological and computational reasons. They hold out the hope of offering computationally sufficient and psychologically accurate mechanistic accounts of the phenomena of human cognition which have eluded successful explication in conventional computational formalisms; and they have radically altered the way we think about the time-course of processing, the nature of representation and the mechanisms of learning (McClelland, Rumelhart and Hinton, 1986am p.11).

In what follows, I'll try and say something about all of these alleged advantages of the approach.

Typically, and as the name suggests, a connectionist model is built out of a collection of neuron-like units that are linked to each other by connections. In just the same way that neurons can fire at different rates, each unit in a connectionist model has a variable activity level: a measure of how 'excited' it is at any given time. Strictly, this activity level is a continuous variable between zero and one, but in practice, most connectionist networks are constructed so that the unit counts as 'on' if its activity level is above a certain threshold, and as 'off' if the level is below that threshold.

Connections between units can be either 'excitatory' or 'inhibitory'. When a connection is excitatory, an increase in activity level in the one unit will tend to increase the activity level in those to which it is connected. By contrast, if the connection is inhibitory, activity in the first unit tends to prevent the second from becoming active. Further, the connections between units can have different strengths (or 'weights') so

```
                    'Input    'Hidden   'Output
                    layer'    layer'    layer'
```

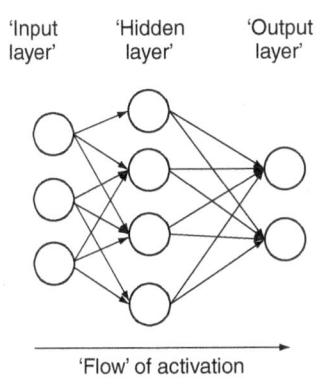

Figure 4.1 A schematic connectionist network

that the degree to which one unit excites or inhibits another varies as a function of both the strength of connection between them *and* their respective levels of activation. So, for example, if unit X is connected to unit Y with an excitatory connection of +0.7 and an excitation level of 0.8, then X contributes $(0.7 \times 0.8) = 0.56$ to Y's overall activity level.

Connectionist models are also usually structured into 'layers' corresponding, roughly, to the input-processing-output sequence that is already familiar from GOFAI (see Figure 4.1 for an impressionistic sketch). The input layer is built out of a collection of units that receive excitation from stimuli outside the system, and become active as a result (much like a transduction mechanism in a sensory organ). Similarly, the output layer is a collection of units that generate behaviour depending on their level of activity (much like neurons that control muscular contraction). In most connectionist models, there are also one or more 'hidden' layers of units in between the input and output layers (indeed, to refer to an earlier example, hidden layers are what allow the computation of the 'exclusive-or' function). These layers are all connected in such a way that activation can 'flow' from input to output; some input excites the first layer, the excitation travels through the weighted connections to the hidden layer(s) which also become active and convey their excitation to the output layer, which cause the system to produce some behaviour.

One of the most significant properties of connectionist models – a structural feature that gives rise to an important functional ability – is their capacity to learn. Recall that the influence of one unit on another is accounted for by the weight of the connection between them. Connectionist models are thus able to learn by *changing* the strengths of the connections between units. There are a number of different ways in which this weight change can be achieved, and they form a spectrum according to the extent to which they require 'supervision' (i.e., the require the modeller to act as 'teacher'). At the unsupervised end of the spectrum are 'associative' forms of learning. If, for example, two connected units are both active at the same time, the weight of the connection between them might be increased by a specified amount. In just the same way that Pavlov's dog famously came to associate two events that were simultaneously presented, association in connectionist models is between two simultaneously active units. This kind of learning – named 'Hebbian' learning after the neuroscientist Donald Hebb – might be characterised with the slogan "neurons that wire together, fire together".

The most obvious form of supervised learning is where a human designer directly specifies the connections and weights. A slightly less direct method – and by far the most common connectionist learning mechanism – is known as *backpropagation*. In this case, after the network gives a response to some input, information about how right or wrong the output was (more specifically, a quantitative measure of the difference between actual and ideal output) is fed back into the network and used to update the weights of the connections. The idea is that on future presentations of the input, the difference between ideal and actual behaviour can be minimised and the response will be closer to the target. The process is much like the children's party game where a supervisor calls out 'hot' or 'cold' depending on how close the players are to finding some object. Clearly, however, this requires someone to know – and calculate deviance from – the correct answer. Thus, supervised forms of learning come with a corresponding decrease in biological plausibility, since many forms of human learning don't always require a teacher.

McClelland et al. (1986a) give a nice example of a simple network constructed according to the principles mentioned thus far. The network is able to recognise four-letter words according to the perceptual features of letters that make them up. So, for example, the units in the input layer increase their activity according to different features of the presented individual letters – one responds to diagonal lines, as in K, R and N, another responds to vertical lines, as in L, E and P and so on. The input layer is connected to a hidden layer that corresponds to letters of the alphabet and the connections are arranged so that, for example, the diagonal-detector has excitatory connections to the hidden units for K, R and N, and inhibitory connections to the hidden units for O, P and L. Finally, the hidden units are connected to output units that represent a small set of four-letter words. The connections are arranged so that, for example, the hidden layer unit for E has an excitatory connection to the output unit for ABLE and TIME, but an inhibitory connection to the output unit for TRAP and CART. Thus, when the input units are presented with a collection of letters such as W, O, R and K, they become active if their feature is present. They consequently excite or inhibit the relevant hidden units, (the letters are 'recognized') and, in turn, the hidden units excite or inhibit the output layer so that the most active output unit is the one representing the four-letter word WORK. Thus, the model demonstrates how very simple units can be arranged to function as a network that can accomplish the cognitive-sounding task of word recognition. It will also be a useful model to return to, in the next section, when I discuss some of the other strengths of connectionist models.

This concludes our brief introduction to the motivation for and architecture of connectionist networks. As we've seen, the motivation can be understood as broadly 'realist' – connectionist models are structured in a way that is deliberately inspired by what we know of the brain's physiology, and this gives rise to some features (including parallelism and the ability to learn) that are clearly significant for cognitive science. In the next section, we'll look at a way in which connectionist models depart significantly from their GOFAI predecessors, and thus permit a kind of 'realism' at the *cognitive* level too.

4.2 Representation reconsidered

As with GOFAI, connectionism subscribes to the idea that the mind works by creating, storing and manipulating *representations*, where these are broadly construed as internal 'stand-ins' for external states of affairs that permit us to reason about what is absent, distal or non-occurrent. Where the two approaches part company, however, concerns the precise *nature* of these representations; the connectionists think that the 'psychological accuracy' of their models arises precisely because of their conception of representation.

Earlier (in Chapter 2.1) we considered the Representational Theory of Mind as a root of the GOFAI approach. We supposed that the mind contained many different 'boxes' – corresponding to beliefs, desires and intentions – and that these boxes could be filled with 'postcards' inscribed with the propositions that are believed, desired and intended. It's no great leap from that 'boxological' conception or mind to the computer architectures of memory registers and symbol-strings that underlie GOFAI. One important feature of this account of processing, however, is that representations are *local* in the sense that each 'stand-in' is a unique inscription stored in a specific place. This kind of information processing and storage system is very familiar in everyday life; dictionaries, filing cabinets, diaries etc. all store information in a precise *location* that is uniquely identified by its *address*.

In connectionist systems, however, a representation is said to be 'distributed' (that's the 'D' in 'PDP'). The internal 'stand-in' for some external state of affairs or piece of information is in fact a pattern of activity that is spread out across a collection of units in a network. This model of information processing and storage is much less familiar in everyday life, but one can clarify it by way of analogy. Consider, for example, an audio spectrum meter (or a graphic equaliser) where different vertical bars correspond to the components of a sound at different frequencies. Here, we might say that the overall sound is *represented* by the total pattern displayed across all of the different bars and one can manipulate different parts of the sound (to emphasise, say, the bassy frequencies at 50Hz or the trebly ones at 14KHz). A 'localist' analogue would be something like an old-fashioned stereo with a single 'tone' dial that simply turns from 'bass' to 'treble'. Or, imagine a choir singing a chord that ranges over several octaves; the total sound depends on the overall pattern of notes and intensities sung by the individual members. Similarly, in a connectionist model, some piece of information (say, the proposition 'Reading Football Club will win the FA cup this year') is represented by a distinctive pattern of activation of a collection of many units somewhere in the network.

This mode of representation gives rise to some of the most significant – and 'psychologically accurate' – abilities of connectionist models. In short, connectionist models are better than GOFAI accounts at capturing what we might think of as the 'soft' aspects of human cognition because they work with representations that are more like statistical averages and continua than the hard-and-fast, all-or-nothing localist rules and representations of GOFAI.

First up, connectionist models are 'damage resistant' in a couple of different respects. A neural network can cope with missing or noisy input data precisely because input representations are distributed. So, to return to the above word-recognition model, suppose that the input is W, O, R and the fourth letter is partially obscured so that it is ambiguous between an R and a K. The network can still give the correct identification of 'WORK'. Here's what happens:

> [T]he activations of the detectors for R and K start out growing together, as the feature detectors below them become activated. As

these detectors become active, they and the active letter detectors for W, O, and R in the other positions start to activate detectors for words which have these letters in them and to inhibit detectors for words which do not have these letters... WORK becomes more active [and] sends feedback to the letter level, reinforcing the activations of the W, O, R and K in the corresponding positions. In the fourth position, this feedback gives K the upper hand over R, and eventually the stronger activation of the K detector allows it to dominate the pattern of activation, suppressing the R detector completely. (McClelland et al., 1986a, pp.21–23)

Putting it anthropomorphically, it's as if the network thinks 'Well, it *could* be WORK or WORR... but since there's no such word as WORR, the correct answer must be WORK'. Needless to say, this kind of 'fault tolerance' is both a notable feature of human cognition and a difficult challenge for localist information storage systems. In the case of the latter, if part of the address for some information is missing, you simply cannot retrieve it: if you don't know how to spell someone's surname, then you cannot find their phone number in the directory.

Similarly, connectionist models can cope with damage to the system itself. In the above example, if one of the units in the input layer were damaged, this would not lead to a total and abrupt cessation in the network's performance. Even if the diagonal-recognition unit ceases to function, the continued operation of units for vertical and horizontal lines etc. still allows the network to recognise the correct word, albeit with a slightly lower activation level in the output units (or, as we might say, with slightly less confidence). The performance of the network *gradually* decreases in proportion to the amount of damage it has incurred. This is known as 'graceful degradation' and, once again, is in marked contrast to the (catastrophic) drop in performance following damage to localist systems. In the case of the latter, if there is damage to the place in which some information is stored, you no longer have any access to that information at all (performance immediately drops to zero): if you spill coffee onto today's page in your diary, then you no longer know what time the meeting is.

Both these aspects of damage resistance – fault tolerance and graceful degradation – are tremendously important for real biological cognitive systems. For one thing, we move around in a noisy, complex and changing world, and the ability to cope with less-than-perfect perceptual data is of paramount importance. Second, the actual hardware out of which our brains are made *requires* graceful degradation. Neurons are pretty unreliable, and they die off with alarming regularity, so it's just as well that such damage does not lead to a catastrophic drop in performance. Indeed, we know for a fact that human cognitive systems display graceful degradation, because performance drops gradually following neurological damage. The brain makes up for the fact that it's built out of shoddy components by having a great number of them work in tandem.

These are, as it were, the ways in which neural networks can overcome obstacles that are put in their paths. But connectionist models also display some positive abilities as a result of their use of distributed representations. Very closely related to fault tolerance is the ability of neural networks to *generalise* (i.e., to respond appropriately to new or unanticipated input; exactly what happened when 'W, O, R, K/R' was presented). This is because both fault tolerance and generalisation are examples of a kind of pattern completion; networks respond to an input pattern that was not in their training set according to its statistical similarity to something that they *have* encountered before. Here are two examples from McClelland and Rumelhart (1986). One network, having learnt how to react to Rover and to Fido, responded in a similar fashion when presented with novel dog stimuli, and was even able to extract a dog 'prototype' from the training data set. Another network learnt to distinguish dogs, cats and bagels, and not only categorised new images correctly, but also treated dogs and cats as *more similar* to each other than either of them is to a bagel.

As a result of the ability to learn and generalise, the type of memory which one finds in connectionist models is quite different from that found in GOFAI. In a standard computer – and, indeed, any localist information storage system – if you want to access some piece of information you must locate the address before retrieving the information stored there. In a computer, this 'address' is the file name and the directory path and in a telephone directory, it's the spelling of the person's name. Thus, information is what we might call 'location-addressable'; you have to know where to look before you can find something. Connectionist models can work, as it were, the other way round; they can retrieve a stored piece of information by using part of its content as a kind of cue for accessing the rest of it. They are thus described as 'content-addressable'.

As we saw in the example of fault tolerance, the distributed representations used by connectionist models allow them to fill in missing pieces of information. In the case of connectionist memory, networks are often able to reconstruct a whole pattern if they are given only part of that pattern as input. But this highlights an interesting point; unlike GOFAI and localist representation storage systems, memory is not really a process of 'retrieval' in a connectionist model. The distinction between 'memory' and 'processing' in Turing-Machine inspired GOFAI (or between gigabytes and gigahertz if you're a computer salesperson) is not really viable in neural networks since both features arise from the activity of the very same set of units with weighted connections. As Bechtel and Abrahamsen (2002, p.50) put it:

> in connectionist networks, remembering is carried out by the same means as making inferences; the system fills in missing pieces of information. As far as the system's processing is concerned, there is no difference between reconstructing a previous state, and constructing a totally new one.

Nonetheless, once again, it's pretty clear that both the ability to generalise and content-addressable memory are ubiquitous and important features of human cognition. We generalise from past experience to new situations with so little effort that it's almost problematic (stereotyping and other well-documented common mistakes in reasoning are an overextension of this natural propensity). Although many people (the present author included) tend to rely on external (localist) memory stores like to-do lists and filing-cabinets – more of which in Chapter 7 – intracranial content-addressable memory is still utterly indispensable. I might be able to recall the name of a student by thinking backwards from which class they took and what grade they got, but to do so with my hard-drive and filing cabinet would be a very difficult task indeed. So, to the extent that neural networks are 'psychologically accurate' in adequately reproducing these features, the connectionist approach appears to be on to something.

It must be noted – especially now that twenty-first century technology is so much more advanced – that none of these features are *impossible* to achieve with a classical computer. We're all now familiar with the way in which Google helpfully points out our search query's spelling mistakes before hazarding a guess at what we *really* meant, and this is surely a display of fault tolerance, pattern completion and generalisation of some kind. Further the development of powerful search algorithms make content-addressable memory *practically* possible on desktop operating systems; some 'productivity' experts even recommend against using a filing system for e-mail because good search techniques within your e-mail client are a quicker way to retrieve something by its content anyway ("Bob + Friday + curriculum + meeting" ought to be enough to find the message without wasting time squirreling it away in a nested system of directories). The point is, however, that though producing content-addressable memory and damage resistance on classical computers is possible, it's also *difficult*; it takes incredibly talented programmers a great deal of financial and computational resources to develop good search-engines, and GOFAI must *fake* the 'softness' of cognition with very many 'hard' rules. By contrast, as I hope to have shown in this section, damage resistance, generalisation and content-addressable memory come easily to neural networks as a *natural* consequence of their architecture. To this extent, connectionists argue, such networks are *better* models of human cognition than those of GOFAI. So, let's take a look at some successful models in action and see what we can learn from them.

4.3 Some connectionist models

The last two-and-a-half decades have seen the publication of literally hundreds of connectionist models dealing with a wide variety of cognitive tasks. The three models I propose to examine in this section may look somewhat dated, so I owe the reader an explanation; all of them exemplify 1986-style connectionism. Exciting recent work has departed significantly from the core of this approach, either by constructing GOFAI-connectionist hybrids, or by using real-time continuous networks and analysing them with the resources of dynamical systems theory (DST). These are matters to which we will return (e.g., in Chapter 6.4). For now, let's restrict ourselves to some famous early cases, in order to see what lessons may be drawn from them.

4.3.1 Pattern recognition: the mine/rock detector

Recall that neural networks are particularly good at pattern recognition and categorisation tasks. One very famous connectionist model, built by Gorman and Sejnowski (1988a,b), used these abilities to construct a network that learnt to distinguish between underwater mines and rocks based on their sonar echo. This is no easy task; with considerable training and practice, human sonar technicians can draw the distinction, but – like the infamous 'chicken sexers' who can tell male from female chicks without really knowing how they do it – the discriminable differences are so subtle that it's difficult to say what exactly is being detected. It turns out that neural networks can learn (or, better, *be taught*) how do it as well as, if not better than, humans.

First, to echo (ha!) my earlier example, the sonar signal was encoded as an input stimulus rather like the graphic equaliser on a stereo system. Each sound is divided up and represented as a set of 60 values, according to the level of energy at different frequencies, so that it has a distinctive 'fingerprint': a distributed representation across the 60 input units of the network. The corresponding activation is then fed forward through sets of weighted connections, to a layer of 24 'hidden' units, and onto the output layer. The output layer consists of only two units – effectively a 'mine' unit and a 'rock' unit – such that, ideally, the network's 'answer' would be <1,0> when a rock is heard and <0,1> when a mine is heard. A sketch of the network and its input stimulus can be seen in Figure 4.2.

Gorman and Sejnowski (1988a) collected several hundred examples of sonar echoes (of both mines and rocks) with which to train the network, and the 'backpropagation' learning technique was employed. The network was presented with the samples one-by-one, and its actual set of output values was compared to what it *ought* to have been, given the input. The difference between actual and ideal output was then calculated and this measure of error was used to make small adjustments to the weights of the connections between units (so, e.g., if the network gives <.31,.82> when the answer should have been <0,1> the connection to

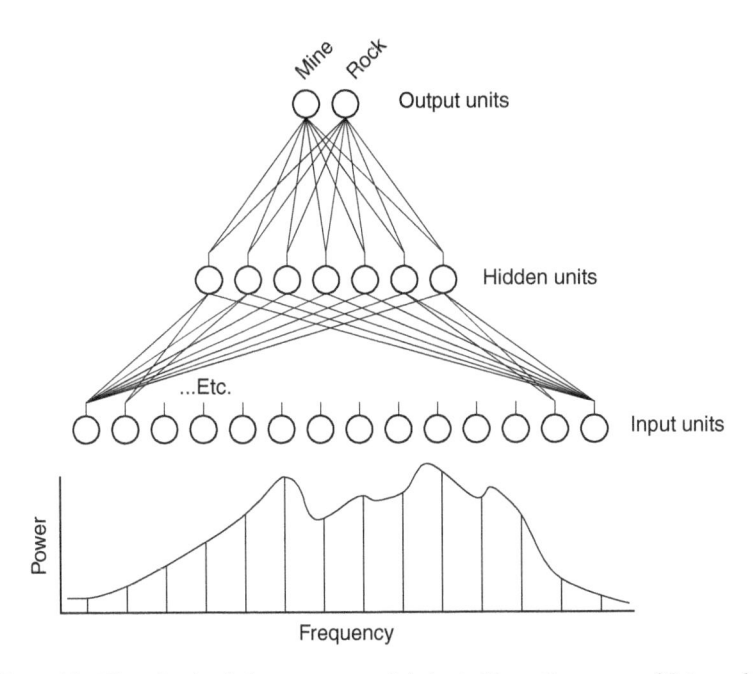

Figure 4.2 The mine/rock detector network (adapted from Gorman and Sejnowski 1988a, p.76)

the first unit might be weakened a little, and the connection to the second strengthened). After several hundred training cycles, Gorman and Sejnowski found that not only could the network classify the training samples themselves with 100% accuracy, but that it could also correctly classify around 90% of *new* samples that it had never encountered before. Further, Gorman and Sejnowski (1988b) report that in a direct comparison between human classifiers and the network, the latter's performance was better by a margin of 100% to 91%.

This example shows that pattern recognition and generalisation are in fact much more broadly applicable than one might have initially thought. Given that a wide variety of human cognitive abilities can be understood as instances of pattern recognition, then, neural networks are naturally equipped with the tools for modelling them. Second, we may be able to gain some insight into what is actually occurring by analysing the weights of the trained network. Churchland (1988, p.160) suggests that the hidden units in the network encode or represent "some fairly abstract structural features of mine echoes, features they all have, or all approximate, despite their superficial diversity". This is borne out by Gorman and Sejnowski's original analysis wherein the hidden units are not responding to some specific frequency ("Rocks are bass-y, mines are treble-y"), but rather to some 'shift-invariant' feature such as the overall proportion of frequencies either side of a variable peak in intensity. Thus, it is quite tempting to make some inferences about what might be going on in the human case. It wouldn't be too much of a leap to say that the hidden units correspond to some unconscious processing; even though humans can't quite tell you how they're doing it, there is an underlying, tractable regularity, hidden from introspective awareness. What's interesting, though, is that even if we can come up with some rule that correctly *describes* the behaviour, the system's performance does not arise as a result of it *following* that rule, since the rule is not encoded anywhere. This is a marked contrast with GOFAI and one that will become especially apparent with the next example.

4.3.2 Language: past-tense learning

Given GOFAI's central emphasis on both the language-like nature of thought and the replication of linguistic performance by computers, it is not surprising that connectionists would try to beat GOFAI at its own game. Indeed, there have been a great many connectionist models of various language-related phenomena, and, given connectionism's emphasis on learning, these often concern linguistic *development*.

Rumelhart and McClelland (1986) developed a connectionist model that learnt to form the past tense of English verbs. As we saw in Chapter 2.1.2, the generative grammar tradition in linguistics was based on the idea that linguistic performance is generated by a subconscious set of rules, much like a computer program. Rumelhart and McClelland (1986, p.217) challenge this claim, arguing that their connectionist approach shows that:

> lawful behavior and judgments may be produced by a mechanism in which there is no explicit representation of the rule. Instead, we suggest that the mechanisms that process language and make judgments of grammaticality are constructed in such a way that their performance is characterizable by rules, but that the rules themselves are not written in explicit form anywhere in the mechanism.

Learning to form the past tense of verbs in English is characterised by what developmental psychologists call 'U-shaped learning'. At an early stage, children use a small number of regular and irregular verbs in the past tense, but they do so mostly correctly. Over time, as a child's vocabulary grows, they use more past-tense verbs, but get a greater proportion wrong. At this second stage, a child is capable of generating a past tense for an invented word (e.g., 'gurk'→'gurked') but incorrectly adds regular past tense endings to verbs that they had previously used correctly (e.g., 'come'→'comed'). Thus, the errors are described as 'over-regularisation' and the performance is taken (especially by classical cognitive scientists) to indicate that the child has implicit knowledge of a rule (something like "add an '-ed' for past tenses") that they're applying across the board. At the final stage (and into adulthood), regular and irregular forms coexist, as if the child has understood both the rule and its exceptions. Thus, it's called 'U-shaped' learning because if you imagine a graph where the horizontal axis is time, and the vertical axis is the percentage of past tenses correctly formed, the resulting developmental plot looks like the letter U; correct, then over-regularised, then correct again.

Rumelhart and McClelland set out to replicate this developmental trajectory with a connectionist model. The details of the network's operation and training are complex (for a very good summary, see Bechtel and Abrahamsen, 2002, pp.120–135), but in short, it involved a four-layer network at the heart of which was a two-layer pattern-associator for learning the association between present and past tense. It was trained on 506 English verbs, divided into high- medium- and low-frequency verbs (depending on how common they are in ordinary speech), and with a mix of regular and irregular verbs in each. A supervised error-correction mechanism was used to compare actual with desired output, and adjust the weights accordingly. In this case, it should be noted, the supervised learning undermines the network's biological plausibility to a much lesser extent, since so much of language learning is indeed facilitated by a parent/teacher.

After ten repetitions of the ten high-frequency verbs (intended to mimic the first stage), the network was "quite good" at producing the correct past tenses. Following the introduction of the 410 medium frequency verbs (mimicking the second stage), performance dropped somewhat, especially for irregular verbs. After 190 more learning trials, the model achieved "almost errorless" performance (stage 3) at which point the low-frequency verbs were added into the mix. To put it briefly, the network did indeed display the U-shaped learning that characterises human language acquisition. Rumelhart and McClelland also found that most of the errors encountered during the second stage were over-regularisations of irregular verbs, just like in the human case. And finally, they were able to make some novel predictions concerning features of human performance that had not been observed at the time; for instance, that 'double inflections' (e.g., where the regular -ed ending is misapplied to a correctly formed irregular past-tense stem, as in 'come'→'camed') will be more common for verbs ending in /p/ and /k/ sounds, for example, 'keep'→'kepted' or 'stick'→'stucked'.[2]

The lesson to be learnt, according to Rumelhart and McClelland, is that the connectionist approach to this aspect of language acquisition is both *viable* in its own right and *preferable* in comparison to GOFAI. On the one hand it is possible to simulate known features of human linguistic performance using the architecture of a neural network. One does not need a computational system of specialised components, since the behaviour can be generated by a network of homogeneous simple units. On the other hand, the model challenges the GOFAI view that linguistic development consists in figuring out and applying a large number of symbolic rules. As Rumelhart and McClelland (1986, p.267) put it:

> We have, we believe, provided a distinct alternative to the view that children learn the rules of English past-tense formation in any explicit sense. We have shown that a reasonable account of the acquisition of past tense can be provided without recourse to the notion of a 'rule' as anything more than a *description* of the language. We have shown that, for this case, there is no *induction problem*. The child need not figure out what the rules are, nor even that there are rules.

4.3.3 Disorders: network models of schizophrenia

One final example of the connectionist approach – less widely discussed, but no less interesting – comes from the insight it may provide concerning various psychological disorders. Given that nobody really attributes genuine intelligence or mentality to the neural networks studied thus far (they're really all examples of *weak* AI), there are no ethical issues concerning inflicting damage upon the networks. So if it's possible to 'injure' neural networks and thereby simulate abnormal cognitions and behaviours, we might derive a better insight into both their aetiology and their prospects for treatment.

One such application comes from a tremendously interesting set of studies from Hoffman and McGlashan (1993, 1997, 2001), concerning schizophrenia. Some of the most well-known of the ('positive') symptoms of schizophrenia include delusions, cognitive disorganisation (disordered thoughts and speech) and hallucinations in all five senses; Hoffman and McGlashan constructed networks that not only replicated some of these symptoms, but also suggested an explanation for how they arise, and provided testable (and confirmed) predictions about the efficacy of certain treatments.

Following both post-mortem examinations and neuroimaging studies, one prominent account of schizophrenia suggests that reduced connectivity between different areas of the cortex may be responsible. This is consistent with the typical age of onset – late adolescence to early adulthood – at which point 'synaptic pruning' (the gradual whittling away of excess neural connectivity developed in childhood) normally ceases. It is hypothesised that schizophrenia may result from a pathological extension of this normal reduction in brain interconnectivity. Hoffman and McGlashan took this theoretical perspective as their starting point and attempted to replicate such changes in neural networks.

In one study, a 'pruning rule' was applied to a network that had been developed to display content-addressable memory. The rule eliminated those connections that were simultaneously both long-distance and low-weight, like a kind of 'neural Darwinism': survival of the fittest connections. At higher levels of pruning Hoffman and McGlashan found that the network began to display behaviours that were similar to the symptoms of cognitive disorder in schizophrenia, including the erroneous 'merging' of distinct learnt memories, the re-creation of patterns of activation that did not correspond to *any* learnt memory, and the exacerbation of these features when the input was particularly noisy or ambiguous.

Concerning the famous auditory hallucinations that occur in around 70% of individuals with schizophrenia, there are two competing hypotheses. One view suggests that auditory hallucinations arise as the result of pathological activity in brain areas that control speech perception. An alternative view is that auditory hallucinations are a pathological misidentification of ordinary 'inner speech'. Hoffman and McGlashan (1997) examined the former hypothesis, using a neural network that had previously been developed as a model of speech perception and that could identify a small set of words from auditory signals. Again, they applied a pruning rule that eliminated any connections between two hidden layers if the weight was below a certain threshold. At lower levels of pruning, network performance actually *increased*; the network got better at 'filling in the gaps' so as to display the kinds of pattern-completion and fault tolerance one would expect. However, Hoffman and McGlashan found that at higher levels of pruning, this 'filling in' became pathological and resulted in the activation of the output layer when no auditory input had been provided (i.e., identification of words that weren't said: hallucinatory speech percepts). Erroneous activation of the word *won't*, for example, occurs predictably after words it had followed during the training set, as if hallucinations non-randomly emerge from specific linguistic expectations.

Whilst the possibility of simulating schizophrenic symptoms in a neural network – in a way that is in accordance with prevailing theories of the disorder – is an important success in its own right, what's most significant is that the model itself also suggests a possibility for therapeutic treatment. Given the consistency between neural network studies and the hypothesis that auditory hallucinations arise from excess activity in brain areas that control speech perception, Hoffman et al. (2000) set out to directly reduce activity in those areas. Using repetitive transcranial magnetic stimulation (rTMS), where a low frequency magnetic field is passed over portions of the left hand side of the brain, it was found that hallucinations in individuals with schizophrenia could be significantly reduced for up to seven weeks following treatment. Thus, not only is the connectionist approach capable of explaining certain types of (pathological) cognitive activity, it can also help in the development of treatments for such disorders.

———◇———

These three relatively simple models present some striking new considerations in our study of the mechanics of mind. Let's wrap up this section by commenting on two: how we might apply the taxonomy of the different varieties of AI (developed in Chapter 1.3) to the models discussed above, and how they exemplify the contrast between connectionism and GOFAI.

In the case of all three examples, Minsky's description of AI – "the science of making machines do things that would require intelligence if done by men" – may be applied here, but with a notably different flavour. It's certainly the case that all three examples accomplish tasks that require intelligence when done by humans. Indeed, in the case of the past-tense generator and the schizophrenic networks, the fact that they replicate human performance *so closely* may be taken as evidence in their favour. At the very least, in these cases, we're dealing with a kind of *weak* AI. This conclusion is further strengthened by the fact that both models make further predictions, either about other linguistic phenomena we might expect to observe, or about treatments we might expect to be efficacious. In the case of the mine/rock detector, however, the model isn't really even supposed to provide any insight into how trained human sonar operators work; it would be a stretch to describe it as weak AI. But neither is the concern with replicating human performance for merely technological ends: doing '4D' jobs so that we don't have to. Rather it's more of a 'proof-of-concept' that shows how such discrimination tasks can be accomplished in brain-like architectures made of many very simple components. In fact, we might also say this for the past-tense generator and the schizophrenic networks, since in both cases, their creators are keen to point out the contrasts between connectionism and the GOFAI approach.

In these network models, there is massive parallelism with no central processor. We've seen that representations are distributed, rather than local, and that it's difficult to speak of them being 'stored' anywhere or 'retrieved' from memory. Rather, a representation just is a kind of disposition for a certain collection of units to take on a particular pattern of activation, and memory 'recall' is more like 'reconstruction', where the very same set of units and connection weights are responsible for 'encoding' (if that's the right phrase) *all* of the different pieces of information that the network processes. Finally, perhaps most importantly, there is no 'program', so to speak. The sense in which networks could be described as 'following' rules is very different from the way in which the same could be said of GOFAI systems. The latter do so – like a chef following a recipe – by consulting the algorithm and following its orders. Connectionist systems are better seen as *instantiating* rules, rather than *following* them (see Hatfield, 1991). The 'rules' are more like a description – rather than a cause – of the cognitive phenomena.

4.4 Connectionism and the mind-body problem

What does the connectionist approach to AI show concerning the mind-body problem and the various positions on it? If all of the phenomena of human cognition were reproducible in neural networks (say, if connectionists obtained a complete wiring diagram of the brain, and subsequently constructed one), then this would undoubtedly point to the truth of some kind of physicalism. But *which* kind of physicalism? There are considerations in favour of three quite different strands.

First, as I hinted at the end of the previous Chapter when considering the systems reply to Searle's Chinese Room thought experiment, we might be tempted to describe the cognitive properties of connectionist models as 'emergent' in some sense. This is because the concept of emergence is often construed as a way of trying to make philosophical sense of the old aphorism 'the whole is greater than the sum of its parts' and in neural networks, we find *systems* displaying properties that are not possessed by their *components*. Whilst a network, suitably constructed and trained, may display fault tolerance, content-addressable memory or hallucinations of a sort, the same can not be said for *any* of the units of which it is composed. Thus, perhaps, like the sponginess of a cake (that is absent from the eggs, flour, sugar and butter that compose it), it might be claimed that cognitive properties of a network (or, indeed, of the brain) are 'emergent' properties that are absent from the parts.

Such a claim – though attractive in some respects – is problematic for at least two reasons. Emergentism is usually understood to be a kind of *non-reductive* physicalist position on the mind-body problem. For it claims that whilst mental properties *depend on* physical properties, they cannot be explained (or explained *away*) as such. If mind is emergent, in this sense, cognitive science would require autonomous 'cognitive-level' laws that cannot be re-formulated in (i.e., reduced to) the concepts and properties of neurophysiology. This is clearly not the case for the sponginess of a cake; whilst it's true that eggs, flour etc., don't *display* sponginess, we can nonetheless fully explain how sponginess comes into being by noting that the batter created by mixing these ingredients tends to incorporate small bubbles of air, which expands upon heating and becomes trapped as the cake mix sets. Note that here, we have actually provided a reductive explanation; we've shown how the 'higher level' property of sponginess arises with an account in 'lower level' terms. The same should be said for connectionist models. Whilst it's true that the network displays properties that the units do not, in all three cases above the model is construed as providing an *explanation* of the overall system behaviour; if you want to know *why* hallucinations occur in individuals with schizophrenia, Hoffman and McGlashan's network is one possible answer.

To the extent that networks provide explanations of cognitive phenomena, then, it may be better to regard connectionist models as supporting a kind of reductive physicalism. The classic example of reduction given in philosophy of science concerns the fact that the temperature of a gas can be fully explained in terms of its mean molecular kinetic energy (hence, thermodynamics is reducible to statistical mechanics). Similarly, we might say, if cognitive phenomena (like content-addressable memory and hallucinations) are fully explained in terms of neural (network) structure, then intelligence is reducible to neurophysiology.[3]

If we want to draw this conclusion about the relation between the *human* mind and brain on the basis of connectionism's relative successes, however, we face a problem. Whilst connectionist models share many similarities with neural structure (parallelism, changing degrees of activity of large numbers of homogeneous units etc.), there are many important differences. The biological *im*plausibility of 1986-style connectionism may thus lead us to reject it as an argument for reductive physicalism about the mind.

Bechtel and Abrahamsen (2002, p.341ff) provide an excellent discussion of some of the respects in which the structure and function of connectionist models depart from those of biological neural systems. Whereas connectionist 'units' are assigned activation values, real neural activity is in terms of spiking frequencies. Biological neural connections are intricately mediated by a wide variety of different neurotransmitters, unlike the simple summation carried out by units in neural nets; the role of neurochemistry is ignored by connectionists. But perhaps the most obviously biologically implausible aspect of connectionism is its use of the 'backpropagation' learning method (discussed above on page 82). Biological neurons do not compute error signals because they do not know the 'correct' answer in order to calculate the difference between actual and ideal output. And even if they *did*, the brain (with the possible exception of the cerebellum) does not contain the recurrent connections needed to transmit an error signal back through the network. Given these differences, the possibility of using the success of connectionism to motivate a reductionist mind-brain identity theory looks decidedly slim.

In response, some have formulated a kind of 'microfunctionalism' (see, e.g., Clark, 1989; Smolensky, 1988), whereby one claims that although real and artificial neural networks do have significant *physical* differences, their causal-functional profiles are sufficiently similar to warrant conclusions about the former drawn on the basis of the latter. On this view, even if connectionism is totally wrong about how backpropagation is *achieved*, since various kinds of learning by error correction *are* found in biological cognitive systems, there's enough of a functional similarity that we needn't worry about the physical differences. On this view, connectionist models are, like GOFAI models, an abstraction from the actual physical machinery of real biological cognitive systems. They're not *as much* of an abstraction – they are, after all, more similar to the brain than Turing Machines – but to reiterate a point made earlier on, they're supposed to be more than just accounts of neurophysiology.

In the next chapter, we'll explore some of these issues construed as criticisms of the connectionist approach. On the one hand, it has been argued that connectionism implies something even stronger than reductive physicalism: eliminativism – the view that there are *no such things* as mental states like beliefs, desires and intentions. Others have argued that since connectionist models cannot display or explain some language-like properties of thought, GOFAI remains the best account of cognition *as such*, with connectionism relegated to a story about how GOFAI systems could be *implemented*.

5
Criticisms and Consequences of the Connectionist Approach

In this chapter, I want to examine two famous discussions of philosophical consequences of the connectionist approach. Naturally, these two discussions are but a small selection of the responses and criticisms that in fact have been made to the development of connectionism. But I have selected these two discussions in particular because they touch on themes that have already been – and will continue to be – important to the particular account being presented in this book. They concern connectionism's implications for the mind-body problem, and the relationship between connectionism and GOFAI (with the latter *also* setting the stage for a subsequent discussion of connectionism's relationship to the dynamical systems approach to cognitive science and AI).

I describe these arguments as 'discussions' because whilst they are often understood as *criticisms* of PDP, such a reading is not mandatory; one could agree wholeheartedly with their premises and conclusions, and still think that connectionism is a powerful, pursuitworthy and preferable alternative to GOFAI. That's to say that we're left in the interesting rhetorical position whereby one could *embrace* the conclusions of both discussions, without actually viewing those conclusions as problematic. One philosopher's reason is another's *reductio*, as they say... or in this case, *vice-versa*.

5.1 Connectionism, folk psychology and eliminativism

If connectionism is correct, then there are no such things as beliefs and we should remove references to them from our scientific and commonsense vocabulary. This is the striking conclusion of an argument put forward by Ramsey, Stich and Garon (1990), that connectionism entails 'eliminativism' about the propositional attitudes postulated by folk psychology. Before turning to how they propose to support and defend this claim, let's pause to clarify some of the philosophical terminology.

'Eliminativism' in general is the view that some class of entities does not exist, and that in virtue of this fact, references to them should be eliminated from our scientific and common-sensical vocabulary. In eighteenth-century chemistry, for example, it was widely held that heat consisted of a substance called 'caloric fluid' that would flow from hotter to colder objects, and would thus explain the thermal properties of objects. Modern chemists are eliminativists about caloric fluid; they hold that it does not exist – and cannot be identified with or explained as something else – and thus has no place in our accepted ontology. Eliminativism in philosophy of mind has a similar flavour and is usually applied to certain classes of mental states. It is the claim that a mature neuroscience will have no need for such concepts (even as a kind of linguistic shortcut), and thus will permit us to remove them from our scientific and everyday ontology. The view is famously associated with the philosophers Paul and Patricia Churchland, and in a recent interview with them, we are given a glimpse of what it might be like if eliminativism took hold. Patricia arrives home from a stressful faculty meeting, and says:

> Paul, don't speak to me, my serotonin levels have hit bottom, my brain is awash in glucocorticoids, my blood vessels are full of adrenaline, and if it weren't for my endogenous opiates I'd have driven the car into a tree on the way home. My dopamine levels need lifting. Pour me a Chardonnay, and I'll be down in a minute. (Quoted in MacFarquhar, 2007, p.69)

It's also worth pausing to be a bit more explicit about what we mean by 'folk psychology'. I mentioned it earlier in passing as a kind of 'common-sense' psychology (indeed, the two expressions are often used synonymously), but to be more precise, let's say that it's the set of (mostly implicit) laws and principles that we ('the folk') use to explain our own and other people's behaviour in everyday life. Suppose you see somebody running across the university campus and you ask why. A folk-psychological explanation might say something like 'She wants to get to class on time, and thinks that she won't make it unless she runs.' Independently of whether this particular explanation is actually correct, it's the *kind* of (everyday, natural) account that we mean when we refer to folk psychology.

In addition to its common-sensical feel, notice three further features of the above example. First, the explanation is framed in terms of what the person *believes* (that she won't make it unless she runs) and what she *desires* (to get to class on time). For this reason – its being couched in terms of propositional attitudes – folk psychology is also sometimes referred to as 'belief-desire psychology', and these beliefs and desires are the entities targeted for removal by eliminativists. Second, it should be noted that folk-psychological explanations are, more often than not, tremendously successful. Their predictions are correct far more often than can be attributed to chance and are far better than could be achieved with any other theory of psychology. We make arrangements to meet friends, or predict the actions of other drivers on the motorway, based on an attribution of beliefs and desires to them, and our predictions are usually right. They're right far more than they would be if we tried to make them on the basis of the behaviourist principles of conditioning and reinforcement histories, or the Freudian account of interactions between id, ego and superego. Folk psychology, by these lights, is a pretty good theory.[1]

Further, it's no accident that the beliefs and desires (i.e., the propositional attitudes) of folk psychology bear a striking resemblance to the representations that are created, manipulated and stored according to GOFAI. The 'representational theory of mind' (RTM; see Chapter 2.1.3) is a picture of cognitive processing that's common to folk psychology *and* classical cognitive science. Indeed it would be fair to say that, in its infancy, cognitive science was often viewed as a way of making folk psychology scientific. Earlier, I suggested that theories of mind have a tendency to mirror the hottest technology at the time of their formulation, hence the mind-as-computer picture that emerged in the 1950s after the development of the computer itself. But, given the close similarity between RTM/GOFAI and folk psychology, it's at least arguable that the influence goes the other way around in this case; maybe we built computers that way because that's how we, the folk, *already* think the mind works. If I may be permitted to quote myself again:

> the roots of RTM go back long before the computer revolution. RTM is a picture of human nature that's implicit in folk psychology. Maybe the similarity between computers and RTM is due to the fact that we constructed computers to function after our own image of ourselves: having set out to build thinking machines, we were guided by our own theories of what it is to think. (Kukla and Walmsley, 2006, p.139)

Finally, Ramsey, Stich and Garon point out that they are only attempting to defend a *conditional* claim: *if* connectionism is correct, then eliminativism about propositional attitudes follows. They state that they are not attempting to argue for the truth or falsity of either connectionism or eliminativism; they are just concerned with the relationship between the two. Thus, even if the argument is sound, its significance could run in one of two directions. If you think eliminativism is false, then the fact that it follows from connectionism would be a *reductio ad absurdum* of the latter. By contrast, if you think eliminativism is true (on some other grounds), then the fact that it follows from connectionism would be a mark in *favour* of the latter. Either way, if Ramsey, Stich and Garon's argument is sound, then we have an interesting consequence for the mind-body problem that follows directly from consideration of a particular approach to AI.

The argument that Ramsey, Stich and Garon put forward requires an even closer look at the entities postulated by folk psychology. In short, Ramsey, Stich and Garon's argument is that; (a) according to folk psychology, propositional attitudes have a certain set of features, but (b) connectionist networks lack these features. The mismatch between connectionism and folk psychology, they argue, means that if one is correct the other has to go, hence their conditional conclusion and the possibility of reading it as a criticism of connectionism if one wishes to preserve or substantiate folk psychology.

According to Ramsey, Stich and Garon the most crucial tenets of folk psychology can be captured by the conjunction of three claims. First, propositional attitudes are supposed to be *functionally discrete* in that they can be lost, gained or activated one at a time, independently of each other. Second, they are *semantically interpretable* in that folk psychology makes law-like generalisations based on the semantic properties of beliefs (like what they *mean* or are *about*), and thus pick out natural kinds (such as the set of all individuals who believe that snow is white) on that basis. Finally, propositional attitudes are viewed as *causally efficacious* in that one's beliefs and desires cause other mental states and behaviour, and can be identified as such. Ramsey, Stich and Garon group these three properties together under the heading of 'propositional modularity'.

In order to support their argument that connectionist models *lack* all of these features, Ramsey, Stich and Garon use the example of a connectionist model that can provide judgements of the truth of various learnt propositions. The network had sixteen input units with which to encode a proposition under consideration, four units in the 'hidden' layer, and one output unit (where an activation close to 1 was interpreted as 'true' and close to 0 was interpreted as 'false'). Using the backpropagation method, they taught the network to give correct 'true' or 'false' answers to a set of sixteen different propositions (e.g., 'Dogs have fur', 'Cats have paws', 'Fish have legs'). Interestingly, as one might expect, the network was also able to give correct answers to propositions that it had not previously encountered, for example, returning 'true' for 'Cats have legs' and 'false' for 'Cats have scales'.

Given the discussion of the previous chapter, whilst it is presumably correct to say that the network stores information about the truth value of various propositions, *locating* that information in a way that corresponds to functional discreteness, causal efficacy or semantic interpretability is very difficult. Because the network stores information in a distributed and holistic way – that is, the very same set of units and connection weights is responsible for *all sixteen* learnt propositions – there is no way of saying which state or part of the network represents any *particular* proposition. Ramsey, Stich and Garon thus write that, concerning the connectionist net,

> Whenever information is extracted from [the network], by giving it an input string and seeing whether it computes a high or a low value for the output unit, *many* connection strengths, *many* biases and *many* hidden units play a role in the computation. And any particular weight or unit or bias will help to encode information about *many* different propositions. It simply makes no sense to ask whether or not the representation of a particular proposition plays a causal role in the network's computation. (1990, p.513)

To emphasise their point, and to highlight the absence of functional discreteness, Ramsey, Stich and Garon also trained up a second network with exactly the same architecture, the same sixteen propositions, and one *additional* proposition ('Fish have eggs', as it happens). In a GOFAI or RTM-type model, such an addition is a straightforward matter of having one more postcard in the belief box, or one more bit-string in a memory register. In the connectionist network identifying such a difference is just not possible. There are, of course, many widespread differences between the two networks, but that's the point. There are *so* many differences in connection weights, biases and so on that – because the additional information is encoded in a holistic and distributed way – the difference is *the whole network*. Thus, there are no identifiable sub-structures that can be semantically interpreted as representations of particular propositions, or that can be seen to play a unique causal role in the generation of behaviour. The stored information about fish being oviparous, Ramsey, Stich and Garon claim, is simply not functionally discrete in the way that folk psychology requires. The two networks are very different, but working out how that difference amounts to the inclusion of an additional semantically interpretable and causally efficacious belief is just not possible.

On the other hand, the contrast between the two networks also makes it difficult to say what the two have in *common* such that they both 'believe' that dogs have fur. Folk psychology, as we noted, treats the set of individuals who believe that dogs have fur as a natural kind, but it seems that connectionism cannot. We could train up many different networks on the sixteen or seventeen propositions, plus or minus a handful, and we could end up with many networks that are substantially different from each other, even though they *all* represent the information that dogs have fur. Ramsey, Stich and Garon conclude that "the class of networks that might model a cognitive agent who believes that dogs have fur is not a genuine kind at all, but simply a chaotically disjunctive set" (p.515). Connectionist modelling cannot, therefore, generate the kinds of law-like regularities that are at the heart of folk psychology (or, for that matter, cognitive scientific developments of it.)

Suppose that Ramsey, Stich and Garon are right about connectionist networks lacking these features. What does this show? We might grant them a slightly different conditional; if connectionism is correct, then folk psychology is mistaken. This still isn't enough to entail their stronger, *eliminativist*, conclusion. The history of science is full of examples of mistaken theories, but not all have led to eliminativism about the entities thus postulated. Whilst we *have* eliminated caloric fluid – the hypothetical substance of heat postulated in the eighteenth Century – from our scientific ontology, the same cannot be said for the planets of Ptolemaic geocentrism; we still think the latter *exist*, it's just that we now think they behave *differently* to how they were described in the first century.

Ramsey, Stich and Garon thus introduce a useful distinction. When the entities and processes of an old theory are retained, or reduced to those of a new one, we are looking at a case of what they call *ontologically conservative* theory change. When theory change results in the entities and processes of an old theory being thrown out entirely, this is a case of *ontologically radical* theory change. In order for the strong version of their conclusion to follow from the considerations adduced thus far, then, Ramsey, Stich and Garon need to show that the relationship between folk psychology and connectionism is of the ontologically *radical* kind.

Why should we think that the relation between folk psychology and connectionism (or the transition from the former to the latter) is a case of ontologically radical theory change? Ramsey, Stich and Garon admit that there is no general theory in philosophy of science that gives us a precise account of when theory change is to be understood as ontologically conservative and when it is not. They suggest that the posits of a new theory being "deeply and fundamentally different" from those of an old theory is indicative of radical theory change, but go on to admit that "since there is no easy measure of how 'deeply and fundamentally different' a pair of posits are, the conclusion we reach is bound to be a judgment call" (Ramsey, Stich, and Garon, 1990, p.503).

This admission is what permits a wide variety of objections and replies to Ramsey, Stich and Garon's position. If it's a "judgment call" as to whether the conclusion is warranted, perhaps eliminativism needn't follow *even if* connectionism does show folk psychology to be mistaken. We might express this by saying that perhaps connectionism doesn't show folk psychology to be wrong *enough*; maybe, for example, a reductionist view might follow instead of an eliminativist one. We might *retain* the concepts of belief and desire but *explain them* as activation vectors, patterns of activity, and sets of weight biases, in just the same way as we have retained the concept of temperature even though we explain it in terms of statistical mechanics (i.e., reduction without elimination). Once you admit that the matter is a judgement call, you permit others to *make* the call differently.

An alternative response, arguably preferable to the indecisive calling of different judgements, is to take Ramsey, Stich and Garon's argument head on, and show that connectionism does not in fact lack the features of propositional modularity, semantic interpretability and causal efficacy. Something like this strategy is adopted by Clark (1990), who argues that "connectionist models are actually more structured than Ramsey *et al.* think, and hence visibly compatible with the requirements of propositional modularity" (p.90). Clark's reply asks whether Ramsey, Stich and Garon are really entitled to the claim that the networks they discuss lack the *functional* discreteness required by folk psychology.

It's certainly the case that the two networks lack *physical* discreteness in the requisite sense; when one looks at the connection weights and activation levels, there's simply no way of identifying a particular belief or of 'pointing to' similarities and differences. But that's not the same as saying that there's no *functional* discreteness on display. Clark points out that there are certain analytical techniques that one can perform on connectionist models that reveal regularities characteristic of functional discreteness. One such technique is known as 'cluster analysis' and involves examining the activation levels of a network's hidden units in order to uncover statistical similarities and differences between different distributed representations. Such analysis permits the grouping (or clustering) of the activity patterns in the hidden units in ways that are, in fact, semantically interpretable; Churchland (1989, p.175) points out that in the mine/rock detector network, cluster analysis of the hidden units after training revealed that their 'space' of possible activation patterns had been partitioned into areas roughly corresponding to 'metal' and 'non-metal'. Thus, regularities that correspond to folk psychology's propositional modularity may be revealed at higher levels of analysis, even if they are not obvious from a simpler examination of the physical components of a network. Clark (1990, p.101) concludes,

> If we are forced to consider only a units-and-weights style description of networks, the compatibility [between connectionism and folk-psychology] is indeed elusive. But well-motivated higher levels of description are not only possible, they are, as the case of [cluster analysis] shows, actual.

One final thought about Ramsey, Stich and Garon's argument makes for a nice transition to a second criticism of connectionism, from Fodor and Pylyshyn (1988), with which we'll be concerned next. Ramsey, Stich and Garon write: "we'd not be at all surprised if trenchant critics of connectionism, like Fodor and Pylyshyn, found both our conditional and the argument for it to be quite congenial" (p.500). Such a similarity comes from taking the cogency of the argument at face value, and viewing it as a *reductio ad absurdum* of connectionism. When viewed in this fashion, the arguments of both Ramsey, Stich and Garon and Fodor and Pylyshyn (1988) have a similar flavour; they both note some feature or property that is, *prima facie*, an essential component of cognition, and go on to argue that since connectionism lacks – or cannot explain – that feature, connectionism is not a good theory of cognition. Thus construed, both arguments exemplify a variant of the general anti-AI argument I put forward at the beginning of Chapter 3, thus:

1. Nothing could be a genuine account of cognition without X;
2. But, connectionist systems cannot display or explain X;
3. THEREFORE, connectionism cannot be a genuine account of cognition.

If we read Ramsey, Stich and Garon as a *reductio* of connectionism (not that they explicitly recommend doing so), then we might substitute 'propositional attitudes' for X. In the case of Fodor and Pylyshyn, we are going to substitute 'representations with combinatorial structure'. Again, such technical terminology will need to be explained carefully, but since Fodor and Pylyshyn are trying to present an argument for preferring GOFAI to connectionism, consideration of their critique will also lead us nicely to a position where we can examine the relation between connectionism and GOFAI, and from there move on to more recent dynamical and embodied approaches.

5.2 Connectionism and compositionality

Recall that GOFAI views cognition as essentially language-like: the rule-governed manipulation of interpretable strings of symbols. Fodor's 'language of thought' hypothesis (mentioned earlier on p.32), which conceives of mental representations as syntactically structured in just this way, is one attempt to explain how certain features of cognition arise *because* of its language-like structure. The most important feature of thought, thus explained, is its *composite structure*; you can build up complex thoughts by adding together simpler thoughts, in just the same way that words can be put together to form sentences, with the whole thing governed by the well-defined grammatical rules of language and/or cognition. So, if you can form the simple ideas of 'Romeo', 'Juliet', and 'love', then you can compose the more complex thoughts 'Romeo loves Juliet' or 'Juliet loves Romeo'.

The idea of composite structure can be made clearer by analogy with chemistry. The difference between atoms and molecules is that, let's say, atoms are the basic building blocks of ordinary matter, whereas molecules are complex structures that are built up out of collections of atoms. So, for example, the water molecule H_2O is built out of two hydrogen atoms and one oxygen atom. More generally, the laws of chemistry specify which atoms can be combined, and in what proportion, in order to form molecules. The language of thought hypothesis may be understood in similar terms. The sentence or thought 'Romeo loves Juliet' is like a molecule composed of three atoms, and the sentence 'Juliet loves Romeo' is a *different* molecule composed of an alternative arrangement of the same atoms – like an isomer. The laws of grammar specify the ways that words may be joined to form sentences, and the laws of cognition specify how the corresponding atomic ideas may be combined into molecular thoughts with composite structure.

It's pretty clear that cognitive *operations* are going to have to be sensitive to the composite structure of the thoughts that they process; there's a world of difference between the thought 'Romeo loves Juliet' and the thought 'Juliet loves Romeo' even though the two molecules are composed of the same atoms. GOFAI systems are very good at displaying this kind of sensitivity, since the 'laws' they obey – their programs – can be set up so that the operations are sensitive to the structure of the symbol-strings they manipulate. For example, there might be a rule that says "If 'X loves Y' is a permissible sentence, then so is 'Y loves X'". More generally, rules could be written so that certain atoms are labelled as nouns, others as verbs, and the computer program specifies the way in which they can be combined.

At the heart of Fodor and Pylyshyn's argument is the claim that, whilst GOFAI systems can process representations in a way that is sensitive to their composite structure, connectionist systems cannot. Their argument proceeds in two stages. First, they give some examples of the sorts of things that connectionist models cannot do (but that minds and GOFAI models *can*). If their argument is correct, this leaves GOFAI as a better candidate for describing, explaining and displaying the essential features of cognition. They then move on to examine why people have (perhaps mistakenly) been attracted to connectionism, and conclude that all of these 'lures' are either (a) features that are not *essentially* absent from GOFAI, or else (b) are really directed at the neural or implementational level. Thus, they conclude, connectionism's appeal can either be accommodated by GOFAI, or else undermines its claim to be a *cognitive*-level theory.

Two features of thoughts (and of *thought*) that seem to result directly from their composite structure are what Fodor and Pylyshyn call *productivity* and *systematicity*. What they mean by the productivity of thought is that just as there are indefinitely many molecular sentences that can be composed from a language with only a finite set of atomic words, so can a person compose and entertain any of an indefinite number of molecular *thoughts* which are composed from a finite number of atomic representations. We do this, presumably, by recursively combining atomic ideas in such a way as to produce a vast number of molecules. With only a handful of atoms, such as 'Romeo', 'Juliet', 'Mercutio', 'Tybalt', 'Paris', 'loves', 'kills', 'fights', we can specify rules of combination that enable us to produce a huge variety of molecular thoughts: 'Romeo loves Juliet', 'Juliet loves Romeo', 'Tybalt fights Mercutio', 'Tybalt kills Mercutio', 'Romeo kills Tybalt', 'Paris fights Romeo', 'Romeo kills Paris', 'Romeo kills Romeo', and 'Juliet kills Juliet'. If you add in a logical connective like 'and', and allow the embedding of one proposition inside another, the number of possible thoughts becomes strictly infinite. As Pinker (1997, p.124) puts it:

> We humans can take an entire proposition and give it a role in some larger proposition. Then we can take the larger proposition and embed it in a still larger one. Not only did the baby eat the slug, but the father

saw the baby eat the slug, and I wonder whether the father saw the baby eat the slug, the father knows that I wonder whether he saw the baby eat the slug, and I can guess that the father knows that I wonder whether he saw the baby eat the slug, and so on.

By systematicity, Fodor and Pylyshyn mean that there is often an intrinsic and essential relationship between molecules composed of the same atoms such that the ability to produce or understand some sentences is *systematically* related to the ability to produce or understand others. So, for example, the molecular thoughts 'Romeo loves Juliet' and 'Romeo loves cake' both contain the atomic representation 'Romeo'. Thus you will be unable to entertain *either* molecular thought if you lack the common atom. Similarly if you are capable of entertaining the thought 'Romeo loves Juliet' then you are also capable of forming the thought 'Juliet loves Romeo' (even if, like Capulet, you *believe* the former but not the latter). Psychologists have never found a person who could think the thought 'Romeo loves Juliet', but could *not* think the thought 'Juliet loves Romeo' because the two thoughts are *systematically* related.

GOFAI systems are, of course, very good at displaying productivity and systematicity. On the one hand, this is because their representations *are* strings of symbols and can thus be combined, split, copied and moved in just the way required. Moreover, the rules they follow – their algorithms – can be set up such that they are very good at *processing* molecules in a way that is sensitive to their atomic structure. GOFAI can therefore offer an explanation of why it is that human thought displays productivity and systematicity; we are such computers and our programs are set up in just that way. But, Fodor and Pylyshyn argue, the same is not true of connectionist systems because, in effect, their representations *do not have* composite structure.

Recall that a distributed representation, in a connectionist model, is just a unique pattern of activity across the set of units that make up a 'layer' in the network. Because of this holistic mode of representation networks process such representations by, in effect, treating them as *atomic* structures; a distributed representation of 'Romeo loves Juliet' does not *literally* contain representations of 'Romeo' and 'Juliet' as proper parts in the way that language, the 'language of thought' and GOFAI symbol strings do. A network might compare 'Romeo loves Juliet' and 'Romeo loves cake' and calculate their statistical similarity, but the representations are nonetheless regarded as atoms rather than as composite molecules with some atoms in common. A virtue of doing so, as we've seen, is that connectionist networks can display fault tolerance and graceful degradation: if part of the representation is faulty or damaged, then its similarity to a previously learnt representation is enough to allow the network to give a sensible response. However, in some cases, very similar representations should give rise to very *different* responses; what a tragedy would have been avoided if it were 'Romeo loves cake' rather than 'Romeo loves Juliet' that fate conspired to thwart.

In effect, the way that connectionism and GOFAI deal with such cases might be schematically represented in the following way. In a connectionist model, we're comparing [Romeo loves cake] and [Romeo loves Juliet] whereas in a GOFAI system, the difference is between [Romeo]+[loves]+[cake] and [Romeo]+[loves]+[Juliet]. In the former case, because the representations are treated as atoms, Fodor and Pylyshyn argue, there can be no structure-sensitive processing, productivity or systematicity. In the latter case the differences in one of their atoms would be enough for these representations to generate appropriately different behaviours (that's the structure-sensitive processing). Further, there *is* an essential relationship between the two representations (that's systematicity). And finally, because the 'object' atom could be switched with many alternatives ([Juliet], [cake], [pie] or even [Romeo]) an enormous number of other representations may be generated (that's productivity).

Putting this all together, Fodor and Pylyshyn (1988, p.33) write:

> these features of cognition are, on the one hand, pervasive and, on the other hand, explicable only on the assumption that mental representations have internal structure.... an empirically adequate cognitive theory must recognize not just causal relations among representational states but also relations of syntactic and semantic constituency; hence... the mind cannot be, in its general structure, a Connectionist network.

In accordance with the general argument structure to which we keep returning, Fodor and Pylyshyn argue: productivity and systematicity are essential features of human cognitive processes, but since connectionism cannot display them, it cannot be a good model of cognitive processes. This leads them to pursue their second set of considerations concerning the 'lure' of connectionism. In short, they argue, whatever is attractive about connectionism can be accommodated by viewing it as an account of how cognitive processes are *implemented* in the brain. So, contrary to the claim we encountered earlier from McClelland, Rumelhart and Hinton (see p.80 above), connectionism according to Fodor and Pylyshyn is only of interest insofar as it explains the physiological mechanisms underlying a cognitive level story that is better told by GOFAI.

Consider a handful of reasons – often advanced, surveyed earlier – for preferring connectionism to GOFAI:[2]

1. The speed of cognitive processes in relation to neural speeds requires parallelism (the 'hundred-step' argument).
2. GOFAI systems are not naturally good at pattern completion, content-addressable memory, graceful degradation, fault tolerance etc., whereas connectionist models are.
3. Brains are physically structured more like connectionist models than computers or Turing Machines.
4. Though 'rules' might *describe* cognition and its results, it is not necessary that cognitive systems explicitly encode those rules.

Fodor and Pylyshyn argue that each of these – and other – reasons given for preferring connectionism is either a criticism of some feature that is not essential to GOFAI, or else is really an advantage for connectionism as an account of how cognition is *implemented*. Take (1) for example. As I pointed out earlier, GOFAI does not necessarily rule out parallelism; cognitive processes might be made up of several Turing Machines running at once. Further, nobody in GOFAI claims that cognitive architectures are *implemented* in the brain in the same way that they are implemented in standard computers. So either (1) is something that GOFAI can accommodate, or else it's a concern about the machinery underlying GOFAI programs. In the case of (2) the expression 'naturally good' alerts us to the fact that, as I mentioned earlier, these abilities of connectionist models *can* be replicated by GOFAI systems. To the extent that connectionist models are *better* at displaying these features, that's a matter, once again, of the speed and efficiency of a neural implementation. (3) explicitly concerns an implementational issue; we are invited to prefer connectionism to GOFAI because neural nets look like the brain whereas computers don't. But Fodor and Pylyshyn point out that while this might be a reason for *neurophysiologists* to prefer connectionism, it's not obvious that we should say the same about *cognitive* scientists:

> The point is that the structure of 'higher levels' of a system are rarely isomorphic, or even similar, to the structure of 'lower levels' of a system. No one expects the theory of protons to look very much like the theory of rocks and rivers, even though, to be sure, it is protons and the like that rocks and rivers are 'implemented in'. (Fodor and Pylyshyn, 1988, p.63)

Finally, Fodor and Pylyshyn remind us, whilst GOFAI systems certainly *permit* the explicit encoding of rules-to-be-followed within the system that follows them, this is not a universal requirement. Just like connectionist systems, in fact, some of what a classical system does may be 'rule-implicit'. Some features might be 'hard wired' (the breakdown voltage of a capacitor or a particular state-transition) in a way that 'following' a descriptive rule doesn't require the *consultation* of its explicit encoding. So, once again, what appears to be an advantage to connectionism is in fact possible with GOFAI too.

At the end of this argumentative pincer movement – the simultaneous attack on both connectionism's abilities and its allure – Fodor and Pylyshyn conclude that the best hope for connectionism is as an implementation theory. They describe this result as if it were a defeat for connectionism, and they're certainly right that their conclusion would warrant a significant toning down of some of early pro-connectionist rhetoric. But in the voluminous literature that now exists, various researchers have explored other options. Some have attempted to construct connectionist models that *do* display systematicity and productivity, whilst others have argued for and constructed connectionist-GOFAI hybrid models that contain both neural network and classical structures.[3] Yet others have tried to increase the biological realism of artificial networks by constructing, for example, 'spiking' neural networks that reproduce the trains of pulses that characterise activation levels of real neurons, or dynamical neural networks that include continuous temporal factors rather than the discrete time-steps of 1986-style connectionism (more on this later). But whatever the status of this burgeoning neural network literature, it seems to me that Fodor and Pylyshyn's 'implementationalist' conclusion is *not* a defeat for connectionism. Even if connectionism can only tell a story about how cognition is physiologically implemented, that would still be a significant accomplishment for cognitive science. Brian McLaughlin writes:

> If connectionism implements classicism, connectionism gets to be quantum mechanics, and classicism only gets to be chemistry. If there were a Nobel Prize in psychology, an account of how a connectionist network in the brain implements a classical cognitive architecture would surely win it. (1993, p.184)

Echoing the title of McLaughlin's paper ("The Connectionism/Classicism Battle to Win Souls") we might conclude by saying that whilst there have been successes and failures on both sides in various *battles*, nobody has yet won the *war*. And this might lead us to speculate as to *why*...

———◇———

It's tempting to see the relationship between connectionism and GOFAI as the struggle between competing Kuhnian 'paradigms'. That's certainly an oversimplification, not least because on the Kuhnian view, the post-revolutionary paradigm is supposed to *explain away* the successes of the pre-revolutionary one. Since connectionists haven't been much interested in building theorem-provers and chess players, for example, it would be a stretch to see their approach as subsuming the successes of GOFAI. Nonetheless, it's a common way of viewing things and leads well into a view of the dynamical approach to cognitive science and AI (the subject matter of the next chapter) as a 'third contender' (see, e.g., Eliasmith, 1996).

But this may not be the best way of looking at the relationship. Philosopher Tim van Gelder has likened the category 'connectionist' to the category 'Macintosh-user'. One could, if one really wished, divide cognitive scientists into Mac-users and non-Mac-users. But such a division would be of almost no *theoretical* interest. He provocatively writes:

> If we suppose that the term *connectionism* refers to some reasonably coherent research program standing as an alternative to mainstream computational cognitive science, then connectionism has *no* interesting implications for cognitive science. This is because there is, in fact, *no such* thing.... Much of connectionist work has significance for the philosophy of mind, but not *as connectionism*. The most significant theoretical division in cognitive science is not between computationalists and connectionists. Rather, it is the related but importantly different division between computationalists and *dynamicists*. (Van Gelder, 1997, p.245)

Summing up my earlier discussion, and moving forward to the subject matter of Chapter 6, van Gelder and Port write:

> there is a much deeper fault-line running between the computational approach and the dynamical approach. In our opinion, connectionists have often been attempting, unwittingly and unsuccessfully, to straddle this line: to use dynamical machinery to implement ideas about the nature of cognitive processes which owe more to computationalism.... Since its heyday in the mid- to late-1980s, this style of connectionist work has been gradually disappearing, either collapsing back in the computational direction (hybrid networks, and

straightforward implementations of computational mechanisms), or becoming increasingly dynamic (e.g., the shift to recurrent networks analyzed with dynamical systems techniques). Connectionist researchers who take the latter path are of course welcome participants in the dynamical approach. (Van Gelder and Port, 1995, pp.33–34)

So it's to the latter we turn next...

6
The Dynamical Approach

6.1 Motivation

Imagine it's the late eighteenth century – during the industrial revolution – and you're a cotton-mill owner in the north of England who has just acquired a new-fangled rotative steam engine to replace the horses and water-wheels driving your loom. In order to continue producing smooth woven cotton, you need a power source that is highly uniform; the engine's flywheel must rotate at a constant, unvarying speed. But steam engine output can fluctuate quite widely depending on the pressure of the steam and the load under which it is placed. So you need some device – a widget or machine known as a *governor* – that can regulate the flywheel speed, despite variations in steam pressure and workload.

Van Gelder (1995) begins his discussion with this little just-so story because it enables us to frame a problem, and to think about different ways we might go about solving it. We need to open and close the valve in the steam pipe running from the boiler – at just the right time, and by just the right amount – in order to adjust the speed of the piston that drives the flywheel, and van Gelder points out that, nowadays, we immediately think up *computational* solutions to the problem. It's tempting to specify the solution in algorithmic form:

1. Measure the speed of the flywheel.
2. Compare the actual speed against the desired speed.
3. If there is no discrepancy, return to step 1. Otherwise,
   a. measure the current steam pressure;
   b. calculate the desired alteration in steam pressure;
   c. calculate the necessary throttle valve adjustment.
4. Make the throttle valve adjustment.
   Return to step 1. (Van Gelder, 1995, p.348)

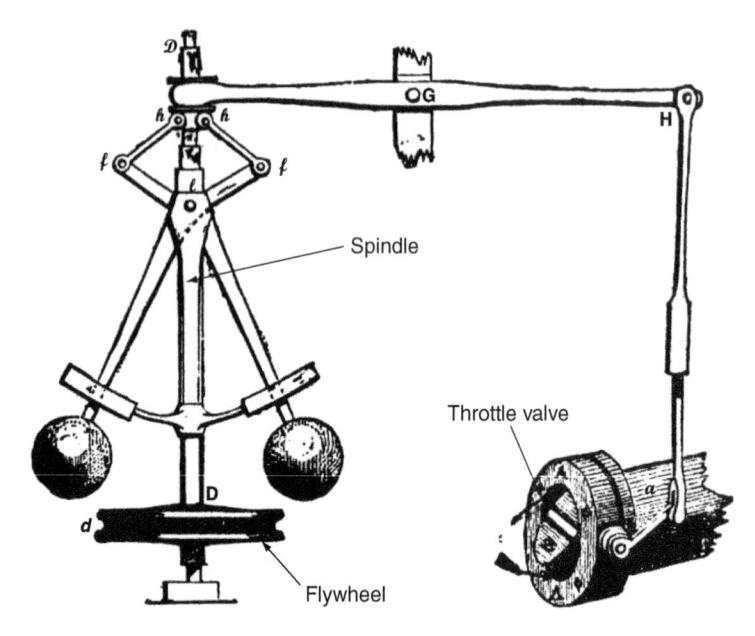

Figure 6.1 The centrifugal governor

Notice all the hallmarks of computer science here; an algorithmic process creates a representation, compares it against other representations stored in memory, and issues output instructions accordingly. *Voilà*. But, of course, such a solution was not available to engineers of the eighteenth century. The solution – usually attributed to the engineer James Watt – was to develop the 'centrifugal governor' (depicted in Figure 6.1).

In the centrifugal governor, a vertical spindle with two weighted hinged arms is attached to the flywheel. The spindle rotates at the speed of the flywheel and as the speed varies, the weighted hinged arms are caused to rise and fall due to centrifugal force. By an arrangement of levers and hinges, the motion of these arms is linked to the throttle valve of the engine. If the speed of the flywheel increases, the arms raise, causing the throttle to close, and restricting the flow of steam. If the speed decreases, the arms fall, and allow the throttle to open, thus increasing the flow of steam. Consequently, the engine maintains a constant flywheel speed with no fluctuations caused by the varying pressures and loads on the engine. In short, rather than a *computational* solution in terms of representations and algorithms, the problem is given a *dynamical* solution in terms of interacting forces that change in real time.

As the title of his famous paper ("What might cognition be, if not computation?") suggests, van Gelder wants to use this little tale to inspire some lessons for cognitive science and AI. His aim is two-fold. On the one hand, he wants to undermine a sort of 'only game in town' or 'what else could it be?' argument – the former attributed to Fodor (1975), the latter identified by Haugeland (1998) – for classical cognitive science and GOFAI. In just the same way that the *computational* governor is not the only possible approach to solving the cotton-weaving problem, van Gelder wants to suggest that there are viable alternatives to GOFAI in the case of cognitive science. He writes that "our sense that a specific cognitive task must be subserved by a (generically) computational system may be due to deceptively compelling preconceptions about how systems solving complex tasks must work" (Van Gelder, 1995, p.358). On the other hand, van Gelder wants to suggest a new widget for thinking about mind and machine; perhaps cognitive systems are more like the Watt governor than the Turing Machine.

The lessons to be learnt from the specific case of the Watt governor are quite specific, and I shall return to them a little later. But insofar *as the Watt governor can be* analysed using the mathematical apparatus of Dynamical Systems Theory (DST), the conceptual toolbox opened up by this alternative approach is well stocked. Let's take a peek inside...

6.2 Dynamical systems theory

There are many different definitions of what actually counts as a dynamical system in mathematics in general, let alone for the purposes of the dynamical hypothesis in cognitive science and AI. Van Gelder (1998) notes that "there is no single official definition waiting to be lifted off the shelf" (p.618). Some general features can nonetheless be drawn out of the various definitions.

The single most obvious feature of DST (especially DST as characterised by philosophers and cognitive scientists) is the emphasis on time and how systems change in time. Van Gelder (1998) cites a number of characterisations of the expression 'dynamical system' that take this aspect as primary. Hirsch (1984) provides perhaps the broadest definition, stating "A dynamical system is one which changes in time" (p.3). Luenberger (1979) elaborates on this, writing "The term *dynamic* refers to phenomena that produce time-changing patterns...the term is nearly synonymous with time-evolution or pattern of change" (p.1). Whilst other issues – particularly the conviction that everything of interest can be characterised and explained by numerical (rather than, say, representational) states – are sometimes mentioned, the issue of time and timing is the most visible and motivating factor for cognitive scientists. I will return to this issue in the next section.

It should also be noted that the term 'dynamical system' is often used in a way that is ambiguous between a dynamical system *in the world* (say, the solar system), and a dynamical system, as it were, *on paper* (say, the set of equations that describe the motions of the planets of the solar system, or the abstract mathematical model of the motions of the planets). It is useful, therefore, to introduce some terminological refinement to help avoid conflating such ontological and epistemic aspects. Giunti (1997) distinguishes between what he calls *real* dynamical systems ("any real system that changes over time") and what he calls *mathematical* dynamical systems ("an abstract mathematical structure that can be used to describe the change of a real system as an evolution through a series of states"). Bearing such distinctions in mind will be particularly important when evaluating the claim 'cognitive systems are dynamical systems' since, as in connectionism, one may describe a system as behaving in accordance with rules, but where those rules need not be explicitly encoded in – or consulted by – the system itself.

There are quantitative and qualitative ways of characterising the way dynamical systems change in time, and both will be useful when applying DST to cognitive science. Given that a mathematical dynamical system is partly made up of a set of time-dependent variables, a system's state at any instant can be given as a list of the values of those variables, and the way in which that state changes over time can be expressed as a differential equation. Such equations show how the values of the variables change with time in relation to various system *parameters* (values that affect, but are not affected by, the system's temporal evolution). The famous 'logistic equation' for modelling population growth is a good example. If x is the variable representing population, whilst r is a system parameter corresponding to the maximum growth rate, and time is treated as a continuous variable, then the system can be described with the equation $\frac{dx}{dt} = rx(1 - x)$. This states that the rate of change of population with respect to time is equal to a function of the population itself; the rate of population growth depends on how big the population already is, and a graphical representation gives a classic s-shaped curve where the population initially increases exponentially, until competition for resources results in its self-limiting.

Given that the state of a dynamical system is constituted by the values of its variables, and in some cases there may be so many variables that solving such differential equations is very difficult, it is sometimes more

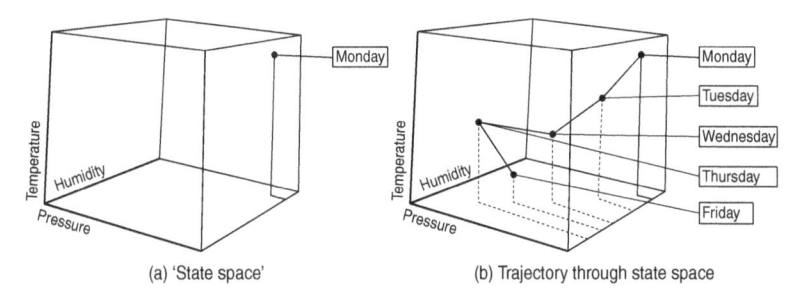

Figure 6.2 Qualitative tools of DST

convenient to describe the system's temporal change in terms of a spatial metaphor. This is where one makes use of the terminology of *state space*, *trajectories*, *attractors*, and so on. Thus, in tandem with the quantitative tools provided by differential equations, there are also some qualitative tools of DST that are of use.

The 'state space' of a system is a hypothetical space with one dimension for each variable of the system. Such a system is easy to visualise when limited to three or fewer dimensions. Imagine that one is keeping track of the weather, and recording the values of three variables: temperature, pressure and humidity. The system in question can then be visualised as a three dimensional space (say, a cube) such that, at any point in time, the total state of the system corresponds to a unique point in that space (see Figure 6.2a). We might then visualise the *change* a system undergoes over time; if we want to see how the weather changes over the course of a week, we could plot points for each day and then 'join the dots'. The resulting line – the *trajectory* through state space – would represent system behaviour (see Figure 6.2b).

Finally, plotting the values over the course of several years might reveal long-term trends in the system; the trajectory might cluster in a certain region (say, high values for all three variables) at certain times of the year (say, summer). Such a feature is sometimes known as an 'attractor' because it looks as if a region of state space is attracting the trajectory towards it. More specifically, an attractor may be defined as a point, or set of points, in state space toward which the system will evolve from any of various other points; a variety of different starting points will converge on (or close to) the same final state. Plotting all of these different *possibilities* results in something that looks like an undulating landscape – known as a *phase portrait* – that corresponds to a complete picture of the different tendencies a system might have.

We can thus reconstruct – in both quantitative and qualitative terms – many of the features that would be required by an account of cognition (and that are found in both GOFAI and connectionism). We have new notions of the current state, system behaviour, general trends and regularities and the laws that govern them all. Moreover, we have all of this in a way that foregrounds the temporal aspects of these features. It's this latter feature in particular that seems to motivate the application of DST to cognitive science and AI.

6.3 Dynamical cognitive science: time and timing

How can DST be applied to *cognition*, whether natural or artificial? In Chapter 6.4, we will examine that question with reference to some of the most successful models of cognitive performance produced using the tools of DST. Before that, it is worth taking a look at the theoretical motivations that have prompted the use of such a toolkit.

On at least one reading, the claim that cognition is a dynamical phenomenon is hardly radical. A dynamical system is a system that changes in (or over) time. All cognitive activity is temporal in this way; perception, planning, imagination and so on, all take place in time. In fact, one is hard pushed to think of anything cognitive that is not dynamic in this sense. On this reading, the dynamical approach to cognitive science is simply the willingness to acknowledge the seemingly obvious, yet surprisingly neglected, fact that cognition is a temporal phenomenon. Dynamicists claim that since cognition is a process which 'unfolds in time', it should be studied as such.

Of course, most of cognitive science is compatible with this insight, so such a proposition, as a *hypothesis*, might seem to be trivially true. Since everything in the universe is a dynamical system, so the objection claims, then *of course* cognitive agents are dynamical systems. Everything changes continuously in time; rivers flowing, planets orbiting around the sun, weather patterns and even computers are all systems which change in time. It is therefore not surprising that cognitive agents also change quantitatively in time. So, the objection concludes, the dynamical hypothesis is true of cognitive agents because it is true of *everything*.

In response to this, we might note that whilst everything in the universe might *be* a dynamical system, that does not mean that everything in the universe should be studied *as such*. The dynamical hypothesis in cognitive science and AI is the much more specific claim that the tools of DST are the best ones available for describing and explaining cognition. Thus, van Gelder distinguishes between two versions of the dynamical hypothesis. Echoing Giunti's earlier distinction, one is metaphysical (the 'nature hypothesis') and the other is epistemological (the 'knowledge hypothesis'). As van Gelder puts it:

> The *nature* hypothesis is a claim about cognitive agents themselves: it specifies what they *are* (i.e. dynamical systems). The *knowledge* hypothesis is a claim about cognitive science: namely that we can and should *understand* cognition dynamically. (1998, p.619)

This distinction between ontological and epistemic versions of a hypothesis has some precedent in psychology; most notably, it can be found in the distinction between 'metaphysical' and 'methodological' versions of behaviourism. Metaphysical behaviourism is a claim about the nature of agents; it is the (radical) claim that mental states do not exist, only behaviour does. Methodological behaviourism is the more modest claim that the discipline of psychology should proceed behaviouristically (in terms of experiments using stimuli and responses, reinforcement, conditioning etc.) The latter makes no pronouncement about what agents actually are. The dynamical hypothesis is similarly divided, with the nature hypothesis claiming that we are dynamical systems (rather than 'computational' systems), and the knowledge hypothesis claiming that cognitive science should proceed dynamically (using the theoretical resources of differential equations, state space, trajectories and attractors). The latter is surely immune from the charge of trivial truth.

There is at least one further sense in which the dynamical approach constitutes a significant ripple in the fabric of cognitive scientific orthodoxy. As we've seen before, the dominant philosophical view in cognitive science is functionalism. The most common characterisation of functionalism is the view that mental states are individuated by their causal roles (rather than, say, by the substance that they are made of). Now, functionalism may well be compatible with the insight that mental states and processes have an essentially temporal character (I do not wish to suggest that functionalism is *non*-temporal, or committed to a conception of mental states as static; after all, it might be argued that cause itself is an intrinsically temporal notion). But functionalism, as often advanced is *a*temporal; it makes no reference to the issue of the time course of cognitive processes. Given that many cognitive processes *are* in fact temporal, adding considerations of time and timing to functionalism would be a significant achievement. Even Eliasmith (1996), a strong critic of some aspects of the dynamical approach, agrees on this point:

> If the dynamics of some aspects of mental life are central to their nature, then an atemporal functionalism is not warranted. Standard functionalism in philosophy of mind is clearly atemporal. And, I take it, some (if not many) aspects of mental life have their character in virtue of their dynamics (e.g., shooting pains, relaxed conversations, and recognizing friends). So, a 'temporal' functionalism is necessary for properly characterizing minds. In other words, input, outputs, and their time course must all be specified to identify a mental state. (1996, p.519)

Eliasmith's point here is that a temporal functionalism would need a kind of temporal *metric* for the inputs and outputs, not merely a temporal ordering. But why is functionalism seen as atemporal? Examining this question provides us with a nice way to compare the dynamical approach to its classical, GOFAI, predecessor.

Recall that, at the end of Chapter 2, we noted two versions of functionalism that Block (1980) describes as 'metaphysical' and 'computation-representation' functionalism. Recall also that the latter aims to analyse mental processes as algorithmically calculable (i.e., Turing computable) mechanical processes. *This* is why functionalism, in its various guises, is seen as atemporal. The analysis of Turing Machines ignores the *geometry* of their temporal behaviour, and deals only with its *topology*[1] because the analysis of a Turing Machine's behaviour orders, but does not quantify amounts of time; it counts temporal steps without assigning metered time to those steps.

As we saw earlier, the Turing Machine is an imaginary device designed to help us get a grip on the notion of effective computability; it is an informal way (in terms of tape, a machine, a controller and so on), to understand a formal mathematical theory. We might be tempted to describe the processing of a Turing Machine by saying 'At t_1, the machine is in S_1, at t_2, the machine is in S_2' and so on. But as Van Gelder (1999) notes:

> We talk about time steps, but the numbers 1, 2, etc., are being used as nothing more than indexes [sic] for imposing orders of the states of the system. More generally, the time set of abstract Turing machines is always a *mere* order. The integers are the most familiar and convenient ordered set we know of, and so we use the integers as the time set. However, none of the properties of the integers, over and above their constituting an ordered set, have any relevance to the Turing machine.

Of course, we can stipulate a metric by specifying the amount of time each processing step of a Turing Machine takes. This would allow us to speak in terms of how long it would take a Turing Machine to compute a function and so on. But, van Gelder argues, doing so is not equivalent to making a temporal Turing machine. In fact, van Gelder calls this "ersatz time", because "the 'time' of the Turing Machine bears only a passing resemblance to the genuine article". Here, van Gelder may be overstating his case. There is a large literature in theoretical computer science (especially algorithmic complexity theory) that concerns the number of steps various algorithms take to run. Given the intended practical applications of these algorithms, and given the real physical constraints on how quickly a step can be computed, it would be unfair to charge computer science with being uninterested in time. It is probably better to say that, in these cases, time is measured, but it is measured in units of steps rather than in real time. This seems vastly closer (though admittedly not identical) to 'real' time than the 'passing resemblance' that van Gelder mentions.

One might also be tempted to think that this problem is due to the 'time' steps of a Turing Machine being discrete: that it makes no sense to ask what state the machine was in at $t_{1.5}$. But the important distinction at issue here is not the one between discrete and continuous systems (for one *can* have discrete dynamical systems, modelled by difference equations), but rather the one between *quantitative* and non-quantitative systems. Van Gelder (1999) writes:

> Note also that for the purpose of understanding the Turing machine as carrying out effective computation, the *amount* of time it spends in any given state, and the *amount* of time it takes to change from one state to another, are utterly irrelevant.

This is the reason it makes no sense to enquire about the state of the Turing Machine at $t_{1.5}$. The Turing Machine's time course is not *quantitative*, and so there is *no* state defined for fractions of integers of time. This enables us to formulate a significant refinement to the earlier characterisations of dynamical systems that I discussed above. A dynamical system here is best understood as a system in which time is a *quantity* (i.e., a system that has a temporal geometry and, not just a temporal topology).

This gives us a good sense of the contrast – the 'major fault line' – we earlier saw drawn between GOFAI and dynamical approaches. Let's sum up by noting that there are, in fact, two parts to the claim that cognitive processes are best understood in the temporal terms of DST. The first is that real time is a quantity best measured by real numbers, and for every point in time there is a corresponding state of the cognitive system (note: this doesn't rule out the possibility of *discrete* dynamical systems – those that are characterised by difference equations – since even if time is a quantity, it need not be mathematically represented *continuously*). The second is that *timing* matters; issues about durations, rates, periods, synchrony and so on are important (and will be important in the consideration of real cognitive processing). Van Gelder and Port (1995, p.2) describe this as the 'flagship' argument for the dynamical approach to cognitive science and AI:

> The heart of the problem is time. *Cognitive processes and their context unfold continuously and simultaneously in real time.* Computational models specify a discrete sequence of static internal states in arbitrary 'step' time (t_1, t_2, etc) ['ersatz' time]. Imposing the latter onto the former is like wearing shoes on your hands. You can do it, but gloves fit a whole lot better.

In its contrast with computational models, this again seems to overstate the case. What is at issue is not whether the system in question unfolds continuously in real time (which, if it is actual, it must), but whether the *analysis* of the system makes reference to the continuous measure of time, or merely to abstract issues of order (whether discrete or continuous). Nonetheless, with this conception of what is important about cognitive dynamics, we will take a look at some of the 'gloves' actually on offer in Chapter 6.4

6.4 Dynamical cognitive science in action

There are a great many examples of the application of DST to cognitive science. These span the full range of 'levels' that may be of interest to cognitive scientists; from the 'low level' functioning of the rabbit olfactory bulb (Skarda and Freeman, 1987), to the modelling of infant behaviour on simple object retrieval tasks (Thelen et al., 2001; Thelen and Smith, 1994), to 'high level' decision-making with beliefs and preferences (Busemeyer and Townsend, 1993; Townsend and Busemeyer, 1995). In what follows, I'll take a look at three (successful) dynamical models with a view to drawing out some common themes which we can then address – in Chapter 6.5 – in terms of the consequences and criticisms of the dynamical approach.

6.4.1 Finger wagging: the 'HKB' model

Given the emphasis that the dynamical approach places on time and timing, it seems appropriate that one of the most widely cited dynamical models concerns the kind of co-ordinated limb movement required by pianists and drummers. This is exactly the kind of account that is provided by the so-called 'HKB' model of rhythmic finger tapping, named after its originators, Haken, Kelso and Bunz (1985). In what follows, I shall examine the exegesis put forward by Kelso (1995).

The HKB model is based upon the simple observation that, when asked to place their hands palm-down and oscillate both index fingers from left to right with the same frequency, people are reliably and stably able to reproduce only two basic patterns. One is where the left index finger and right index finger are both to the left or to the right at the same time (Kelso calls this 'antiphase' motion; it is the kind of parallel motion normally exhibited by windscreen wipers). The other is where one finger is to the left, whilst the other is to the right, or *vice-versa* ('in phase' or symmetrical motion).

If people are asked to gradually increase the oscillation frequency in time with a metronome, two interesting results are found. First, people who start working with parallel motion will, at a certain frequency of movement, spontaneously switch to the symmetrical mode. Second, people who start symmetrically would exhibit no such switch – the symmetrical motion will remain stable through and beyond the critical region. Thus, Kelso (1995, p.49) writes: "while people can produce two stable patterns of low frequencies, only one pattern remains stable as frequency is scaled beyond a critical point". In the language of DST, there are two stable attractors at low frequencies with a bifurcation at a critical point, leading to one stable attractor at high frequencies.

The specifics of the HKB model of finger movement can be elegantly captured using the mathematics of DST. The HKB model focuses on the nature of one collective variable – that of 'relative phase', designated as ϕ – and how it varies as a result of the control parameter: frequency of oscillation (inversely proportional to the ratio b/a indicated in equation 6.1). Since we are concerned with the way relative phase changes over time, the co-ordination law may be expressed as a differential equation, in terms of the derivative of ϕ, thus:

$$\frac{d\phi}{dt} = -a\sin\phi - 2b\sin 2\phi \qquad (6.1)$$

In short, this equation states that the rate of change of relative phase is equal to a periodic function of current relative phase and the frequency of oscillation. It shows how, as $\frac{b}{a}$ decreases (i.e., as the frequency of oscillation is increased), the system goes from having two stable states (corresponding to symmetrical and parallel motion), to only having one stable state (symmetrical motion).

It is worth noting two features of the model that Kelso takes to be philosophically significant. First, he notes that the model is able to account for the observed switch as the oscillation frequency passes through a critical range, without positing any special kind of inner 'switching mechanism'. He writes:

> one of the main motivations behind these experiments was to counter the then dominant notion of motor programs which tries to explain switching (an abrupt shift in spatio-temporal order) by a device that contains 'switches'. This seems a cheap way to do science. (1995, p.57)

In fact, the switching occurs as a natural product of the normal, self-organising evolution of the system without reference to any kind of 'central executive'.

Second, the HKB model was capable of making predictions of behaviour which had not yet been observed in human subjects at the time the model was developed, but were nonetheless subsequently confirmed in further experiments. Using the model, Haken, Kelso and Bunz were able to predict the results of selective interference with the system. If one finger is unexpectedly and temporarily forced out of its stable phase relation (by applying a small electrical pulse to one of the oscillating fingers), the model correctly predicts both how long it would take for the relative phase to return to a stable state, and whether (if it occurred when the frequency of oscillation was close to the critical region) such a perturbation would lead to a transition from one attractor to the other.

6.4.2 Beer on bugs

The work of Randall Beer (1995, 1997) on the abilities of artificial insects provides an excellent example of the kind of overlap between connectionist and dynamical approaches that I mentioned at the end of the previous chapter. Beer used a connectionist network to synthesise the walking behaviour of an artificial insect, and subsequently analysed the behaviour using the (qualitative) resources of DST (i.e., the language of state spaces, trajectories and attractors). Beer was especially interested in examining different walking strategies in terms of the relationship between motor output and sensory feedback, with a view to determining which would be the most adaptively successful for a creature to adopt.

Each insect had six legs, each of which had a foot at one end and a joint connecting it to the body at the other. The insect was controlled by a 30-unit neural network with five units for each leg: three motor controllers (one to determine the elevation of the foot – in the air or on the ground – and two to determine the clockwise and anticlockwise torque about the leg's single joint) and two sensors to determine the leg's angle relative to the body. Three main types of control network (corresponding to different walking strategies) were evolved and examined. Bechtel and Abrahamsen (2002) call these 'coupled networks' (where the motor controllers have full access to the sensors), 'autonomous networks' (where the sensors provide no input to the motor controllers) and 'mixed networks' (where the sensors are enabled only intermittently).

As a side note for the anthropomorphically inclined, Beer's description of the unsuccessful agents is quite heart-breaking:

> Very early on, agents appeared that put down all six feet and pushed until they fell.... In the next stage, agents evolved the ability to swing their legs in an uncoordinated fashion. Such agents made forward progress, but they fell quite often. Finally, agents using statically stable gaits began to appear, but their co-ordination was still sub-optimal. Subsequently, the efficiency of locomotion slowly improved. (1995, p.191)

Beer found that all three types of network were eventually able to make the insect walk using the 'tripod gait' that is characteristic of biological insects; the front and back legs on one side are down at the same time as the middle leg on the other side, and the insect is stably supported when the triangle formed by the planted legs underlies the body's centre of gravity. But the degree of success – or evolutionary 'fitness' – displayed by each of the networks was quite different, and is illuminated well by the qualitative resources of DST.

Coupled networks, Beer found, develop a walking strategy which depends on the sensors. Consequently, if the sensors are later removed or damaged, the insect fares badly. Autonomous networks are capable of generating the requisite rhythmic control signals, but produce a stereotyped output which can make no use of sensory feedback to fine-tune its operation. The 'fittest' insects are the ones which evolve with intermittently available sensors (i.e., 'mixed networks'). Such insects are able to perform autonomously (and can thus overcome sensory damage), but are also capable of using sensory feedback to improve their performance if it is available.

To employ the qualitative resources of DST, imagine a space of three dimensions corresponding to one leg's position (up or down), 'forward swing' controller activity, and 'backward swing' controller activity. All three types of network produce trajectories through this state space that

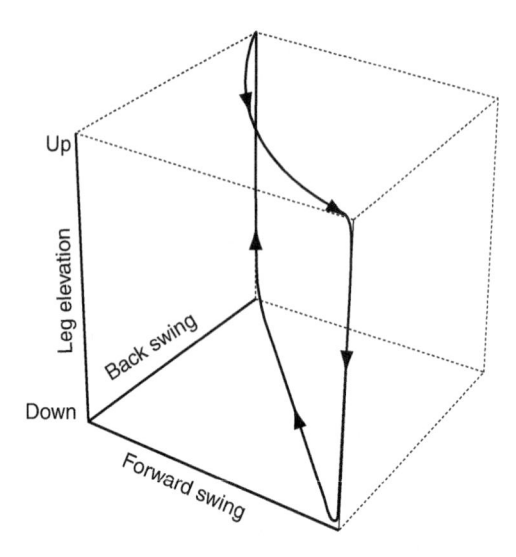

Figure 6.3 Trajectory through state space for an artificial insect. (Much simplified and generalised from those found in Beer, 1995)

are superficially similar, as depicted in Figure 6.3. Broadly speaking, the front-bottom-right of the space is where a leg first hits the ground and then as backswing increases with the leg still planted, the insect is moved forward. At this point, the leg raises (and the cycle is in the back-top-left corner) and swings forward as the insect prepares to plant it for another step. Thus the cyclical movement of the leg is effected.

However, the *reason* for this trajectory is different for each of the three types of control network. In the case of the *autonomous* network, there are no *attractors* in state space; the leg just goes through the motions, resulting in the stereotyped ('robotic' it's tempting to say) behaviour mentioned above. In the case of the *coupled* network, the trajectory is generated by point attractors in the front-bottom-right and back-top-left corners of state space. These point attractors – arising because of the constant availability of sensory feedback concerning leg angle – ensures that as the leg cycles through the different values of its variable angles, it is always moving towards either being planted at the front (the 'stance attractor'), or swinging at the back (the 'swing attractor'). As noted above, however, the coupled network is not able to withstand damage when the sensory feedback becomes unavailable. Bechtel and Abrahamsen (2002, p.246) put it nicely:

the reliance on sensory feedback... has a price. If the coupling is broken by turning the sensor off, the network will get stuck on one trajectory leading to the stance attractor and, once it reaches that state, will have no way to move out of it. The insect will stand forever.

The *mixed* networks, recall, were the most successful. This is because whilst they result in the same trajectory (and therefore reproduce a gait that is largely the same), in the case of mixed networks the path of the trajectory itself is the attractor. In the terminology of DST, it's known as a 'limit cycle' since any other path through state space will eventually converge onto it. What this means is that the network does not get stuck if sensory feedback is removed, and moreover, the network can adapt by returning to the limit cycle if it is temporarily knocked out of phase (say, if the insect steps on a rock and loses its footing), or if the sensory feedback signal changes more slowly than normal (as it would, say, following leg growth). This ability to cope with a noisy environment, Beer says, "arises as a natural consequence of the dynamics of the mixed controller and its coupling with the body" (1995, p.203).

It's clear here that there are explanatory advantages that come with the dynamical approach that would not be available to a 'pure' neural network approach. The possibility of analysing the insect's behaviour in terms of trajectories and attractors in state space helps us to get a grip on quite subtle differences between the types of control network, especially concerning the evolutionarily salient features of fitness within an environment and robustness in the face of change and/or damage. This emphasis on organism–environment relations leads Beer to draw a further philosophical conclusion that will be of special interest as we start to consider varieties of AI that attempt to take into account the way in which an agent's body and local environment – its 'situatedness' – contribute to and shape its cognitive processes.

Beer (1995, p.204) notes that embodiment and environmental embeddedness are fundamental to both the design and the analysis of his insect robots. The goal of his framework is to focus "on the problem of generating the appropriate behavior at the appropriate time as both an agent's internal state and external environment continuously change". As a consequence, one of the key ideas of the framework is "that an agent and its environment must be understood as two coupled dynamical systems whose mutual interaction is jointly responsible for the agent's behaviour". Elsewhere, Beer (1997, p.266) makes an even stronger claim; not only is situatedness necessary for *understanding* behaviour, but it is also (at least partially) *constitutive* of behaviour: "Strictly speaking, behavior is a property only of the coupled agent–environment system; it cannot in general properly be attributed to either the agent or the environment alone." In other words, not only is the dynamical approach advanced as a more appropriate framework for understanding agent–environment interaction, but according to Beer that interaction is part of what it is to behave. We will return to this issue in Chapter 6.5 below.

6.4.3 Perceptual categorisation

So far, the kinds of examples of dynamical cognitive science and AI we've been considering seem a long way from the chess playing, problem solving and language-use exemplified by GOFAI and connectionist models. One might complain that finger-wagging and insect leg co-ordination are hardly the stuff of *intelligence* proper; they're more like kinesiology and ethology than psychology. This concern is tackled head on in another study from Randall Beer (2003), who advocates the construction of systems that display what he calls *minimally cognitive behaviour*: "the simplest behavior that raises issues of genuine cognitive interest" (p.210). In the particular case we'll examine, he investigates 'categorical perception' – the ability to divide up the world into specific objects according to their properties – as a case study of dynamical AI. But more interesting than the model itself, are the lessons for cognitive science and AI that he proposes to draw from it.

In Beer's study, the simulated agent was controlled by a fourteen-unit neural network. It was trained to 'visually' discriminate between circles and diamonds falling from the top of a two-dimensional environment (much like a good old-fashioned game of 'Space Invaders'), so that it would move left and right in order to 'catch' circles and 'avoid' diamonds. Its behaviour was completely described by a complex set of differential equations (I shan't go into the details – even Beer describes them as 'tedious') that describe the interrelated changes over time of the agent's neural activity and its horizontal position together with the object's vertical position and shape.

The most successful agents (selected by an artificial 'evolutionary' process) were over 97 per cent accurate, and achieved this by deploying a strategy of 'active scanning'. When the falling object initially appears, the agent positions itself directly under it, before repeatedly moving from left and right to scan the object and finally 'deciding' either to stay in the object's path (if it is a circle) or make a large avoidance movement (if it is a diamond). Even this relatively simple strategy is theoretically significant. Each agent's 'visual perception' consisted of seven rays distributed over a small section of the visual field above it; a ray intersecting with an object resulted in the activation of one of the sensory input units with a value that was inversely proportional to the distance between the agent and the object. Thus, the agent's bodily movement would accentuate the small perceptual differences between a circle and a diamond in a way that would compensate for the low resolution of its perceptual equipment. Perception, in this case, is intimately bound up with *action*; perception is something an agent *does*, not something that simply *happens* to it. Thus to analyse them separately in the way that both GOFAI *and* connectionism do, with their emphasis on the input-processing-output cycle occurring over discrete time steps, would be to miss the way that their *interaction* contributes to performance.

Following on from this, Beer once again proposes to analyse the model by seeing the agent, its body and its environment as intertwined. He writes:

> we will decompose the agent-environment dynamics into: (1) the effect that the relative positions of the object and the agent have on the agent's motion; (2) the effect that the agent's motion has on the relative positions of the object and the agent. (2003, p.228)

In Beer's approach, brain, body and environment are all conceived of as 'coupled' dynamical *sub*systems that are part of an overall brain-body-environment whole. Echoing the claim of his that we saw earlier, he writes: "an agent's behavior arises from this interaction between these subsystems and cannot properly be attributed to any one component in isolation from the others" (Beer, 2003, p.211). Continuing in this vein, Zednik (2011) suggests a useful reading. The set of differential equations that describe the agent's behaviour may be divided into two subsets – call them B and E – that correspond to the embodied brain and to the environment respectively. Importantly, however, B and E are, in the language of DST, 'coupled'; both B and E contain variables that track features of the agent's body, and so what's happening in the brain can alter what's happening in the environment *and vice versa* in a continuous and integrated feedback loop. The body acts, as Zednik (2011, p.252) puts it, as a "two-way interface...that mediates between the brain and the environment", and DST is the common language in which this situatedness can be described.

6.5 Taking stock: consequences and criticisms of the dynamical approach

Having examined some of the motivations for, and examples of, dynamical cognitive science and AI, we are now in a better position to take stock.

In this section, I want to examine a handful of consequences and criticisms of the dynamical approach. Oddly enough, however, each of the areas I'll look at is a double-edged sword; advocates of the approach view these consequences as *advantages*, whereas sceptics about the approach view them as *problems*. Thus, even though coming to a resolution will not be possible, given the controversies that these consequences engender, it would seem that van Gelder's point – that there *is* an alternative and that GOFAI is not the 'only game in town' – is well established.

6.5.1 Explanation

Given its emphasis on the provision of differential equations, one might object that the dynamical approach (or, rather, the DST employed by cognitive scientists) only really *describes* the phenomena of interest without actually *explaining* them. Van Gelder (1998, p. 625) anticipates this, noting that such an objection claims that "dynamical models are at best descriptions of the data, and do not explain why the data take the form they do". The thought behind this objection is that, given any set of points in state space, one could construct a trajectory that connects them, and *any* line can be described (to an arbitrarily close approximation) by *some* equation or other. Thus, if we already know the data, we could engage in a 'curve-fitting' exercise to connect the dots, calculate the equation which describes this line, and offer the result as an 'explanation' of the phenomenon that generated the data.

Explanation in dynamical cognitive science and AI can, I think, do better. The differential equations in question may be more than just a concise redescription of the data. Recall that the HKB model of finger-wagging in fact made predictions of behaviour that had not been observed at the time it was developed, but were subsequently confirmed. Thus the HKB model can 'go beyond' the data by supporting counterfactual claims about how the system *would* behave in various non-actual circumstances (i.e., making *predictions*). This gives us good grounds for saying that the model provides a genuine explanation.

The close tie between explanation and prediction, the ability to support counterfactuals, and the formulation of regularities (laws?) in the form of differential equations, suggests that we might fruitfully view dynamical cognitive science as providing a kind of 'covering law' explanation. Very briefly, this account of explanation comes from Hempel and Oppenheim (1948), and views explanations as having the form of a sound deductive argument where a law of nature occurs as a premise, and the conclusion is the thing-to-be-explained. As Hempel (1965, p.337) puts it:

A [covering-law] explanation answers the question '*Why* did the explanandum phenomenon occur?' by showing that the phenomenon resulted from certain particular circumstances...in accordance with the laws.... By pointing this out, the argument shows that, given the particular circumstances and the laws in question, the occurrence of the phenomenon *was to be expected*; and it is in this sense that the explanation enables us to *understand why* the phenomenon occurred.

Elsewhere, I have argued that the HKB model conforms to this account of explanation (see Walmsley, 2008). The two stable states of the system are the ones where $\frac{d\phi}{dt}$ (i.e., the rate of change of relative phase) is zero. The bifurcation point – i.e., where one switches from parallel to symmetrical motion – is the one where $\frac{d\phi}{dt}$ is at a maximum. So, depending on our interests, we can insert the values we know into the equation, and solve the equation in order to find the values we do not know. Finding the values for *a*, *b*, and *ϕ* when $\frac{d\phi}{dt}$ is zero would constitute an explanation of *why* $\frac{d\phi}{dt}$ takes the value it does, or a prediction that the system would be stable at these values of *a*, *b* and *ϕ*.

For various reasons (e.g., concerning relevance, the 'direction' of explanation, and the difficulty in formulating psychological 'laws'), the covering-law model of explanation has fallen out of favour or been rejected entirely in philosophy of science. So, to the extent that dynamical cognitive science adopts a flawed model of explanation, this may be a problem for the approach. However, I think there are two possible responses we can make here. First, as Zednik (2011) notes, dynamical explanations are not *exclusively* covering-law in form. In the case of the two models from Randall Beer we examined above, the explanations *also* make substantial reference to the actual *mechanisms* (i.e., neural networks) that give rise to the behaviour in question. It seems most likely that the kind of explanation appropriate to the dynamical approach will be a pluralistic one that incorporates elements of both covering-law *and* mechanistic explanation.

Further, one *strength* of the covering-law account of explanation is that it is able to abstract away from the componential details of implementation. Van Gelder (1991, pp.500–501) notes:

> In its pure form, dynamical explanation makes no reference to the actual structure of the mechanism whose behaviour it is explaining.... Dynamical explanation, which proceeds in terms of parameters, equations and state spaces, takes place at one level of remove

from the actual mechanisms which produce the behaviour quantified and explained in the dynamical account.

The variables that feature in a dynamical covering-law need not correspond neatly to a component or part of the cognitive system in question, but instead can track properties that are internal, external or both: for example, the central feature of the HKB model, ϕ (the relative phase of the fingers), is a relational property between two parts of the agent's body. This is particularly useful given dynamical cognitive science's interest in 'situated' cognitive phenomena, where the constraints on a system extend beyond the physical boundaries of the system itself; covering-law explanations are better able to cope with this kind of thing-to-be-explained, since there is no limit as to what the variables in the law can refer to, and thus they may track properties that obtain in the relation between an organism and its environment. Andy Clark puts this nicely:

> much of the distinctive power and attractiveness of these approaches lies in the way they can fix on collective variables – variables whose physical roots involve the interactions of multiple systems (often spread across brain, body and world). (1996, pp.119–120)

This leads nicely to our next consequence; the dynamical approach's relation to 'situated' phenomena.

6.5.2 Situation

We've seen the dynamical approach's concern with the temporal features of cognition, as well as its emphasis on the embodied and environmentally embedded nature of cognitive activity. I see these two features as different sides of the same coin; they're both ways of being 'situated' – either temporally, or physically. It is no accident that these two aspects often go hand in hand; advocates point out that DST is well suited to explaining (and therefore integrating) mind, body and world with a common language. Van Gelder (1995, p. 379), for example, writes:

> that within which cognition takes place (the brain, the body and the environment) demand dynamical tools in their description. A dynamical account of cognition promises to minimize difficulties in understanding how cognitive systems are real biological systems in constant, intimate dependence on, or interaction with, their surrounds.

We've already seen Beer emphasising this strong 'coupling' between brain, body and world. To the extent that it provides tools for explaining organism–environment coupling, the dynamical approach shares an ideological – if not always methodological – concern with other approaches to cognitive science and AI that emphasise 'situatedness'. Everybody knows that time, the body and the environment are important for cognition. You would not get much thinking done if you were not in a sufficiently oxygen-rich environment or if your body did not operate so as to deliver that oxygen to your organs in just the right quantities at just the right times. In addition, it is almost a truism that what we do with our bodies and environments is tremendously important for mental life; we all rely on diaries and shopping lists to help supplement our notoriously unreliable memories, and even adults sometimes resort to counting on their fingers in order to speed up calculations. The situated approach to cognition simply takes this recognition a step further. The practical significance of the body and the environment is seen as amounting to a kind of *theoretical* significance for cognitive science; an agent's body, environment and temporal coordination are more than (mere) implementation details. Brian Cantwell Smith (1999, p.769) sums up this new *zeitgeist*, by noting that the situated approach

> views intelligent human behaviour as engaged, socially and materially embodied activity, arising within the specific concrete details of particular (natural) settings, rather than as an abstract, detached, general purpose process of logical or formal ratiocination.

Two things are, therefore, worth noting. First, such a conception of cognition warrants a move away from AI as traditionally conceived, and towards robotics and *A-Life*. Second, the contrast with GOFAI (and to a lesser extent, connectionism) should also be clear. Let's deal with these in turn.

One movement – 'situated' or 'behaviour-based' robotics – takes the intimate relation between mind and world as a starting point for what it sees as a much more biologically realistic approach to AI. One of the movement's pioneers, Rodney Brooks (1991), for example, argues that AI really started in the wrong place by building machines for chess and logic out of functionally specialised subsystems. Instead, his approach is to start with the construction of relatively low-level 'creatures' and to build them from an architectural hierarchy of relatively autonomous, behaviour-generating and situated 'layers'. He claims that his approach

> makes no distinction between peripheral systems, such as vision, and central systems. Rather the fundamental slicing up of an intelligent system is in the orthogonal direction dividing it into *activity*

> producing subsystems. Each activity, or behavior producing system individually connects sensing to action. We refer to an activity producing system as a *layer*. (1991 p. 146)

The idea here is that, just as in the 'incremental' process of biological evolution, each layer should actually be able to *do* something in the real world, with more sophisticated behaviours grafted on top of behaviourally complete lower layers. With these principles in mind, Brooks and colleagues built a series of robots, the first of which were named Allen and Herbert (after Newell and Simon). In the case of Allen, for example, the lowest layer ('level 0') was a straightforward 'obstacle avoidance' system. This enabled the robot to exist in a changing environment: if it was placed in an empty room, it would sit still; if someone walked up to it, it would move away; if it moved towards another object it would halt. On top of this, Brooks constructed a 'wander' layer ('level 1') that would randomly generate a direction of movement for the robot from time to time, but that could also suppress the 'obstacle avoidance' layer. Finally, the top layer ('level 2') is described as an 'explorer' module; it identifies distant places and then tries to reach them. It can suppress the lower layers, but also observes how the bottom layer avoids objects and corrects for divergences until the goal is achieved.

Such simple but situated abilities combine to generate behaviour that is relatively complex, reminiscent of actions at about the level of a pet rodent, for example. Here's Brooks's (1986, p.22) description of Allen in operation:

> Under level 0 control, the robot finds a large empty space and then sits there contented until a moving obstacle approaches. Two people together can successfully herd the robot just about anywhere – through doors or between rows of disk drives, for instance.
>
> When level 1 control is added the robot is no longer content to sit in an open space. After a few seconds it heads off in a random direction...
>
> Under Level 2 a sonar-based corridor finder usually finds the most distant point in the room. The robot heads of in the direction [sic]. People walking in front of the robot cause it to detour, but the robot still gets to the initially desired goal, even when it involves squeezing between closely spaced obstacles.

Bermúdez (2010) nicely summarises three important lessons to be learnt from Brooks's situated approach. First, design is 'incremental' in that new, higher-level, subsystems are grafted on to lower layers in a way that is supposed to mimic evolution. We'll return to this issue shortly, in Chapter 6.5.4. Second, the sub-systems are 'semi-autonomous' in that they operate relatively independently even though some may override others; there is no 'central executive'. Third, there are direct perception–action links at all levels; motor responses are immediately issued upon sensory input in order to attain real-time control of action. Thus, the robot is 'situated' both temporally and physically.

This all stands in marked contrast to previous approaches. Given the Turing Machine's essentially idealised character (and arguably because of cognitive science's Cartesian legacy), GOFAI (and, to a lesser extent, connectionist) approaches inherited the view that mind and cognition are things to be studied apart from the body and the world. Of course, the mind–world interface (the mechanisms of sensory transduction and, to a lesser extent, muscular activity) *are* still studied by classical cognitive scientists, but only insofar as they are (mere) implementation details concerning how the self-sufficient mind gets hooked up with the body and the world. Chess playing machines don't actually move artificial arms to pick up pieces, and logic-crunchers don't actually put chalk to blackboard to sketch out their proofs (as Ronnie de Sousa, 1991, p.176 puts it, "It is a pregnant irony that computers are now relatively good at some of the reasoning tasks that Descartes thought the secure privilege of humans, while they are especially inept at the 'merely animal' functions that he thought could be accounted for mechanically").

Whilst this 'individualist' conception of cognition *does*, as it were, disconnect mind and world, that's arguably a reflection of one of the mind's most important features; you can think about things that are spatio-temporally distal or even non-existent (you can sit in a darkened room with your eyes closed and plan next year's summer holiday). Thus, to the extent that the situated robotics movement *requires* its 'creatures' to be in constant causal contact with the objects of its thought, it neglects the fact that humans are often able to think 'off line'. This contrast represents an interesting and deep tension between different aspects of human nature. On the one hand, we are biological creatures, situated in bodies and environments, and subject to the selection pressures afforded by these facts. But on the other hand, we are thinkers who are able to reason, make plans, remember and imagine precisely because we can (temporarily) 'detach' our minds from the immediate physical surroundings.

The latter ability is, on reflection, a tremendous achievement, and the representational theory of mind can explain it; we think about things that are distal or non-actual by manipulating internal 'stand-ins' for them. So the debate about situatedness goes hand in hand with a much deeper – and more controversial – debate about the necessity of representations. Theorists like Brooks (as the title of his (1991) paper "Intelligence Without Representation" suggests) flat-out deny that representations are necessary for intelligence, and thus seek to avoid them in the development of AI. Dynamicists have either advocated, or been accused of advocating, a similar position. So it is to that issue I now turn.

6.5.3 Representation revis(it)ed

The anti-representationalist tendency in dynamical approaches to cognitive science and AI, as I suggested, goes hand in hand with the emphasis on situatedness and the intimate interaction between mind and world. As Bechtel writes

> [O]ne of the functions of representations is to stand in for things outside the system; once a system has representations, it can operate on them and not need the world... Getting rid of representations thus facilitates reconnecting cognition and the world. (1998, p.297)

Further, this conceptual motivation is bolstered by evolutionary considerations; the situated robotics movement takes 'the world is its own best model' as a slogan because agents can *economise* by offloading some storage or processing onto the environment. Storing and processing information internally is costly – literally for roboticists who have to buy memory drives, and figuratively in terms of time and energy for biological creatures – and so we might expect complex creatures to have evolved ways of exploiting local environmental resources to do some of this work for them. I'll return to this issue in the next chapter.

Representations, as we've been using the notion in GOFAI and connectionism, are usually understood as internal 'stand-ins' for environmental features. If we want to explain the success of an organism in negotiating its environment we can construe some of its internal processes as carrying information about (and thus 'standing in for') some aspect of its body or environment that needs to be taken into account. Van Gelder emphasises this understanding of representation, concerning which

> pretty much any reasonable characterization [is] based around a core idea of some state of a system which, by virtue of some general representational scheme, stands in for some further state of affairs, thereby enabling the system to behave appropriately with respect to that state of affairs. (1995, p.351)

The trouble is that the 'stand-in' conception of representation is ambiguous between two senses of 'representation', both of which are important for cognitive science. The difference, as Clark puts it, is between, inner systems that operate only so as to control immediate environmental interactions, and ones that use inner resources to model the world so as to obviate the need for such continual environmental interaction. (1997 p.464)

The former, Clark calls 'weak internal representation'. A weak internal representation is a 'stand-in' in the sense of being an adaptive or functionally intended correlation between some internal state and some aspect of the environment. The latter he calls 'strong internal representation'. A strong internal representation is a 'stand-in' in the sense of being an internal model, which the agent can use *instead of* the real world, for various cognitive purposes. Bearing this distinction in mind will be important in the forthcoming discussion, for the claim that cognitive systems can operate without weak internal representations is clearly much less controversial than the claim that cognitive systems can operate without strong internal representations, not least because we often think of strong internal representations as partially constitutive of cognition. So what is it about dynamical cognitive science that could motivate anti-representationalism, and what are the specifics of that position?

Anti-representationalism seems to derive from van Gelder's discussion of the Watt centrifugal governor. Van Gelder emphasises the fact that explanations of the Watt centrifugal governor are not normally spelt out in terms of representations:

> A noteworthy fact about standard explanations of how the centrifugal governor works is, however, that they never talk about representations. This was true for the informal description given above, which apparently suffices for most readers; more importantly, it has been true of the much more detailed descriptions offered by those who have actually been in the business of constructing centrifugal governors or analyzing their behaviour. (1995, p.352)

There *is* a debate to be had about the representational status of the Watt governor. Indeed, the dynamicist literature contains such a debate: Van Gelder (1995) puts forward four arguments for the conclusion that the Watt governor is non-representational and Bechtel (1998) counters these arguments and comes to the conclusion that the Watt governor's arm angle is best understood as representing engine speed. This debate – however interesting – is a distraction from our concerns here, for at least three reasons.

First, we should note that what is at stake in the Watt governor example is only the issue of weak internal representation; that is, the less controversial notion. The Watt governor, as Clark might say, operates only so as to control immediate environmental interactions. So the claim that the Watt governor is non-representational amounts to the claim that the Watt governor can adapt its behaviour to its local environment *directly*, without the mediation of any kind of 'stand-in.' An observer could *use* arm angle as a sign or index of engine speed, but from the point of view of the Watt governor, as it were, no stand-in is even necessary. Nobody would claim that the Watt governor has or needs *strong* internal representations, since it does not, in Clark's phrase, "use inner resources to model the world so as to obviate the need for such continual environmental interaction". So even if Bechtel-style representationalism about the Watt governor stands up, the anti-representationalist can still claim that the representations in the Watt governor are of the *wrong kind*.

Second, this construal of the non-representational character of the Watt governor stands to reason. After all, nobody contends that the Watt governor is doing anything *cognitive*: even van Gelder is only advancing it as a suggestive example in order to undermine 'only game in town' arguments that see computational solutions for everything. One could claim that the Watt governor has no strong internal representations precisely because strong internal representations are constitutive of cognition, and the Watt governor is totally non-cognitive.

Third, I do not believe that the kind of anti-representationalism that van Gelder advances in his discussion of the Watt governor is reflective of his view of representation in cognitive science in general. Van Gelder's view is more of a 'revisionary representationalism', since he seeks a reconception of what representations are. He writes:

> While the Watt governor is clearly a non-representational dynamical system... in fact there is nothing preventing dynamical systems from incorporating some form of representation; indeed an exciting feature of the dynamical approach is that it offers opportunities for drastically reconceiving the nature of representation in cognitive systems, even within a broadly noncomputational framework. (1995, p.376)

Representational status may be assigned to various features of a given dynamical account, such as variables or parameters, or even trajectories and attractors. Rockwell (2005, p.37), in discussing the work of Thelen and Smith (1994) and Skarda and Freeman (1987), argues that "identifying mental representations and functions with attractor basins is the most effective way of understanding perception". Indeed, it seems that van Gelder and Port would agree with this kind of *non-eliminative* reconception, since they write:

A wide variety of aspects of dynamical models can be regarded as having a representational status: these include states, attractors, trajectories, bifurcations, and parameter settings... The crucial difference between computational models and dynamical models is that in the former, the rules that govern how the system behaves are defined over the entities that have representational status, whereas in dynamical models, the rules are defined over numerical states. That is, dynamical systems can be representational without having their rules of evolution defined over representations. (Van Gelder and Port, 1995, p.12)

But van Gelder is frequently interpreted as being an eliminativist about representation. Eliasmith (1996, p.452), for example, quotes van Gelder as saying "it is the concept of representation which is insufficiently sophisticated" for understanding cognition. But then, only two sentences later, Eliasmith attacks a straw man of the dynamicist position by writing: "Notably, the dynamicist assertion that representation is *not* necessary to adequately explain cognition is strongly reminiscent of the unsuccessful behaviorist project." Eliasmith's interpretation of van Gelder is inadequate, if not misleading: van Gelder says that representation is not *sufficient* for cognition; Eliasmith's straw man says that representation is not necessary. The real van Gelder does not deny that there is still room for representations in cognitive science. His view is simply that we must reconsider what we mean by the term 'representation'.

Dennett similarly attributes a radical anti-representationalist position to (at least one half of a split-personality) van Gelder. He writes:

There seem to be two van Gelders: the 'Hard Line van Gelder' says, in effect, There are no representations at all, anywhere in the brain, in any useful sense – down with representationalism! The 'Soft Line van Gelder' says, in effect, We must replace misshapen ideas of representation... with more perspicuous, biologically sound versions. (Dennett, 1998c, p.636-7)

It is a mystery where Dennett has met Hard Line van Gelder for he is certainly not a character that appears in print. Van Gelder does not express the 'Hard Line' view anywhere; as we have seen above, he rejects it. Van Gelder's response is illuminating: he says that the most plausible explanation for Dennett's (and others') mistaken belief in Hard Line van Gelder is that "prior belief in van Gelder's supposed antirepresentationalism biased their interpretation" (Van Gelder, 1998, p.658).

Where could this 'prior belief' have come from? I suspect that the explicit, and much more radical, anti-representationalism espoused by other dynamical cognitive scientists, coupled with the belief that there was some unity to the dynamical approach, could generate the view that 'the' dynamical approach to cognitive science is antirepresentational across the board. The work of Brooks (1991) – considered in the last section – is a case in point. He claims that "explicit representations and models of the world simply get in the way" of very simple level intelligence, and that "Representation is the wrong unit of abstraction in building the bulkiest parts of intelligent systems" (p.150). Skarda and Freeman (1987, p.184) present a similarly strong form of anti-representationalism in describing their model of the rabbit olfactory bulb, writing:

> The concept of 'representation'...is unnecessary as a keystone for explaining the brain and behaviour. This is because the dynamics of basins and attractors can suffice to account for behaviour without recourse to mechanisms for symbol storage.

In both Brooks' and Skarda and Freeman's cases, such anti-representationalism is driven by a desire similar to van Gelder's; the authors wish to contrast their view with the 'dominant' or 'orthodox' view – classical cognitive science and GOFAI. Brooks' motivation is largely methodological and spawned by practical attempts to build model robots. Skarda and Freeman (1987, p.184) express a *goal*: "cognitivists have written repeatedly for some years that rule-driven, symbol manipulating devices are the only realistic hope for mimicking and explaining behaviour. We submit that the brain can do much better."

For one thing, Skarda and Freeman appear to be committing a confusion of levels in the above quotation; after all, the claim that *cognitive* level explanations require formal symbol manipulation is quite compatible with the *neural* level claim that the brain does not traffic in representations. But both Brooks and Skarda and Freeman seem to run dangerously close to throwing the baby out with the bathwater, as it were. Eliminativism about representations is not a necessary condition for being opposed to classical cognitive science; connectionism, despite being opposed to GOFAI, simply seeks to reconceive representations in distributed terms. Similarly, van Gelder's dynamical hypothesis is explicitly contrasted with the 'computational hypothesis', but yet, as I have argued (and as van Gelder claims), it only leads to a revisionary view of representations. In striving to contrast their views with the 'classical' cognitive scientific approach, then, Brooks and Skarda and Freeman may have gone too far.

With that said, Beer (2003, p.239) (in his discussion of the dynamical account of perceptual categorisation), points out that there comes a point at which the revisions to the concept of representation are so extensive as to render the latter concept vacuous. He writes:

> If 'representation' comes to mean nothing more than correlated internal state...then a computational theory of mind loses its force...if the mechanisms underlying situated, embodied cognitive behavior look nothing like representations, and they act nothing like representations, then they are *not* representations, and continuing to call them representations is just going to confuse everyone.

Thus, revisionary and radical (i.e., eliminative) conceptions of representation in the dynamical approach seem to form something of a spectrum, and it's no easy matter to say where the line is drawn regarding a view of their necessity for cognition. At the very least, we can see that the concept of representation is something about which even dynamicists themselves are not in agreement, and this leads nicely to the fourth consequence of the dynamical approach, and a related criticism.

6.5.4 Incrementalism

The kind of examples that lead to anti-representationalist pronouncements are the same examples that are subject to what I shall call, following Clark (2001), the 'incrementalist' objection. One might object that the motivation for anti-representationalism stems from case studies that are all too peripheral or low-level. Clark and Toribio (1994, p.421), for example, write:

> insofar as the robot insect/governor style cases are meant to illustrate the tenability of a general anti-representationalism, they seem to us to miss the mark. For the problem domains which they negotiate are not (yet, at least) the ones on which the representationalist should rest her case.

The more general anti-representationalist claim does not follow, in Clark and Toribio's view, because the kinds of problems solved by robot insects, olfactory bulbs and Watt governors are not really high-level enough to require *strong* internal representations. This points to a more general objection that comes in two parts: (a) dynamical cognitive science has, as its target, a set of phenomena that are not *genuinely* cognitive, and (b) it is an unargued assumption that the insights from these low-level tasks will 'scale up' to the point where the same kinds of conceptual tools can account for the kind of 'high-level' cognition that was the focus of GOFAI and connectionism. Perhaps *the* most common response to many otherwise successful dynamical models is a feeling of unease concerning the extent to which they may properly be regarded as models of cognitive phenomena.

Such an objection claims that it is premature to conclude, on the basis of the models outlined in Chapter 6.4, that human cognition is best understood in the terms of DST, since the models only demonstrate that some (low-level or peripheral) sensorimotor engagements with the world (such as finger wagging or insect leg-movement) have a complex structure that makes them hard to explain using the standard resources of the GOFAI. Indeed, Van Gelder (1998) calls this the "peripheral objection". The canon of models, it is claimed, does not seem like a strong enough foundation upon which to build a whole cognitive paradigm, since it is aimed at the wrong target.

This building metaphor is apt, as such a notion is present in much of the dynamical literature. Thelen and Smith (1994, p.xxiii), for example, write:

> [T]here is in principle no difference between the processes engendering walking, reaching, and looking for hidden objects and those resulting in mathematics and poetry. Our developmental theorising leads us to a view of cognition as seamless and dynamic.

This view depends on what Andy Clark (2001, p.135) calls 'cognitive incrementalism': the view that "you do indeed get full-blown, human cognition by gradually adding 'bells and whistles' to basic (embodied, embedded) strategies of relating to the present at hand". Thelen and Smith explicitly endorse such a principle, but I think it is also implicitly held by other dynamicists.

Kirsch (1991) captures the incrementalist assumption with a slogan: 'Today the earwig, Tomorrow man.' The question is whether such an assumption is *justified*. Kirsch's own view is that it is not. He writes:

> I am not yet convinced that success in duplicating insect behaviours such as wandering, avoiding obstacles, and following corridors proves that the mobotics approach is the royal path to higher-level behaviours. Insect ethologists are not cognitive scientists. (1991, p. 162)

Clark is equally suspicious of the incrementalist assumption, writing:

> some cognitive functions may depend not on the tweaking of basic sensorimotor processing, but on the development of relatively (functionally) independent and (functionally) novel kinds of neural processes. (2001, p.135).

The charge, then, is that what passes for dynamical cognitive science is in fact merely ethology, kinesiology or physiology, and so, whilst dynamical explanations are important, they are aimed at the wrong target to explain cognition *as cognitive*. It could even be this objection which underlies the emergentist intuitions one finds in the dynamical cognitive scientific literature (more of which shortly); perhaps it is the gap between ethology, kinesiology or physiology and cognition which emergence is supposed to 'leap'.

I think that the objection can be overcome in three ways. First Brooks (1991) provides a *methodological* answer: over the course of evolution, simple adaptively successful sensorimotor behaviour took much longer to evolve than the kind of behaviour with which cognitive science has traditionally been concerned; language and chess-playing arose only in the last few thousand years. In Brooks's own words,

> This suggests that problem solving behavior, language, expert knowledge and application, and reason, are all pretty simple once the essence of being and reacting are available. That essence is the ability to move around in a dynamic environment, sensing the surroundings to a degree sufficient to achieve the necessary maintenance of life and reproduction. This part of intelligence is where evolution has concentrated its time – it is much harder. (Brooks, 1991, p.141)

So Brooks's methodological answer to the objection is that it is an open empirical question whether the incrementalist assumption is justified, and that cognitive science will have to postpone the problem, and focus on building low-level or peripheral models, until such time as we are able to answer it.

Second, then, the dispute can be recast as one concerning what *counts* as paradigmatically cognitive; traditionally, we have thought of problem-solving, language and chess-playing as exemplars, but the dynamical approach, with its embodied/embedded insights, seems to suggest that low-level sensorimotor environmental engagement is the most pressing set of problems. The objection can thus be addressed by recasting it as a dispute over what phenomena constitute the appropriate target for cognitive science in general and AI in particular.

The third and final response is to employ the old maxim; when life gives you lemons, make lemonade (or computer science's nearest variant: 'It's not a bug, it's a feature'). Van Gelder's (1998, p.625) response to the incrementalist objection is that the applicability of DST to a *variety* of different target phenomena is a strength of the dynamical approach. Dynamical systems theory itself is applicable to a wide variety of levels in physics, from quantum mechanics to cosmology, van Gelder argues, so "Similarly in cognitive science: dynamicists develop their explanations at the level of theoretical interest, whatever that might be". Thus, whereas connectionists are committed to low-level, high-dimensional models of the 'microstructure' of cognition, "The dynamical approach is more catholic; it embraces dynamical models of all kinds and at all levels."[2] The ability of DST to apply to ethology (Beer), kinesiology (HKB), physiology (Skarda and Freeman), *and* higher-level phenomena like perceptual categorisation (Beer) and decision making (Busemeyer and Townsend, 1993; Townsend and Busemeyer, 1995) is its unique strength.

As these comments suggest, then, I do think that the incrementalist objection can be met. It is interesting to note that there is no clear consensus, *even amongst advocates* of the dynamical approach, as to the target level of phenomena at which the dynamical approach should be aimed. But as a result, there are dynamical models pitched at many different levels and concerning both central and peripheral cognitive activities, and this breadth of scope does indeed seem like a strength; at the very least, it's the unifying stuff of which cognitive scientific dreams are made.

6.6 The dynamical approach and the mind-body problem

Whether one takes the material in the previous section as favourable to the dynamical approach, or as raising doubts about it, one might nonetheless ask the hypothetical question: 'What implications does the dynamical approach have for the mind-body problem?' One very widespread intuition – perhaps owing to the concern with systemic and temporal properties and processes – is that there's a 'natural affinity' between the dynamical approach to cognition and emergentism about the mind.

Such an intuition appears in literature that ranges all the way from theoretical physics to developmental psychology. Physicist James Crutchfield (1994) refers to dynamics as one of the 'calculi of emergence'. In describing the HKB model of finger-wagging, Van Gelder (1998, p.616) writes:

> The basic insight is that coordination is best thought of not as masterminded by a digital computer sending symbolic instructions at just the right time, but as an emergent property of a nonlinear dynamical system self-organizing around instabilities.

Some make the stronger claim that, not only are dynamics and emergence *consistent*, but the former could even *explain* the latter. Developmental psychologist Jeff Elman (1998, p.504) views DST as "a mathematical framework for understanding the sort of emergentism... found in both connectionism and artificial-life models" and describes "dynamical systems theory as a formal implementation of the old notion of emergent form" (Elman et al., 1996, p.366).

The existence of such intuitions is perhaps hardly surprising, since the language of DST seems to be ideal for describing and explaining many properties that are sometimes understood to be emergent. The most well-developed dynamical models, as we've seen, display behaviours that result from the collective and interactive action of a system's parts, rather than from the action of any single component. This seems to be captured by the emphasis on systemic 'total state' explanations in DST such that DST does seem like a natural way to accomplish the goal of explaining or vindicating emergentism. I certainly feel the force of the intuition. The question is whether such an intuition is a reliable guide to truth.

One immediate cause for concern is that the type of 'covering law' explanation we've seen offered by dynamical cognitive science requires a deducibility relation between the thing doing explaining (e.g., the differential equations and the initial conditions) and the thing being explained (e.g., the cognitive behaviour). But deducibility is a hallmark of the classic treatment of *reduction* offered by Ernest Nagel (1961). According to Nagel's model of reduction, if the laws of theory T_1 can be deduced from the laws of theory T_2, then T_1 is said to be reducible to T_2: reducibility is deducibility. In fact, it is sometimes even said that cases of Nagel-reduction are cases where the reduced theory is *explained* by the reducing theory (Silberstein, 2002, p.85, for example, writes that the Nagelian account of reduction "treats intertheoretic reduction as deductive, and as a special case of [covering law] explanation"). This close relationship between covering-law explanation and Nagel-reduction gives rise to an interesting problem; covering-law explanations require that the thing-to-be-explained is deducible from the conjunction of laws and initial conditions, whereas most theories of emergence (insofar as they're non-reductive views) require the *absence* of such deducibility (see Walmsley, 2010, for a more detailed discussion).

An alternative reading of the dynamical approach, then, embraces the parallel between dynamical explanation and Nagel-reduction, and thus jettisons talk of emergence. Even though he does not describe it in this way, the view put forward by Kelso (1995) can be understood as such, because it seeks to characterise different 'levels' (in this case cognitive and neural) using the same vocabulary. Beer (2000, p.97) argues that dynamical cognitive science aims to provide a "common language for cognition, for the neurophysiological processes that support it, for non-cognitive human behaviour, and for the adaptive behaviour of simpler animals" and a "unified theoretical framework for cognitive science." Kelso (1995, p.289) follows suit, writing:

> My aim here was to join together neural processes at one end of the scale and mental or cognitive processes at the other, in a common language. This is the language of dynamic patterns, not the neuron *per se*. But more than a language, shared principles of self-organisation provide the linkage across levels of neural and cognitive function.

Such a view can be understood as advocating a *kind* of reductionism: not Nagel-reduction, but what Silberstein (2002, p.88) has called the 'semantic approach' to reduction, wherein the "reduction relation might be conceived of as some kind of 'isomorphism' or 'expressive equivalence' between models". Kelso uses just this terminology to tie together the technical vocabulary of DST and the traditional language of the mind-body problem:

> an order parameter isomorphism connects mind and body, will and brain, mental and neural events. Mind itself is a spatiotemporal pattern that molds the metastable dynamic patterns of the brain. Mind-body dualism is replaced by a single isomorphism, the heart of which is semantically meaningful pattern variables. (Kelso, 1995, pp.288–289)

Recall the distinction we drew earlier, following Giunti (1997), between a *real* dynamical system (a concrete entity which changes in time) and a *mathematical* dynamical system (a set of equations used to characterise the changes in a real system). One interesting feature of this distinction is that it allows for more than one real dynamical system to be described by the same mathematical dynamical system. The *same* equations might also describe a number of *different* concrete systems. Given that dynamical explanations are able to abstract away from implementation details, this amounts to the claim that mathematical dynamical systems are multiply realisable. So Kelso's form of reductionism could be understood as the claim that what unifies mind and brain is the fact that both are described by the same differential equations. This claim is not so much that cognition can be reduced to neurophysiology, but rather that *both* can be 'reduced' to the same, shared, underlying dynamics. Thus Kelso (1995, p.287) argues that "Instead of trying to *reduce* biology and psychology to chemistry and physics, the task now is to *extend* our physical understanding of the organisation of living things".

Kelso clearly does not want to call this 'reductionism,' but it sits well with an alternative account of reduction – 'functional reductionism' – advanced by the philosopher Jaegwon Kim (1997, 2000). Very briefly, a Kim-style functional reduction consists of two stages. The first is a specification of the target (i.e., reduced) property or behaviour in terms of its functional role (i.e., its law-like causal relations) with respect to other properties or behaviour. An example that Kim gives of this kind of functional reconstrual is the gene. Instead of thinking of a gene in terms of its intrinsic properties, Kim argues, we need to specify its causal/nomic relations by saying something like "the gene is that mechanism in a biological organism which is causally responsible for the transmission of heritable characteristics from parents to offsprings" (Kim, 2000, p.25). The kinds of equations provided by the canonical dynamical models in cognitive science can be viewed as analogous; they specify the causal-nomic relationships between the important variables in a cognitive system.

The second stage is to "find properties or mechanisms, often at the microlevel, that satisfy these causal/nomic specifications and thereby fill the specified causal roles" (Kim, 2000, p.25). In the case of the gene, the DNA molecule fills the causal role of being responsible for the transmission of heritable characteristics from parents to offspring. According to Kim, this is why we can justifiably say that the gene has been reduced to DNA, even though this kind of reduction allows the possibility of multiple realisability; the functional role could (in another world, or in another organism) be played by some other lower-level structure. In the case of dynamical cognitive science, this kind of functional reductionism would require that we find brain systems which obey the same equations as those which govern higher-level behaviours. This would make Kelso's (and Silberstein's) repeated use of the term 'isomorphism' literal; the equations which characterise both cognitive and neural dynamics would have the same form. If that were possible, we could say that the dynamics of cognition had been (functionally) reduced to the dynamics of the brain, whilst allowing that the dynamics of cognition could be implemented by some other (perhaps non-biological) kind of concrete system, so long as its components were arranged in such a way as to fill the requisite functional role.

This kind of two-step process could be what Kelso is hinting at. If we could find the differential equations which governed both high-level behavioural *and* low-level neural aspects of a given task, we might well find that they were (literally) isomorphic. Thus the job of dynamical cognitive science – one which Van Gelder (1998) admits, when he describes the approach as 'catholic' – is to investigate the same phenomena at multiple levels of explanation with a view to effecting this kind of unification. This is the kind of stuff of which cognitive scientific dreams are made, but would require abandoning the hope that cognitive science and AI would justify a non-reductive, or emergentist, position on the mind-body problem. Of course, it's too early to say whether dynamical cognitive science will evolve in this way. But we might say that we presently stand at a bifurcation point, and, although the direction in which our trajectory will be pushed is not clear, we can at least see the shape of some of the attractors ahead.

7
The Future: Mind and Machine Merged

> Soul and body, body and soul – how mysterious they were! There was animalism in the soul, and the body had its moments of spirituality... Who could say where the fleshly impulse ceased, or the psychical impulse began?
>
> Oscar Wilde (1890) *The Picture of Dorian Gray*

I start with this quotation, because in this Chapter I intend to turn back and examine one of our initial questions from a slightly different angle. In addition to the question of the possibility of thinking machines, we have also had at the back of our minds the question of whether *we* are such machines. In this chapter, I want to consider some ideas in cognitive science and AI that either dispute the legitimacy of the mind–machine distinction, or else blur the boundary between mind and world (or between 'psychical' and 'fleshly' impulses). The topics I shall discuss are all regarded as 'speculative' (as is appropriate for a Chapter concerned with the future of a discipline). The extent to which this tag is intended as derogatory is not clear – I leave it to the reader to adopt their own view on this matter – but I shall treat the topics in ascending order of 'speculativity'.

We'll start by looking at a set of arguments – both philosophical and scientific – that follow on from our earlier consideration of situated robotics and give rise to the 'extended mind' hypothesis in cognitive science. Very briefly, the idea is that the 'boundaries' of the mind do not correspond to the skin/skull boundary, and thus, that the mind is extended in the sense that parts of the body and the world are also parts of the cognitive system. This leads us into a consideration of 'cognitive technology' and the human-machine hybrid systems that Andy Clark (2003) has called "natural-born cyborgs". As we'll see, despite sounding like the stuff of science fiction, the idea might *already* apply to us. Finally, we'll see how these kinds of considerations lead to a set of different futuristic scenarios, described as 'The singularity', in which human-made machines (or human-machine hybrids) achieve a level of intelligence superior to that of the 'naked' human brain, and thus return us to a question of 'supra-psychological' AI.

Many of these considerations have their roots in a field known as *cybernetics*. Cybernetics came into being in the 1940s as an interdisciplinary enterprise involving engineers, biologists, mathematicians, psychologists and neuroscientists, all of whom found common ground in the study of systems that use informational feedback to control and govern their actions. The word *cybernetics* itself derives from the Greek for *pilot* or *steersman* and thus the subtitle of Norbert Wiener's (1948) book *Cybernetics* – in which we've already seen him characterise Pascal and Leibniz as the 'patron saints' of AI – is "control and communication in the animal and machine". In the preface (p.vii), Wiener writes "The role of information and the technique of measuring and transmitting information constitute a whole discipline for the engineer, for the physiologist, for the psychologist, and for the sociologist". In another seminal introduction to the subject, Ashby (1956) describes cybernetics as a field with co-ordination, regulation and control as its main themes, and one that is "essentially functional" (p.1). He writes:

> Cybernetics stands to the real machine – electronic, mechanical, neural, or economic – much as geometry stands to a real object in our terrestrial space... Cybernetics is similar in its relation to the actual machine. It takes as its subject-matter the domain of 'all possible machines', and is only secondarily interested if informed that some of them have not yet been made, either by Man or by Nature. What cybernetics offers is the framework on which all individual machines may be ordered, related and understood. (1956, p.2)

This provides a nice link – both in terms of its overarching functionalism, and in terms of its concern with *possibility* rather than *actuality* – to our first port of call: the 'extended mind' hypothesis.

7.1 The extended mind hypothesis

In the previous chapter (especially Section 6.5.2), we considered some of the empirical or experimental motivation for adopting a 'situated' approach to cognitive science and AI. The construction of artificial insects (Beer) and mobile autonomous robots (Brooks) led to the conclusion that cognition must be understood as intertwined with the body and the environment in which an agent finds itself. So, we might ask (along with Clark and Chalmers, 1998), "where does the mind stop and the rest of the world begin?" What are the 'boundaries' of the mind that would need to be included (respected or reproduced) in cognitive science and AI?

In their famous paper, Clark and Chalmers (1998, p.8) come to the striking conclusion that "cognitive processes ain't all in the head" by advancing a thought experiment designed to show that the privilege often accorded to intracranial aspects of cognition is in fact a misguided prejudice. They invite us to consider two parallel cases in which, despite superficial differences in intra- and extra-cranial location, cognitive processes are, they claim, identical in other important respects. For the purposes of exposition, I'll restrict the discussion to the case of belief. Inga, so the story goes, is a 'normal' adult human who happens to store her memories intra-cranially. Otto, by contrast, suffers from an impairment in memory that results in him having to write information in a notebook that he carries with him everywhere he goes (note: the characters' names reflect the differing locations of their information stores: Inga, inner; Otto, outer). In this sense, Otto's repository of information is extra-cranial.

When Inga hears about an exhibition that she wants to see, she thinks for a moment, remembers that the museum is on 53rd street, and then goes there. By contrast, when Otto hears about the exhibition, he checks his notebook, finds that it says that the museum is on 53rd street, and then goes there. Our folk-psychological notions of belief suggest that there is an important difference between Otto and Inga; we are tempted to say that Inga has beliefs about the location of the museum, but Otto does not (at least, not until after he has consulted his notebook). But according to Clark and Chalmers, this is a mistake; if we were to follow him around for a while, we would notice that Otto's (external) notebook functions in just the same way as Inga's (internal) memory. Thus, Clark and Chalmers conclude that,

> In all *important* respects, Otto's case is similar to a standard case of (nonoccurrent) belief. The differences between Otto's case and Inga's are striking, but they are superficial. (p.14, emphasis in original)

The motivation for coming to this conclusion is what Clark (2010) has described as a 'parity principle', which says something like 'as within the skull, so without'. The parity principle has been interpreted as the claim that there is no significant, non-question begging difference between intra-cranial and extra-cranial systems involved in cognition. Elsewhere, Clark (2005, p.4) has advanced this claim about mental *content*, writing: "I do not believe that there is any non-question-begging notion of intrinsic content that picks out all and only the neural in any clear and useful fashion." Here, Clark and Chalmers are concerned to establish a similar conclusion for the vehicles that carry those contents. In their own words,

> If...a part of the world functions as a process which, *were it done in the head*, we would have no hesitation in recognizing as part of the cognitive process, then that part of the world *is* (so we claim) part of the cognitive process. (p.8, emphasis in original)

Notice here that Clark and Chalmers attempt to motivate their position by redeploying the functionalism of classical cognitive science and GOFAI. Recall that the most general kind of metaphysical functionalism defines mental states according to the causal role they play with respect to (sensory) input, (behavioural) output and other mental states, rather than by the substance out of which they are made; we saw Clark (1989, p.21) characterise functionalism with the slogan "It ain't the meat, it's the motion". Thus, functionalism allows that there could be *psychological* similarities between systems that are *physically* very different; according to functionalists, you, your brother, your dog, a Martian and a thinking super-computer could all have an identical belief (despite the drastic differences in your *physical* make-up), so long as your *functional* structure is sufficiently similar. Functionalism permits the kind of multiple-realisability that makes AI possible in principle.

But once one accepts the view that mental states are multiply realisable and defined by their function, then one might ask why the material that performs those functions has to be located *within* the boundaries of skull and skin. If how you are functionally organised is all that matters for cognition, then there seems to be no good reason to restrict that functional organisation to the *inside* of agents. The functionalist parity principle permits a kind of multiple-*locatability*.

This general principle may then be re-deployed in the analysis of particular cases. Consider the 2001 film *Memento*, in which the character Leonard suffers from an inability to form new memories. To compensate for this, he writes notes to himself, takes Polaroid pictures, and tattoos important information onto his body. According to the advocates of the extended mind hypothesis, since Leonard's notes, pictures and tattoos play the same kind of functional role for him as *internal* memory storage does for normal adults, then we must count the notes, pictures and tattoos as *part* of Leonard's cognitive apparatus; his mind is, quite literally, not wholly inside his head. Leonard's notes, polaroids and tattoos, on this view, are the kind of 'cognitive technology' that might permit describing him as a 'natural-born cyborg' (more of which in the next section) because constitutive parts of his cognitive system are located outside of his head.

Despite claims like those made by Clark and Chalmers sounding like something from science fiction (Wilson, 2010, calls them 'cyborg fantasy arguments') they are in fact motivated by a more general, evolutionarily inspired, approach to studying the mind as a biological phenomenon. Wilson and Clark (2009) argue that it is natural to take the extended mind hypothesis in cognitive science as continuous with the emphasis on extendedness elsewhere in biology. They claim that Dawkins' famous 'extended phenotype' theory, views such as Turner's (2000) 'extended physiology' and the extended mind hypothesis, all share a central premise: that "The individual organism is an arbitrary stopping point for the scientific study of at least a range of relevant processes in the corresponding domain" (Wilson and Clark, 2009, p.60).

These considerations take evolutionary constraints on biological systems to be paramount. Offloading one's information-processing tasks onto the environment is one way of freeing up inner resources that can subsequently be dedicated to the evolutionarily salient 'four Fs' (feeding, fighting, fleeing and reproduction). Clark points out that this principle may apply to any kind of processing – whether it is advanced information processing or low-level food-processing. Presumably, one reason we cook food is because heating it serves to break it down in ways that avoid the costs of doing so internally. Similarly, Clark (1989, p.64) describes what he calls the '007 principle,' according to which

> evolved creatures will neither store nor process information in costly ways when they can use the structure of the environment and their operations upon it as a convenient stand-in for the information processing operations concerned. That is, know only as much as you need to know to get the job done.

One might characterise the inspiration thus; if I write my shopping list on an external piece of paper, then I can dedicate my internal resources towards not dying on the way to the supermarket. Further, this all sits well – both theoretically and empirically – with Brooks-style situated robotics and its emphasis on biological/evolutionary realism.

All this is not to say, however, that the extended mind hypothesis is uncontroversial. Far from it. Two interesting objections will tie it in to material we've considered in earlier chapters. First, recall the problem of 'original meaning' that we first encountered in Chapter 1. There, we saw that Hobbes ran into a problem, for whilst his account sees thought as language-like, we cannot say that thoughts get their meanings via the same process as linguistic items. Words in a public language (and other signs) acquire their meaning in a derivative or conventional fashion, but (on pain of circularity or regress) we cannot tell the same story concerning the meanings of the components of thought.

Adams and Aizawa (2001), for example, contend that this original meaning (or 'non-derived content' as they call it) is in fact a 'mark of the cognitive': for something to *count* as a cognitive state, it must involve intrinsic or non-derived content. They write:

> Strings of symbols on the printed page mean what they do in virtue of conventional associations between them and words of language... [but] it is not by anyone's convention that a state in a human brain is part of a person's thought that the cat is on the mat. (Adams and Aizawa, 2001, p.48)

In the case of Otto, they point out, retrieving an item 'from memory' requires thumbing through his notebook to find the relevant entry. But, they claim, the marks in Otto's notebook – since they are written in a public language – only have derived content, whereas whatever is going on in Inga's brain has non-derived content. Thus, they conclude, there *is* a significant and relevant difference between Otto and Inga, despite their recall processes being functionally similar. They conclude: "it is hard to see how these differences could be scientifically unimportant or irrelevant, save by adopting a behavioural conception of cognition" (p.56) and thus, that "Whatever is responsible for non-derived representations seems to find a place only in brains" (p.63).

Clark's (2010) response is enough to avoid Adams and Aizawa's objection, even though it does not – and does not attempt to – *solve* the problem of 'original meaning'. He points out that even if we take non-derived content to be the mark of the cognitive, we are still not committed to the (much stronger) claim that *every part* of a cognitive process should have non-derived content; perhaps all that's required is that cognitive processes should include *some* states with non-derived content. This much is true of Otto, for when he reads his notebook, presumably the marks therein (with derived content) *trigger* neural goings-on with non-derived content. Clark (2010, p.49) thus concludes that the writing in Otto's notebook "can be properly poised in any larger cognitive economy that includes states with intrinsic content". Given that Adams and Aizawa (2001, p.50) actually admit that "it is unclear to what extent each cognitive state of each cognitive process must involve non-derived content" it seems that Clark has the upper hand.

A second objection – to the Clark and Chalmers argument in particular, but also to more mundane examples such as the use of diaries, shopping lists, and counting on one's fingers – connects with our earlier discussion of 'coupling' in dynamical systems. Adams and Aizawa (2010) argue that whilst these examples show how a cognitive agent may be reliably coupled to various local environmental features (such as notebooks and shopping lists), that insight alone does not warrant the further inference to the conclusion that the agent's cognitive processes are *constituted* by the local environmental features. Adams and Aizawa regard this argumentative move as fallacious – dubbing it the 'coupling-constitution fallacy', and writing:

> If you are coupled to your pocket notebook in the sense of always having it readily available, use it a lot, trust it implicitly, and so forth, then Clark infers that the pocket notebook constitutes a part of your memory store... Yet coupling relations are distinct from constitutive relations, and the fact that object or process X is coupled to object or process Y does not entail that X is part of Y. (Adams and Aizawa, 2010, p.68)

Adams and Aizawa attempt to defend this claim using several examples that are supposed to be importantly similar to the Otto/Inga case, but in each of which (they claim) the move from coupling to constitution is more clearly illegitimate. First, consider the coupling relationship between the different parts of a neuromuscular junction. Adams and Aizawa write:

> The neurons leading into a neuromuscular junction are coupled to the muscles they innervate, but the neurons are not a part of the muscles they innervate. The release of neurotransmitters at the neuromuscular junction is coupled to the process of muscular contraction, but the process of releasing neurotransmitters at the neuromuscular junction is not part of the process of muscular contraction. (Adams and Aizawa, 2010, p.68)

But considering this case explicitly in terms of systems and processes, it is tempting simply to deny the claim made in the above quotation. The release of neurotransmitters *just is* a constitutive part of the process of muscular contraction – counterfactually, if the neurotransmitter had not been released, the muscles would not have contracted; the release of neurotransmitters is a necessary component of the process of contraction. A similar point can be made regarding Adams and Aizawa's second example, concerning the role of the kidney within the circulatory system. They write:

> The kidney filters impurities from the blood. In addition, this filtration is causally influenced by the heart's pumping of the blood, the size of the blood vessels in the circulatory system, the one-way valves in the circulatory system, and so forth. The fact that these various parts of the circulatory system causally interact with the process of filtration in the kidneys does not make even a prima facie case for the view that filtration occurs throughout the circulatory system, rather than in the kidney alone. (2001, p.56)

In fact, however, the causal interaction between the circulatory system and the kidney is much more tightly coupled than this description would suggest. The kidneys play an essential role in the maintenance of blood pressure throughout the circulatory system, but at the same time, excessively high or low blood pressure can severely impair the kidneys' ability to carry out their function of filtration. It does not seem unreasonable, therefore, to say that the *circulatory system* is one in which the process of filtration occurs; the kidney is a necessary, but not sufficient, subsystem and it is the tight coupling between kidneys, heart, blood vessels and valves that jointly *constitute* the broader circulatory system, blood pressure, filtration and oxygen-delivery included.

These two examples, then, serve neither to illustrate nor to motivate charges of the so-called 'coupling-constitution fallacy'. Quite the opposite in fact. Coupling between neurotransmitters and muscles really does entail the constitution of a *broader* process of muscular contraction, and coupling between the actions of the kidneys, the heart and the blood vessels is exactly what constitutes the broader circulatory system. In both cases, the move from coupling to constitution is not generally fallacious. Indeed, in DST, as we've seen, it is normally the case that coupling between two systems *entails* the joint constitution of a broader system.

Consider, for example, the case of the double pendulum: one pendulum attached to the end of another. Despite the rich chaotic behaviour exhibited by such a system (many animations of which can be found on-line) the double pendulum is really rather simple; in the language I have already been using, it consists of two *coupled* single pendula, which jointly *constitute* the larger double-pendulum. The mathematics of dynamical systems theory (DST) allows for the behaviour of the double-pendulum as a whole to be neatly captured by a coupled pair of ordinary differential equations, each of which describe the behaviour of the individual component pendula under the conditions of physical coupling.

The mathematical details need not concern us here, but what is worthy of note is that, on the one hand, this is a case where coupling between two systems entails the joint constitution of a broader system, and on the other hand, the mathematical framework of DST allows for a fairly straightforward – and integrated – explanation of this relationship.

By adopting the dynamical approach to *cognition*, cases of organism–environment coupling can be seen as importantly similar; they are those cases where the organism and environment jointly constitute a broader system. Recall, for example, that Beer (1997) conceptualises the relationship between nervous system, body and environment as a set of nested dynamical systems, whereby the coupling between each level leads to the constitution of a broader system, and argues that it is this jointly constituted agent–environment system that is the proper object of study for cognitive science. He writes (p.266): "Strictly speaking, behaviour is a property only of the coupled agent–environment system; it cannot in general properly be attributed to either the agent or the environment alone" (p.266). So, not only is the move from coupling to constitution a legitimate inference, but here such a step is essential; by switching to the broader view in which the agent is but a sub-component of the whole agent-body-environment system, one is afforded a better picture of situated cognition, and the common language of DST to describe it.

In the Otto/Inga case, therefore, one may conceive of the different components as *coupled* dynamical systems. On the one hand, Otto's internal cognitive resources could be described and explained in dynamical systems terms. On the other hand, his notebook and the way it changes over time could be described using a similar formalism. Then, the coupling between Otto and his notebook could be explained – very naturally – along the same lines as the integrated mathematical explanation of the double pendulum. In doing so, we would have to note that the broader Otto-notebook system is itself a further dynamical system, newly constituted by the coupling that obtains between its component sub-systems, but different from either of them taken in isolation.

The extended mind hypothesis, then, can be defended against its most prominent objections, particularly when combined with some of the insights from the dynamical approach to cognitive science and AI. For present purposes, however, what's most interesting is that, in blurring the traditional boundary between mind and *world*, the extended mind hypothesis permits the merging of mind and *machine*. In the next section, I'll take a look at the line of thought that runs from tool-use, through the extended mind hypothesis and 'cognitive technology' to the rather surprising conclusion that we humans are already, to use Andy Clark's phrase, 'natural-born cyborgs'.

7.2 Cognitive technology and human-machine hybrids

The term 'cyborg' was coined in an article by Manfred Clynes and Nathan Kline (1960) as an acronym for 'Cybernetic Organism'. In it, they argued that extraterrestrial travel and habitation would be better accomplished with the technological modification of human bodily function rather than the construction of earth-like environments in space. Thus, despite sounding like the stuff of science fiction, their own description of the cyborg fits very well with what we have already encountered in the literature on the extended mind; they write:

> For the exogenously extended organizational complex functioning as an integrated homeostatic system unconsciously, we propose the term 'Cyborg'. The Cyborg deliberately incorporates exogenous components extending the self-regulatory control function of the organism in order to adapt it to new environments. (Clynes and Kline, 1960, p.27)

On reflection, the idea of an "exogenously extended organizational complex" is not terribly surprising. My cat, Trim, is implanted with a microchip about the size of a grain of rice. When passed under a scanner, it can transmit a small radio-frequency ID signal that carries sufficient information that *my* phone number and address can be retrieved from a database, and Trim can be safely returned home if lost. But Trim doesn't count as a cyborg by Clynes and Kline's definition; his microchip has no homeostatic control function and even though it is an information-carrying device, Trim is not its user. Trim doesn't even know he has the chip and it's really just a slightly more sophisticated version of the very old technological practice of farmers painting ID numbers on sheep.

By contrast, though, my grandfather *is* implanted with an 'exogenous component extending his self-regulatory control': a pacemaker. Since his body's own biological pacemaker does not make his heart beat as it should, that homeostatic function is accomplished by a small metal-and-plastic widget that sits just below his collar-bone, and is wired up to his heart. The first ever implantable pacemaker was developed and employed in 1958 (its owner ended up outliving both its inventor and the surgeon), and so it's reasonable to assume that Clynes and Kline may have had this sort of thing in mind when they formulated their definition. But it's still not the sort of thing that would be of interest to *cognitive* scientists or those concerned with artificial *intelligence*. For that, we might instead consider exogenously extended organisational complexes that extend the ability of a user to process *information*.

Examples of artificial ways of enhancing our sensory abilities abound; from the humble pair of reading glasses, to the more sophisticated cochlear implant, we have developed ways of, as it were, amplifying the signal strength for incoming information. But one particular – and fairly well-known – example is a good case where a technological add-on not only enhances, but transforms, sensory information: the case of tactile-visual sensory substitution (TVSS). In a series of pioneering studies, neuroscientist Paul Bach-y-Rita developed a system whereby visual information could be obtained from tactile stimulation.

In the typical set up, a head-mounted camera is connected to an array of vibrating prongs pressed against the back (in the original study: Bach-y-Rita et al., 1969) or to an electrotactile array placed on the tongue (see, e.g., Bach-y-Rita et al., 2003). Blind individuals who have learnt to use TVSS systems report that initially, they feel the bodily tactile sensation. But after a while, with extensive practice, they begin to experience quasi-visual (or at least 3D spatial) sensations that permit them to perform a stunning range of 'normal' visual-related and hand-'eye' co-ordination tasks, including "facial recognition, accurate judgment of speed and direction of a rolling ball with over 95% accuracy in batting a ball as it rolls over a table edge, and complex inspection-assembly tasks" (Bach-y-Rita et al., 2003, p.287). Subjects will duck if a ball is thrown at the head, note things looming in on them, and even experience some visual illusions, such as the waterfall effect (Bach-y-Rita, 2002). Finally brain imaging studies have revealed that it is actually the visual cortex – not the somatosensory cortex – that was activated in cases of sensory substitution. Though somewhat controversial, it would seem defensible to conclude that, both phenomenologically and physiologically, blind people using a TVSS system can see (and not just 'see'). Further, Bach-y-Rita and Kercel (2003) do not shy away from describing TVSS as a 'human-machine interface', and on Clynes and Kline's definition, it would not be too much of a stretch to apply the label 'cyborg' to this mind-machine merger.

Whilst the use of TVSS is largely non-invasive, there are other instances of man-machine hybridity that – in virtue of their more invasive nature – seem to bring science-fiction to life. In a series of experiments, Kevin Warwick (Professor of Cybernetics at Reading University) received a number of subcutaneous microchip implants that explicitly took him on a quest to become a cyborg (his 2002 book is entitled *I, Cyborg*). In 1998, in what he describes as 'Project Cyborg 1.0', he had a small radio transmitter surgically inserted into his arm. This chip sent signals to various receivers located around his department so that doors would open as he approached, lights and heaters would turn on as he arrived and so on. This initial stage was more of a proof-of-concept, however; similar results could have been achieved using a transmitter carried in a pocket or on a lanyard or key-chain. There was not really a proper 'interface' between Prof. Warwick and the chip such that he could, at this stage, properly be described as a cyborg.

'Project Cyborg 2.0', however, was a much more significant development. In this case, Warwick had a small array of 100 electrodes implanted into the median nerve of his left arm. It was able to measure the impulses sent along this nerve, and copy them via a radio signal to a computer *and vice-versa*. Using this bi-directional connection, Warwick was able to control a robotic hand to manipulate an unseen object, and even able to do so via a transatlantic internet connection between New York and Reading (Warwick et al., 2003). Finally, in what must surely count as the most intimate scientific collaboration on record, a similar array was implanted in the arm of Irena Warwick (Prof. Warwick's wife). By exploiting the bi-directional nature of the connection, they were each able to perceive when the other was flexing their arm muscles with over 98 per cent accuracy! (Warwick et al., 2004)

These experiments are, of course, quite remarkable. Perhaps unsurprisingly, they generated a lot of publicity, and even the briefest twirl around the internet reveals them being described as presenting a futuristic kind of 'telepathy' and 'empathy'. Prof. Warwick really is an exogenously extended organisational complex, and through this bi-directional information exchange, he can send and receive signals to and from external objects, including other people. His self-professed desire is to be a cyborg, and by Clynes and Kline's definition, it's reasonable to say that he has fulfilled it.

Clark (2003, p.22), has an interesting take on the matter. Reflecting on the Warwick case, he argues, shows that

> what we should really *care about* is not the mere fact of deep implantation or flesh-to-wire grafting, but the complex and transformative nature of the animal-machine relationships that may or may not ensue.

The exchange of information between Prof. Warwick and the robot arm – or between Prof. Warwick and his wife – is not, as it were, *direct*, but rather mediated (by the machinery itself and the interface). But we're already very familiar with technologies that give us improved-but-mediated information exchange between humans and machines, or between each other. Language – especially written language – is an example of one of the very earliest cognitive technologies that augments and transforms the information processing activities of the agents that employ it.

One might thus sketch out a progression of increasingly sophisticated cognitive technologies that, whilst different in terms of their engineering, are identical in terms of the cognitive information transfer that they facilitate. Language (especially as embodied with pen and paper) is one. The clock (especially the wrist-watch) is another, for its development shifted a whole lot of freedoms and responsibilities away from one party (an employer or a town crier) and onto the individual. Nowadays, a great many people in the developed world carry always-on internet-ready devices with them at all times so that pretty much any piece of factual information can be more-or-less instantaneously accessed with an iPhone, 3G-enabled tablet or pocket-PC. In combination with the video camera, GPS system and accelerometer embedded in these devices, we now even have real-time 'augmented reality' applications (such as 'Wikitude') that allow the user to access additional information about the things they're looking at. You're standing at the base of the Eiffel tower, so you point your smartphone camera at it, whereupon the *Wikipedia* entry is pulled up, you're given the option of paying for a ride in the elevator, and a list of nearby places for lunch appears.

What lessons can we learn from these examples, then, about what it takes for mind and machine to become symbiotically intertwined? First, to go back to the 'unconscious' element of Clynes and Kline's definition, it seems that the technological augmentation must become 'transparent'. When writing, we don't have to think about the pen; it becomes invisible to us and we concentrate on the words that are formed with its ink. When I want to know the capital of Chile, I simply type it into *Chrome*'s 'omnibar' and without me having to think about how it works, I am told "Best guess for Chile Capital is Santiago". In a similar fashion, when I'm walking, I don't think about my legs, and when I'm talking, I don't think about my tongue. As with my biological body, the very best cyborg technologies are those that we barely notice ourselves using. Of course, when these systems break down, we *do* notice them as objects in their own right. When the pen runs out of ink and I can't write, my internet connection is down and I can't go online, I sprain my ankle and can't walk, or I bite my tongue and can't talk, then these technologies go from being, in Heidegger's terms "ready-to-hand" to "present-at-hand". It's no accident that the move to dynamical, embodied, embedded and situated approaches has sometimes been called the 'Heideggerian Turn' in cognitive science and AI; the ready-to-hand/present-at-hand distinction is just one way in which Heidegger's understanding of being-in-the-world is often seen as importantly consonant with the most recent developments in cognitive science and AI.

Second, cyborg technologies must be appropriately 'poised' for the information exchange to occur smoothly and, as we might say, naturally. Clark gives a neat example; when stopped on the street and asked 'Do you know the time?' most of us would answer 'Yes...' even before we had consulted our watches (not 'No, but I can find out very quickly'.) I am inclined to think that we might say the same kind of thing in other cases; just the other day, a student asked me if I knew what room our Tuesday class would take place in, and my answer, as I wiggled the mouse to wake the computer, was "Sure... let me just look". As our cyborg technologies become more ubiquitous and more sophisticated, the question 'Do you know X?' now means 'Can you find out X fairly promptly?' The more I have to mess around to access the information, the less poised it is and therefore the weaker the symbiosis.

Finally, to complete the comparison between our on-board (internal) information processors and our cyborg extensions, we should note that we must *trust* the latter for the two classes to be truly equivalent. If I have some reason to suspect that my watch is faulty, this undermines both its poise and its transparency; I am hesitant about reporting what it says, and I am forced to consider the watch as an object in its own right. This is not normally the case with my diary: I see the appointment at 10.30 in my handwriting, and that's good enough for me. The case of ubiquitous access to internet resources unfortunately lies somewhere in-between; one must constantly remind oneself that although *Wikipedia* seems to have immediate answers to almost any factual question one can formulate, it is, after all, written by other humans who may have an axe to grind or mischief to make.

I have chosen these three characteristics – transparency, poise and trust – because they closely resemble the criteria that Andy Clark advances for when an external (non-biological) artefact may be included as part of the 'extended mind.' According to Clark (2010), they are (a) that the resource be reliably available and typically invoked, (b) that its informational content is more-or-less automatically invoked, and (c) that the information should be easily accessible as and when required. Thus, it's only a short step to go from the extended mind hypothesis of the previous section, to the conclusion that *we* are, in Clark's phrase 'natural born cyborgs'. He writes:

> I am slowly becoming more and more a cyborg. So are you.... Perhaps we already are. For we shall be cyborgs not in the merely superficial sense of combining flesh and wires but in the more profound sense of being human-technology symbionts: thinking and reasoning systems whose minds and selves are spread across biological brain and nonbiological circuitry. (2003, p.3)

Given the close parallel to the extended mind hypothesis, and the fact that the latter is defensible, it seems plausible to conclude that we do indeed *already* meet Clynes and Kline's definition of cyborgs.

7.3 'The singularity'

It is well known that the machines we can build, especially computers, are growing bigger in capacity and faster in speed at well-defined rates. Turing's predictions were relatively conservative – in his 1950 paper, he discussed machines that he predicted would have, by 2000, "a storage capacity of about 10^9" (just shy of what we would now call 125MB) – but in fact, according to variants of what is known as 'Moore's Law', many measures of digital technological capacity (e.g., size, speed, cost etc.) are changing at exponential rates.[1] Computer capacity is not just increasing; its rate of increase is also increasing. Computer technology is *accelerating*.

In his obituary for the computer science pioneer John von Neumann, Stanislaw Ulam recalls that

> One conversation centered on the ever accelerating progress of technology and changes in the mode of human life, which gives the appearance of approaching some essential singularity in the history of the race beyond which human affairs, as we know them, could not continue. (Ulam, 1958, p.5)

This expression – 'The singularity' – has since come to designate a cluster of concepts concerned with the point at which human-made machines will exceed human levels of intelligence. This, in turn, could lead to an intelligence- or rate-of-change- 'explosion' that would make predictions about future machine performance impossible. It seems to me that this final, and perhaps most speculative, consideration for the future of AI and its relation to human cognitive activity follows nicely from previous sections concerning the extended mind and the possibility of cyborg hybrids. Thus, it will be instructive to consider arguments concerning why the singularity is thought (by some) to be imminent, and where that would leave us. (There are, of course, numerous related ethical and political considerations that I shall not go into. For an excellent overview, see Chalmers, 2010.)

At the heart of arguments concerning the singularity is that, if we ever successfully create AI, then one of the things it will be able to do is design intelligent machines (since, by hypothesis, that's something we can do, and the machine can do everything that we can). If such a machine has any advantage over us (say, because of slightly faster or more reliable hardware) then of course its capacity for designing intelligent machines will be greater than ours; it will be an AI+ (this notation is from Chalmers). More importantly, though, the intelligent machines that are designed by the AI+ (call them AI++s) will themselves be *even* better at designing intelligent machines than the AI+s were. By this accelerating procedure, we have the basis of an 'explosion' of intelligence as each generation of AI is capable of creating more intelligent machines than itself.

The idea that AI machines could improve themselves was present in the original 1956 Dartmouth Summer School research proposal (McCarthy et al., 1955), with the elliptical suggestion "Probably a truly intelligent machine will carry out activities which may best be described as self-improvement". The *acceleration* argument has been most recently laid out in detail by the inventor and futurologist Ray Kurzweil (2005), and expressed in somewhat apocalyptic-sounding terms by the mathematician and SciFi writer Vernor Vinge:

> When greater-than-human intelligence drives progress, that progress will be much more rapid. In fact, there seems no reason why progress itself would not involve the creation of still more intelligent entities – on a still-shorter time scale. ... This change will be a throwing-away of all the human rules, perhaps in the blink of an eye – an exponential runaway beyond any hope of control. (2003, p.2)

But the *explosion* argument was first set out as early as 1965 in an article by Irving Good:

> Let an ultraintelligent machine be defined as a machine that can far surpass all the intellectual activities of any man however clever. Since the design of machines is one of these intellectual activities,

an ultraintelligent machine could design even better machines; there would then unquestionably be an 'intelligence explosion,' and the intelligence of man would be left far behind... It is curious that this point is made so seldom outside of science fiction. It is sometimes worthwhile to take science fiction seriously. (1965, p.33)

Indeed it is. It seems to me that even with the most conservative estimates about technological developments and the possibility of AI, one can still make a plausible case that the singularity will happen. I am not qualified (or brave enough) to make an estimate of the time-scale, and the practical, political and moral dimensions of the discussion lie beyond the scope of this book, but setting out the case and considering how we (mere) humans fit in, lead us to consider some of the most central and important questions in contemporary philosophy of mind. As Chalmers puts it, these are "the questions of consciousness and personal identity. First, will an uploaded version of me be conscious? Second, will it be me?" (Chalmers, 2010, p.42).

Grant, for the sake of argument, that the Lucas-Penrose argument of Chapter 3.1 is sound, and that the Chinese-Room thought experiment of Chapter 3.3 succeeds in showing that computation is not sufficient for cognition. Technological (and scientific) developments might *still* lead us to the point of an intelligence explosion if they jointly permit the possibility of whole-brain *emulation*. Ordinarily, emulation is understood in computational terms. Sandberg and Bostrom (2008, p.7), for example, describe it as a kind of "one-to-one modelling" of the human brain, where we

> take a particular brain, scan its structure in detail, and construct a software model of it that is so faithful to the original that, when run on appropriate hardware, it will behave in essentially the same way as the original brain.

Such a procedure would be susceptible to the Lucas-Penrose/Searle arguments, for example, if there is some non-algorithmic process underlying mentality that would not be captured by such a procedure. But the concept of emulation itself does not necessarily require that the emulator be a GOFAI system; there could be a much broader sense of 'emulation' in which, having discovered the lowest relevant level of physical process that underlies cognition, we simply replicate *that* in some artificial or non-biological system. In short, whatever kind of machine the brain is (computer, quantum device, neural net, dynamical system etc.,) we build one of *those*. The only scenario in which this broader procedure would fail to emulate the brain is if Cartesian dualism is true (and even then, perhaps we could find a way of mechanically emulating the processes of a non-physical 'soul' – see Chapter 1.5). But at this stage, I think it's safe to assume both physicalism and multiple realisability.

Of course, this is a monumentally challenging method, depending as it does on breathtaking achievements in both neuroscience and engineering. But it seems to me that all it requires is painstaking accumulation of detail and not any fundamental step-change or qualitative difference from the things we are already capable of doing. Indeed, as Sandberg and Bostrom (2008) point out, we have already completely mapped the neuroanatomy of *Caenorhabditis elegans* (a 1mm-long transparent roundworm with a 302 neuron nervous system). Research endeavours such as the *Blue Brain Project*[2] are working towards doing the same thing for humans, with interim successes for functionally specialised portions of the rat brain. In short, it seems plausible that this physical emulation method will eventually lead to AI, given *lots more of the same*. And once we reach *that* stage, only minor improvements in hardware performance and reliability, or the addition of small enhancement modules, would put us at the 'takeoff' point for the swift transition from AI, to AI+ to AI++.

It remains to ask where we (mere, biological, unenhanced) humans would fit into this futuristic scenario. Whole brain emulation is sometimes taken as synonymous with 'mind uploading' (e.g., by Sandberg and Bostrom, 2008 and in the FAQ section on the website of the 'Singularity Institute'.[3]) This is understandable; if perfect whole-brain emulation is possible in non-biological materials, then (because multiple realisability is true) it will be possible to transfer the structure and function of one's *own* brain into this new medium. So, the possibility of uploading raises two questions (as I mentioned earlier). First, if you were to upload in this way, would the resulting AI be conscious *in the same way as you are*? Second, would the resulting AI *be* you?

I think we have to say that consciousness would be preserved after uploading. Various 'neuron replacement' thought experiments (e.g., Pylyshyn, 1980 and Chalmers, 1995) lead to the view that, as J. D. Bernal put it in his 1929 book *The World, The Flesh and The Devil*, "even the replacement of a previously organic brain-cell by a synthetic apparatus would not destroy the continuity of consciousness". Whatever the smallest relevant functional unit in your brain, suppose we were to replace it with an artificial component that perfectly emulated it (replacing a neuron, for example, requires computing power equivalent to a contemporary laptop according to the people at the *Blue Brain Project*). It seems unlikely that the replacement (or removal) of a single neuron would instantaneously turn you into a zombie, so it seems reasonable to say that your consciousness would be preserved, undiminished. We might then run a gradual replacement process, swapping out your neurons one-by-one, until your entire brain has been replaced by nonbiological mechanisms. Since the same conclusion – that your conscious mental life has remained intact – follows at each stage, it seems plausible to conclude that whole brain replacement will preserve consciousness (if only because the alternatives – consciousness disappearing abruptly with the replacement of some 'essential' single part, or consciousness gradually 'fading' – seem so *im*plausible.)

Now, the only difference between the 'replacement' and 'uploading' scenarios (i.e., between whole-brain-replacement and whole-brain-emulation) is that, in the case of the latter, the process might be possible 'non-destructively' (i.e., by *copying* your brain's structure whilst preserving the original you). So even if we agree that your AI-clone is conscious, we still face the tricky question of whether or not it's *you*; is personal identity preserved after uploading?

I have to say, I have no idea. My AI-clone would certainly *feel* like, and *claim* that, he was me (we've concluded that consciousness is preserved, and so his waking up would feel to him just as my waking up feels to me). But given the possibility of non-destructive uploading, the fact that there would subsequently be *two* people who felt like me does violence to our ordinary (logico-mathematical) notion of identity. Perhaps you think, following Parfit (1984), that such 'fission' cases show that *identity* is not the right way of thinking about such matters, and that *survival* (which comes in degrees, and may be indeterminate) is more important. Or perhaps you take the 'instrumentalist' or 'constructivist' view (something like the positions argued for by Donald Davidson and Dan Dennett) that personal identity over time consists in some third party *taking you* to be the same person. I leave it as an exercise for the reader to figure out the best view concerning the relationship between mind uploading and personal identity. But don't take too long; according to the Singularity Institute's website, various estimates put the singularity's occurrence at some time between 2050 and 2150, and at that point questions about the relation between mind and machine will get complicated in a way that goes far beyond the scope of this little book.

Conclusion

> Man is not made into a machine by analysing his behaviour in mechanical terms. Early theories of behaviour, as we have seen, represented man as a push-pull automaton, close to the nineteenth-century notion of a machine, but progress has been made. Man is a machine in the sense that he is a complex system behaving in various lawful ways, but the complexity is extraordinary.
>
> B.F. Skinner (1971) *Beyond Freedom and Dignity*

In a book that has been concerned with various aspects of mentality, intelligence and cognition, I am loath to begin my concluding remarks with a quotation from the twentieth century's most famous behaviourist. But Skinner makes several good points. Although I have judiciously avoided explicitly offering my own view on the two central questions – Could a machine think? Are *we* such machines? – with which this book started, it's probably reasonable to do so by way of summing up.

I think that machines could – indeed *can* – think, precisely *because* I think we are such machines. But I don't think that this conclusion should come as a surprise, because it follows from premises that are already widely accepted more-or-less independently of the material covered in this book. Further, I don't think that this claim should be regarded as 'reductive' in the pejorative sense of 'making crude'. I mentioned in the introduction that I joke with my philosophy of AI class – deliberately to shock them – that I have already created a thinking machine in the form of my three year-old daughter. To the extent that such a joke *does* shock anyone, it's only because they haven't yet embraced the two-fold claim that Skinner makes above: real contemporary machines can be incredibly sophisticated, and, in a sense, any physical system counts as one.

So one should take care to note that we thinking machines are probably not – or are probably not *just* – the sorts of hydraulic or clockwork systems that exercised the imagination of Descartes, Hobbes, Hume, Pascal and Leibniz. If the last 400 years of technological progress have taught us anything, especially given the past 60 years of *information* technology, it's surely that 'mere machines' are capable of things that are, on reflection, *astounding*: flying to the moon, real-time video conferencing with people in five continents, holding 40,000 recorded songs on a device that's smaller than a bar of soap... all three at once, even. The historical track record demonstrates that the actual capacities of 'machines' far outstrip our capacity to imagine them, and I certainly don't mind being a machine with *that* degree of sophistication.

Further, I think that Skinner's broad notion of 'machine' – "a complex system behaving in various lawful ways" – is intended as a statement of physicalism: the thesis that we are (just) matter in motion. Thus, to deny that we are such thinking machines is to deny physicalism, or to say that we are something *more*. And that option – most obviously instantiated in some kind of metaphysical dualism – is simply untenable. Of course, this is not something I have proved in the present volume. But physicalism has come to be the dominant position in contemporary philosophy of mind, and it's in that sense that we are thinking machines. The examples of AI in action that we've examined over the course of this book – the use of language and logic, chess playing, perceptual categorisation and even pathological extensions of these abilities – surely do show that an awful lot can be accomplished by machines that are an awful lot simpler than us, however piecemeal and incremental that demonstration may be. And the different approaches to AI – GOFAI, connectionism, dynamical and embodied/embedded – have simply added more and more conceptual and technical resources for fleshing out this demonstration.

So I think that Brooks (2008) is about right, when he provocatively writes, "I, you, our family, friends, and dogs – we all are machines". But he goes on:

> We are really sophisticated machines made up of billions and billions of biomolecules that interact according to well-defined, though not completely known, rules deriving from physics and chemistry. The biomolecular interactions taking place inside our heads give rise to our intellect, our feelings, our sense of self.

So much for *us*. But what of 'artificial' thinking machines (in the sense of 'artificial' that means 'genuine, but produced by non-standard means' like 'artificial light')? Again, I think this possibility follows from a more general physicalism. Brooks (2008) again:

> Accepting this hypothesis opens up a remarkable possibility. If we really are machines and if – this is a big *if* – we learn the rules governing our brains, then in principle there's no reason why we shouldn't be able to replicate those rules in, say, silicon and steel. I believe our creation would exhibit genuine human-level intelligence, emotions, and even consciousness.

This doesn't, by itself, make any precise claim about what *kind* of machine thinkers are or must be. And neither does it weigh in on the 'big if' of whether such projects will be practically (or morally) pursuit-worthy. For these reasons, the debates discussed in this book are still live ones. Are we computational machines in the sense envisaged by Turing? Or would the 'rules' have to be replicated in (or followed by) a neural network structure? Are the rules best described in the language of algorithms? Or in terms of differential equations? Are these options mutually exclusive? Are they exhaustive? What is the relationship between the thinking machinery and the bodily and environmental machinery? I've tried to suggest answers to these questions – albeit tentative ones – but whichever way those debates go, the outcome will not detract from the double positive answer to my two central questions. Machines can think, and we are examples.

———◇———

Notes

Chapter 1

1. These are my translations of Pascal's self-produced pamphlet, the original of which can be seen here: http://history-computer.com/Library/PascalLettreToChancelier.pdf with a transcription here: http://www.fourmilab.ch/babbage/pascal.html

Chapter 2

1. Of course, this glosses over some important metaphysical questions that have only recently arisen in conjunction with computer science; what is it to talk of 'identity' when concerning the entities – programs, files, folders, sub-routines etc. – of computer science? In what sense is a later revision of 'mybook.doc' the *same* file as an earlier draft? For some discussion of these deep issues, see Smith (1996).
2. See http://aturingmachine.com/ for this particular device; the video footage there is breathtaking. See also http://legoofdoom.blogspot.com/ for examples of what one can do with this sort of machine.
3. Randall Munroe's excellent webcomic "xkcd" even has a graphical map of optimal moves for playing the perfect exhaustive game: http://xkcd.com/832/
4. Hodges (2008) suggests that this reference to "mistakes" gives Turing a way out of the kinds of Gödel-style objections that we will consider in the next chapter. Indeed, it does; see page 61.
5. For substantial, but accessible, detail on the former, see Campbell et al. (2002), for material on both aspects written by an IBM insider, see Hsu (2002).
6. IBM Deep Blue FAQs: http://www.research.ibm.com/deepblue/meet/html/d.3.3a.html#ai
7. Ibid.
8. There are many online versions that one can play around with. The best I have found (because it is based closely on Weizenbaum's program, and because it lets you tinker around with the code) is the Javascript implementation found at: http://www.chayden.net/eliza/Eliza.html
9. It should be noted that, whilst the idea that mental states are mutliply realised has been a prominent assumption in philosophy of cognitive science and AI, it has nevertheless recently become a topic of considerable controversy, following Bechtel and Mundale (1999) and Shapiro (2000).

Chapter 3

1. When presented with this robot-system reply, a student in my Philosophy of AI class exclaimed "What more *is* there?" Quite.

Chapter 4

1. XOR = "Either A or B but not both" as in "This soup comes with either side-salad XOR sandwich".
2. I don't know whether this prediction has been confirmed, but one might expect it to be true on independent anecdotal grounds. Given that the most common verbs to which a child has been exposed end in hard consonants ("Stop! Sit! Put that down!"), one who displays good prosody might expect a hard consonant to be followed by an -ed inflection, and thus add one to a correctly produced irregular past-tense verb stem.
3. Note, however, that the similarity with the temperature/statistical mechanics case is not absolute; the latter requires type-identity between the two, and *nobody* claims that connectionist models are type-identical to cognitive phenomena.

Chapter 5

1. It should be noted that this way of putting it is somewhat controversial. Some (e.g., Gordon, 1986; Goldman, 1992) have argued that folk psychology is not really a (proto-)'theory' at all (but rather a set of practical, heuristic, guides to action), and is thus not the sort of thing that could be eliminated as false. This would, of course, rather undermine Ramsey, Stich and Garon's conclusion, but since it would do so in a way that would obviate the need to even *engage* with their argument, I shall set it to one side in what follows.
2. For succinctness, this is just a sampling of the exhaustive list presented by Fodor and Pylyshyn. Both Fodor and Pylyshyn (1988) and Harnish (2002) provide much more comprehensive discussions, though their conclusions apply, *mutatis mutandis*, to what I mention here.
3. For the former, see Chalmers (1990, 1993). For the latter, see Sun (1995); Wermter and Sun (2000)

Chapter 6

1. This terminology comes from Smith (1996), p.12n.
2. Strictly speaking, van Gelder's claim in the latter of these two quotations is false. *Dynamical systems theory* (i.e., the branch of mathematics) is 'more catholic' in the literal sense of 'of interest or use to all'. *Van Gelder's dynamicism*, however, is less catholic, since it prescribes a certain use of DST (in low-dimensional, continuous systems). He repeatedly makes this claim in his 1998 article, arguing that the dynamical hypothesis is "concerned not with low-level systems, but with how agents are causally organised at the highest level relevant to an explanation of cognitive performances" (p.619) and that "cognitive agents instantiate quantitative systems at the highest relevant level of causal organisation" (p.623). As the context of these quotations makes clear, the 'highest relevant level' is intended to denote the psychological level; van Gelder is not, after all, an eliminativist, for whom there is *no* theoretically relevant level above the neural one. But in this case, the normative element in the

dynamical hypothesis restricts it to 'high-level' phenomena, making it narrow rather than 'catholic'!

Chapter 7

1. Strictly, Moore's law concerns transistor density: The number of transistors that can be placed on a certain sized integrated circuit doubles approximately every two years.
2. See http://bluebrain.epfl.ch/
3. See http://singinst.org/singularityfaq#WhatIsWholeBrain

Suggestions for further reading

Historical and theoretical background

In addition to the primary sources discussed in the text, Haugeland's (1985) *Artificial Intelligence: The Very Idea* provides an excellent discussion of the Early Modern precursors of AI, and associated philosophical complexities and consequences. Copeland's (1993) *Artificial Intelligence: A Philosophical Introduction* also provides some interesting details about the birth of both AI and its philosophy, whilst McCorduck's *Machines Who Think* gives an insider's perspective on both technical and sociological aspects of early AI, by providing fascinating interviews with many of the key players.

Classical cognitive science and GOFAI

Chapter 1 of Clark's *Microcognition* gives a good survey of some of the central themes of classical cognitive science, while chapters 2 and 3 of Johnson-Laird's (1989) *The Computer and the Mind* works through some of the ideas concerning symbols, computers and computability in an especially helpful way. Copeland's (2004) edited volume *The Essential Turing* collects all of Turing's most important writings, and provides some excellent editorial commentary, and to see a breathtaking example of a Turing Machine in action (well, a close variant, but with a non-infinite memory), you can visit http://aturingmachine.com/. Many of the original papers outlining GOFAI's early successes are collected in Feigenbaum and Feldman's (1995) *Computers and Thought* and Copeland (1993), once again, provides an illuminating philosophical discussion.

Gödel, the Turing Test and the Chinese Room

The literature on Gödelian arguments against AI, the Turing Test and the Chinese Room thought experiment is vast, but judicious use of a philosophical search engine such as http://philpapers.org/ or David Chalmers's http://consc.net/mindpapers will get the interested reader to the important papers quickly. Nagel and Newman's (1971/2001) *Gödel's Proof* is a very accessible introduction to the metamathematical background to the theorem itself, whilst Millican and

Clark's edited (1996) collection *Machines and Thought* contains many useful essays on the Turing Test and its legacy. Searle's original (1980) Chinese Room paper comes with 27 commentators and his own reply. Preston and Bishop (2002) is a more recent collection of excellent new essays. The entry on "The Chinese Room Argument" in the *Stanford Encyclopedia of Philosophy* (http://plato.stanford.edu/entries/chinese-room/) by David Cole not only gives an excellent concise summary, but goes some way towards providing a way of *classifying* the different replies into various categories.

Connectionism

Chapter 6 of Franklin's (1995) *Artificial Minds* gives a brief but accessible introduction to some of connectionism's major concepts. For a much more detailed and psychology-related introduction, McLeod, Plunkett and Rolls (1998) *Introduction to Connectionist Modelling of Cognitive Processes* is a comprehensive text which comes with a software package that will allow the interested reader to experiment with neural nets themselves. Ellis and Humphreys (1999) *Connectionist Psychology: A Text With Readings* collects many famous connectionist examples with some helpful editorial commentary, and Bechtel and Abrahamsen (2002) *Connectionism and the Mind* is a comprehensive philosophical discussion.

Criticisms and consequences of the connectionist approach

Cynthia and Graham Macdonald's (1995) *Connectionism: Debates on Psychological Explanation* contains many excellent papers on both eliminativism and compositionality. On the latter, Pinker and Mehler's (1988) *Connections and Symbols* collects the original Fodor and Pylyshyn paper together with two prominent replies.

The dynamical approach

Van Gelder's 1995 and 1998 papers are probably the most widely cited philosophical examples of the dynamical approach to cognition, and the latter also features many responses and criticisms, together with van Gelder's reply. Port and van Gelder's (1995) edited volume *Mind as Motion* collects many good examples of the use of DST in cognitive science, and, most recently, Shapiro's (2010) *Embodied Cognition* has an excellent discussion of some of the philosophical aspects of dynamics and their connection to the 'situated' movement more generally.

The Future: Mind and machine merged

There has been a recent explosion of interest in the 'Extended Mind' hypothesis. Clark articulates a more developed version of his view in his (2008) *Supersizing the Mind*, Chemero's (2009) *Radical Embodied Cognitive Science* and Rowlands's (2010) *The New Science of the Mind* take things further, Menary's (2010) edited volume *The Extended Mind* collects many key papers, and Adams and Aizawa's (2008) *The Bounds of Cognition* provides an important dissenting voice.

The question of cognitive technology and mind-machine mergers is addressed philosophically in Clark's (2003) *Natural Born Cyborgs*. Perhaps the most famous (and accessible) discussion of 'The Singularity' is Kurzweil's (2005) *The Singularity is Near*, and the *Journal of Consciousness Studies* has just published a superb collection of responses (Vol. 19, Issue 1–2, 2012) to the original Chalmers paper I discuss in the text.

Works Cited

Adams, Fred and Aizawa, Ken. 2001. "The Bounds of Cognition." *Philosophical Psychology* 14:43–64.
——. 2010. "Defending the Bounds of Cognition." In Richard Menary (ed.), *The Extended Mind*. Cambridge, MA: MIT Press.
Anderson, J. A. and Rosenfeld, E. (eds.). 1998. *Talking Nets: An Oral History of Neural Networks*. Cambridge, MA: MIT Press.
Ashby, W. Ross. 1956. *An Introduction to Cybernetics*. New York: J. Wiley.
Bach-y-Rita, Paul. 2002. "Sensory Substitution and Qualia." In Alva Noë and Evan Thompson (eds.), *Vision and Mind: Selected Readings in the Philosophy of Perception*. Cambridge, MA: MIT Press.
Bach-y-Rita, Paul, Collins, C. C., Saunders, F., White, B., and Scadden, L. 1969. "Vision Substitution by Tactile Image Projection." *Nature* 221:963–964.
Bach-y-Rita, Paul and Kercel, Stephen W. 2003. "Sensory Substitution and the Human–Machine Interface." *Trends in Cognitive Science* 7:541–546.
Bach-y-Rita, Paul, Tyler, Mitchell, and Kaczmarek, Kurt. 2003. "Seeing with the Brain." *International Journal of Human-Computer Interaction* 15:285–295.
Bechtel, William. 1998. "Representations and Cognitive Explanations: Assessing the Dynamicist Challenge in Cognitive Science." *Cognitive Science* 22:295–317.
Bechtel, William and Abrahamsen, Adele. 2002. *Connectionism and the Mind: Parallel Processing, Dynamics, and Evolution in Networks*. Oxford: Blackwell, 2nd edition.
Bechtel, William P. and Mundale, Jennifer. 1999. "Multiple Realizability Revisited: Linking Cognitive and Neural States." *Philosophy of Science* 66:175–207.
Beer, Randall. 1995. "A Dynamical Systems Perspective on Agent-Environment Interaction." *Artificial Intelligence* 72:173–215.
——. 1997. "The Dynamics of Adaptive Behavior: A Research Program." *Robotics and Autonomous Agents* 20:257–289.
——. 2000. "Dynamical Approaches to Cognitive Ccience." *Trends in Cognitive Science* 4:91–99.
——. 2003. "The Dynamics of Active Categorical Perception in an Evolved Model Agent." *Adaptive Behaviour* 11:209–243.
Bermúdez, José Luis. 2010. *Cognitive Science: An Introduction to the Science of the Mind*. Cambridge University Press.
Block, Ned. 1980. "Introduction: What is Functionalism?" In Ned Block (ed.), *Readings in Philosophy of Psychology*, 171–184. Cambridge, MA: Harvard University Press.
Boole, George. 1854/1958. *An Investigation of the Laws of Thought on Which are Founded the Mathematical Theories of Logic and Probabilities*. New York: Dover.
Brooks, Rodney. 1986. "A Robust Layered Control System for a Mobile Robot." *IEEE Journal of Robotics and Automation* 2:14–23.
——. 1991. "Intelligence Without Representation." *Artificial Intelligence* 47:139–159.

———. 2008. "I, Rodney Brooks, Am a Robot." *IEEE Spectrum* Available at: http://spectrum.ieee.org/computing/hardware/i-rodney-brooks-am-a-robot.

Busemeyer, J. and Townsend, J. T. 1993. "Decision Field Theory: A Dynamic-Cognitive approach to Decision Making in an Uncertain Environment." *Psychological Review* 100:432–459.

Campbell, Murray, Hoane, A. Joseph, and Hsu, Feng-hsiung. 2002. "Deep Blue." *Artificial Intelligence* 134:57–83.

Carnie, Andrew. 2006. *Syntax: A Generative Introduction*. Oxford: Blackwell, 2nd edition.

Chalmers, David J. 1990. "Syntactic Transformations on Distributed Representations." *Connection Science* 2:53–62.

———. 1993. "Connectionism and Compositionality: Why Fodor and Pylyshyn Were Wrong." *Philosophical Psychology* 6:305–319.

———. 1995. "Absent Qualia, Fading Qualia, Dancing Qualia." In Thomas Metzinger (ed.), *Conscious Experience*, 309–328. Exeter: Imprint Academic.

———. 2010. "The Singularity: A Philosophical Analysis." *Journal of Consciousness Studies* 17:7–65.

Chomsky, Noam. 1965. *Aspects of the Theory of Syntax*. Cambridge, MA: MIT Press.

Christian, Brian. 2011. *The Most Human Human: What Talking with Computers Teaches Us about What It Means to Be Alive*. New York: Doubleday.

Churchland, Paul M. 1988. *Matter and Consciousness*. Cambridge, MA: MIT Press, revised edition.

———. 1989. *A Neurocomputational Perspective: The Nature of Mind and the Structure of Science*. Cambridge, MA: MIT Press.

Clark, Andy. 1989. *Microcognition: Philosophy, Cognitive Science and Parallel Distributed Processing*. Cambridge, MA: MIT Press.

———. 1990. "Connectionist Minds." *Proceedings of the Aristotelian Society* 90:83–102.

———. 1996. *Being There: Putting Brain, Body and World Together Again*. Cambridge, MA: MIT Press.

———. 1997. "The Dynamical Challenge." *Cognitive Science* 21:461–481.

———. 2001. *Mindware: An Introduction to the Philosophy of Cognitive Science*. Oxford University Press.

———. 2003. *Natural-Born Cyborgs: Minds, Technologies and the Future of Human Intelligence*. Oxford University Press.

———. 2005. "Intrinsic Content, Active Memory, and the Extended Mind." *Analysis* 65:1–11.

———. 2010. "*Memento's* Revenge: The Extended Mind, Extended." In Richard Menary (ed.), *The Extended Mind*. Cambridge, MA: MIT Press.

Clark, Andy and Chalmers, David. 1998. "The Extended Mind." *Analysis* 58(1):7–19.

Clark, Andy and Toribio, Josefa. 1994. "Doing Without Representing." *Synthese* 101:401–431.

Clarke, Desmond M. 2003. *Descartes's Theory of Mind*. Oxford University Press.

Clynes, Mandfred E. and Kline, Nathan S. 1960. "Cyborgs and Space." *Astronautics* September:26–27 & 74–76.

Colby, Kenneth Mark, Watt, James B., and Gilbert, John P. 1966. "A Computer Method of Psychotherapy: Preliminary Communication." *Journal of Nervous and Mental Disease* 142:148–152.
Copeland, B. Jack. 1993. *Artificial Intelligence: A Philosophical Introduction*. Oxford: Blackwell.
———. 1997. "Artificial Intelligence." In Samuel Guttenplan (ed.), *A Companion to the Philosophy of Mind*, 122–131. Oxford: Blackwell.
———. 2000. "The Turing Test." *Minds and Machines* 10:519–539.
———. 2002. "The Chinese Room—A Logical Point of View." In John Preston and Mark Bishop (eds.), *Views Into the Chinese Room: New Essays on Searle and Artificial Intelligence*, 109–122. Oxford University Press.
Copeland, B. Jack (ed.). 2004. *The Essential Turing*. Oxford University Press.
Copeland, B. Jack and Proudfoot, Diane. 1996. "On Alan Turing's Anticipation of Connectionism." *Synthese* 108:361–377.
Cottingham, John, Stoothoff, Robert, Murdoch, Dugald, and Volume 3 including Anthony Kenny. 1988. *The Philosophical Writings of Descartes*. Cambridge University Press. 3 Vols.
Crutchfield, James P. 1994. "The Calculi of Emergence: Computation, Dynamics and Induction." *Physica D* 75:11–54.
Cunningham, Suzanne. 2000. *What Is a Mind?: An Integrative Introduction to the Philosophy of Mind*. Indianapolis: Hackett.
Dascal, Marcelo. 2007. "Hobbes's Challenge." In Andrew Brook (ed.), *The Prehistory of Cognitive Science*, 67–96. Basingstoke: Palgrave Macmillan.
de Sousa, Ronald. 1991. "Does the Eye Know Calculus? The Threshold of Representation in Classical and Connectionist Models." *International Studies in the Philosophy of Science* 5:171–185.
Dennett, Daniel. 1978. *Brainstorms*, Chapter 7: "Artificial Intelligence as Philosophy and Psychology". London: Harvester.
———. 1980. "The Milk of Human Intentionality." *Behavioral and Brain Sciences* 3:428–430.
———. 1987. "Fast Thinking." In his *The Intentional Stance*, 323–337. Cambridge, MA: MIT Press.
———. 1990. "Betting Your Life on an Algorithm." *Behavioral and Brain Sciences* 660:660–61.
———. 1996. *Darwin's Dangerous Idea: Evolution and the Meanings of Life*. New York: Simon & Schuster.
———. 1998a. *Brainchildren: Essays on Designing Minds*, Chapter 11: "Cognitive Wheels: The Frame Problem of AI". Cambridge, MA: MIT Press.
———. 1998b. *Brainchildren: Essays on Designing Minds*, Chapter 1: "Can a Machine Think?". Cambridge, MA: MIT Press.
Dennett, Daniel C. 1998c. "Revolution, No! Reform, Si!" *Behavioral and Brain Sciences* 21:636–637.
Dretske, Fred. 1994. "If You Can't Make One, You Don't Know How It Works." *Midwest Studies in Philosophy* 19:468–482.
Ekbia, H.R. 2008. *Artificial Dreams: The Quest for Non-Biological Intelligence*. Cambridge University Press.
Eliasmith, Chris. 1996. "The Third Contender: A Critical Examination of the Dynamicist Theory of Cognition." *Philosophical Psychology* 9:441–463.

Elman, Jeff L. 1998. "Connectionism, Artificial Life and Dynamical Systems." In William Bechtel and George Graham (eds.), *A Companion to Cognitive Science*, 488–505. Oxford: Blackwell.

Elman, Jeff L., Bates, E. A., Johnson, M. H., Karmiloff-Smith, A., Parisi, D., and Plunkett, K. 1996. *Rethinking Innateness: A Connectionist Perspective on Development*. Cambridge, MA: MIT Press.

Flanagan, Owen J. 1991. *The Science of the Mind*. Cambridge, MA: MIT Press, 2nd edition.

Fodor, Jerry. 1975. *The Language of Thought*. New York: Thomas Y. Crowell.

——. 1981. "The Mind-Body Problem." *Scientific American* 244:114–123.

——. 1991. "Replies." In Barry Loewer and Georges Rey (eds.), *Meaning in Mind: Fodor and His Critics*, 255–319. Oxford: Blackwell.

——. 2008. *LOT2: The Language of Thought Revisited*. Oxford: Clarendon Press.

Fodor, Jerry A. and Pylyshyn, Zenon W. 1988. "Connectionism and Cognitive Architecture." *Cognition* 28:3–71.

Franklin, Stan. 1995. *Artificial Minds*. Cambridge, MA: MIT Press.

Giunti, Marco. 1997. *Computation, Dynamics and Cognition*. Oxford University Press.

Goldman, Alvin. 1992. "In Defense of the Simulation Theory." *Mind and Language* 7:104–119.

Good, Irving John. 1965. "Speculations Concerning the First Ultraintelligent Machine." In F. Alt and M. Rubinoff (eds.), *Advances in Computers*, volume 6, 31–79. New York: Academic Press.

Gordon, Robert M. 1986. "Folk Psychology as Simulation." *Mind and Language* 1:158–71.

Gorman, R Paul and Sejnowski, Terrence J. 1988a. "Analysis of Hidden Units in a Layered Network Trained to Classify Sonar Targets." *Neural Networks* 1:75–89.

——. 1988b. "Learned Classification of Sonar Targets Using a Massively Parallel Network." *IEEE Transactions on Acoustics, Speech, and Signal Processing* 36: 1135–1140.

Haken, H., Kelso, J. A. S., and Bunz, H. 1985. "A Theoretical Model of Phase Transitions in Human Hand Movements." *Biological Cybernetics* 51:347–356.

Harnish, Robert M. 2002. *Minds, Brains and Computers: An Historical Introduction to the Foundations of Cognitive Science*. Oxford: Blackwell.

Hatfield, Gary. 1991. "Representation and Rule-Instantiation in Connectionist Systems." In Terence Horgan and John Tienson (eds.), *Connectionism and the Philosophy of Mind*, volume 9 of *Studies in Cognitive Systems*, 90–112. Dordrecht: Kluwer.

Haugeland, John. 1981. "Semantic Engines: An Introduction to Mind Design." In John Haugeland (ed.), *Mind Design: Philosophy, Psychology and Artificial Intelligence*, 1–34. Cambridge, MA: MIT Press.

——. 1985. *Artificial Intelligence: The Very Idea*. Cambridge, MA: MIT Press.

——. 1998. "The Nature and Plausibility of Cognitivism." In his *Having Thought*, 9–45. Cambridge, MA: Harvard University Press.

Hempel, Carl G. 1965. "Aspects of Scientific Explanation." In *Aspects of Scientific Explanation and Other Essays in the Philosophy of Science*. New York: Free Press.

Hempel, Carl G. and Oppenheim, Paul. 1948. "Studies in the Logic of Explanation." *Philosophy of Science* 15:135–175.

Hirsch, M. 1984. "The Dynamical Systems Approach to Differential Equations." *Bulletin of the American Mathematical Society* 11:1–64.

Hodges, Andrew. 2008. "Alan Turing and the Turing Test." In Robert Epstein, Gary Roberts, and Grace Beber (eds.), *Parsing the Turing Test: Philosophical and Methodological Issues in the Quest for the Thinking Computer*, 13–22. New York: Springer.

Hoffman, R. E., Boutros, N. N., Hu, S., Berman, R. M., Krystal, J. H., and Charney, D. S. 2000. "Transcranial Magnetic Stimulation and Auditory Hallucinations in Schizophrenia." *Lancet* 355:1073–1075.

Hoffman, R. E. and McGlashan, T. H. 1993. "Parallel Distributed Processing and the Emergence of Schizophrenic Symptoms." *Schizophrenia Bulletin* 19:119–140.

———. 1997. "Synaptic Elimination, Neurodevelopment, and the Mechanism of Hallucinated 'Voices' in Schizophrenia." *American Journal of Psychiatry* 154:1683–1689.

———. 2001. "Neural Network Models of Schizophrenia." *The Neuroscientist* 7: 441–454.

Hofstadter, Douglas. 2002. "Staring Emmy Straight in the Eye—and Doing My Best Not to Flinch." In T. Dartnall (ed.), *Creativity, Cognition and Knowledge: An Interaction*, 67–100. Westport, CT: Praeger.

Hsu, Feng-hsiung. 2002. *Behind Deep Blue: Building the Computer that Defeated the World Chess Champion*. Princeton, NJ: Princeton University Press.

Jaynes, Julian. 1970. "The Problem of Animate Motion in the Seventeenth Century." *Journal of the History of Ideas* 31:219–234.

Johnson-Laird, Philip. 1989. *The Computer and the Mind*. Cambridge, MA: Harvard University Press.

Kelso, J. A. S. 1995. *Dynamic Patterns: The Self-Organisation of Brain and Behavior*. Cambridge, MA: MIT Press.

Kidwell, Peggy Aldritch and Williams, Michael R. (eds.). 1992. *The Calculating Machines: Their History and Development*. Cambridge, MA: MIT Press. Translated and edited from Martin, Ernst (1925). *Die Rechenmaschinen und ihre Entwicklungsgeschichte*. Germany: Pappenheim.

Kim, Jaegwon. 1997. "Explanation, Prediction and Reduction in Emergentism." *Intellectica* 25:45–57.

———. 2000. *Mind in a Physical World: An Essay on the Mind-Body Problem and Mental Causation*. Cambridge, MA: MIT Press.

Kirsch, D. 1991. "Today the Earwig, Tomorrow Man?" *Artificial Intelligence* 47: 161–184.

Knuth, Donald. 1997. *The Art of Computer Programming. Volume 1: Fundamental Algorithms*. Reading, MA: Addison-Wesley, 3rd edition.

Kukla, André. 1989a. "Is AI an Empirical Science?" *Analysis* 49:56–60.

———. 1989b. "Nonempirical Issues in Psychology." *American Psychologist* 44: 785–794.

———. 2001. *Methods of Theoretical Psychology*. Cambridge, MA: MIT Press.

Kukla, André and Walmsley, Joel. 2006. *Mind: A Historical and Philosophical Introduction to the Major Theories*. Indianapolis: Hackett.

Kurzweil, Ray. 2005. *The Singularity is Near*. London: Viking.

Langton, Christopher G. 1996. "Artificial Life." In Margaret Boden (ed.), *The Philosophy of Artificial Life*, 39–946. Oxford: OUP.

Lloyd, Dan (ed.). 1989. *Simple Minds*. Cambridge, MA: MIT Press.

Lodge, David. 2001. *Thinks*, 38. London: Secker & Warburg.

Loemker, Leroy (ed.). 1969. *Leibniz: Philosophical Papers and Letters*. Synthese Historical Library. Dordrecht: D. Reidel.

Longuet-Higgins, Christopher. 1981. "Artificial Intelligence—A New Theoretical Psychology?" *Cognition* 10:197–200.
Lucas, John R. 1961. "Minds, Machines and Gödel." *Philosophy* 36:112–127.
Luenberger, D. G. 1979. *Introduction to Dynamic Systems: Theory, Model and Applications.* New York: John Wiley & Sons.
MacFarquhar, Larissa. 2007. "Annals of Science, 'Two Heads'." *The New Yorker* February 12:58–69.
Marshall, John C. 1980. "Artificial Intelligence—The Real Thing?" *Behavioral and Brain Sciences* 3:435–437.
McCarthy, John. 1990. "Chess as the Drosophila of AI." In T. Anthony Marsland and Jonathan Shaeffer (eds.), *Computers, Chess, and Cognition*, 227–237. New York: Springer-Verlag.
McCarthy, John, Minksy, M., Rochester, N., and Shannon, C. 1955. "A Proposal for the Dartmouth Summer Research Project on Artificial Intelligence." Available at: http://www-formal.stanford.edu/jmc/history/dartmouth.pdf.
McClelland, J. and Rumelhart, D. 1986. "A Distributed model of Human Learning and Memory." In D. Rumelhart, J. McClelland, and The PDP Research Group (eds.), *Parallel Distributed Processing: Explorations in the Microstructure of Cognition. Volume 2: Psychological and Biological Models*, 170–215. Cambridge, MA: MIT Press.
McClelland, J., Rumelhart, D., and Hinton, G. 1986a. "The Appeal of Parallel Distributed Processing." In D. Rumelhart, J. McClelland, and The PDP Research Group (eds.), *Parallel Distributed Processing: Explorations in the Microstructure of Cognition. Volume 1: Foundations*, 3–44. Cambridge, MA: MIT Press.
McClelland, J., Rumelhart, D., and The PDP Research Group (eds.). 1986b. *Parallel Distributed Processing: Explorations in the Microstructure of Cognition. Volume 2: Psychological and Biological Models.* Cambridge, MA: MIT Press.
McCorduck, Pamela. 1979. *Machines Who Think.* San Francisco: W.H. Freeman and Co.
McCulloch, Warren and Pitts, Walter. 1943. "A Logical Calculus of the Ideas Immanent in Nervous Activity." *Bulletin of Mathematical Biophysics* 7:115–133.
McLaughlin, Brian P. 1993. "The Connectionism/Classicism Battle to Win Souls." *Philosophical Studies* 71:163–190.
McLeod, P., Plunkett, K., and Rolls, E. T. 1998. *Introduction to Connectionist Modelling of Cognitive Processes.* Oxford: OUP.
Minsky, Marvin. 1967. *Computation: Finite and Infinite Machines.* London: Prentice Hall.
Minsky, Marvin. 1968. *Semantic Information Processing*, P. N. Cambridge, MA: MIT Press.
Minsky, Marvin and Papert, Seymour. 1968. *Perceptrons.* Cambridge, MA: MIT Press.
Moor, James H. 1976. "An Analysis of the Turing Test." *Philosophical Studies* 30:249–257.
Nagel, Ernest. 1961. *The Structure of Science: Problems in the Logic of Scientific Explanation.* New York: Harcourt.
Nagel, Ernest and Newman, James R. 2001. *Gödel's Proof.* New York University Press, Revised edition.
Newell, Allen, Shaw, J. C., and Simon, H. A. 1957/1995. "Empirical Explorations with the Logic Theory Machine: A Case Study in Heuristics." In Edward A.

Feigenbaum and Julian Feldman (eds.), *Computers and Thought*, 109–133. Cambridge, MA: MIT Press.

———. 1958/1995. "Chess-Playing Programs and the Problem of Complexity." In Edward A. Feigenbaum and Julian Feldman (eds.), *Computers and Thought*, 39–70. Cambridge, MA: MIT Press.

Newell, Allen and Simon, H. A. 1956. "The Logic Theory Machine: A Complex Information Processing System." *RAND Corporation Report P-868, June 15, 1956* Available at: http://shelf1.library.cmu.edu/IMLS/MindModels/logictheorymachine.pdf.

———. 1961/1995. "GPS, A Program that Simulates Human Thought." In Edward A. Feigenbaum and Julian Feldman (eds.), *Computers and Thought*, 279–296. Cambridge, MA: MIT Press.

———. 1976. "Computer Science as Empirical Inquiry: Symbols and Search." *Communications of the Association for Computing Machinery* 19:113–126.

Parfit, Derek. 1984. *Reasons and Persons*. Oxford University Press.

Penrose, Roger. 1989. *The Emperor's New Mind*. Oxford: OUP.

———. 1990. "Author's Response—The Nonalgorithmic Mind." *Behavioral and Brain Science* 13:692–705.

———. 1994. *Shadows of the Mind*. Oxford University Press.

Petzold, Charles. 2008. *The Annotated Turing*. Indianapolis: Wiley.

Pinker, Stephen. 1994. *The Language Instinct*. London: Penguin.

Pinker, Steven. 1997. *How the Mind Works*. London: Penguin.

Pullum, Geoffrey K. 1999. "Generative Grammar." In Robert A. Wilson and Frank C. Keil (eds.), *The MIT Encyclopedia of the Cognitive Sciences*, 340–342. Cambridge, MA: MIT Press.

Pylyshyn, Zenon W. 1980. "The 'Causal Power' of Machines." *Behavioral and Brain Sciences* 3:442–444.

Ramsey, William, Stich, Stephen and Garon, Joseph. 1990. "Connectionism, Eliminativism and the Future of Folk Psychology." *Philosophical Perspectives* 4:499–533.

Rockwell, Teed. 2005. "Attractor Spaces as Modules: A Semi-Eliminative Reduction of Symbolic AI to Dynamic Systems Theory." *Minds and Machines* 15:23–55.

Rosenblatt, Frank. 1958. "The Perceptron: A Probabilistic Model for Information Storage and Organization in the Brain." *Psychological Review* 65:386–408.

Rumelhart, D. and McClelland, J. 1986. "On Learning the Past Tenses of English Verbs." In D. Rumelhart, J. McClelland, and The PDP Research Group (eds.), *Parallel Distributed Processing: Explorations in the Microstructure of Cognition. Volume 2: Psychological and Biological Models*, 216–271. Cambridge, MA: MIT Press.

Rumelhart, D., McClelland, J., and The PDP Research Group (eds.). 1986. *Parallel Distributed Processing: Explorations in the Microstructure of Cognition. Volume 1: Foundations*. Cambridge, MA: MIT Press.

Ryle, Gilbert. 1949. *The Concept of Mind*. London: Hutchinson and Co.

Sandberg, A. and Bostrom, N. 2008. "Whole Brain Emulation: A Roadmap." Future of Humanity, Oxford University, Technical Report #2008-3. Available at: http://www.philosophy.ox.ac.uk/__data/assets/pdf_file/0019/3853/brain-emulation-roadmap-report.pdf.

Seager, William E. 2003. "Yesterday's Algorithm: Penrose and the Gödel Argument." *Croatian Journal of Philosophy* 3:265–273.

Searle, John R. 1980. "Minds, Brains and Programs." *Behavioral and Brain Sciences* 3:417–457.
———. 1982. "The Myth of the Computer." *The New York Review of Books* April 29.
———. 1984. *Minds, Brains and Science*. Cambridge, MA: Harvard University Press.
———. 1999. "Chinese Room Argument." In Robert A. Wilson and Frank C. Keil (eds.), *The MIT Encyclopedia of the Cognitive Sciences*, 115–116. Cambridge, MA: MIT Press.
Shannon, Claude. 1950. "Programming a Computer for Playing Chess." *Philosophical Magazine* 41. Reprint available online at http://archive.computerhistory.org/projects/chess/related_materials/text/2-0\%20and\%202-1.Programming_a_computer_for_playing_chess.shannon/2-0\%20and\%202-1.Programming_a_computer_for_playing_chess.shannon.062303002.pdf
Shapiro, Lawrence A. 2000. "Multiple Realizations." *Journal of Philosophy* 97: 635–654.
———. 2010. *Embodied Cognition*. Routledge.
Silberstein, Michael. 2002. "Reduction, Emergence and Explanation." In P. Machamer and M. Silberstein (eds.), *Blackwell Guide to the Philosophy of Science*, 80–107. Oxford: Blackwell.
Sloman, Aaron. 1978. *The Computer Revolution in Philosophy*. Hassocks, Sussex: Harvester Press.
Skarda, C. A. and Freeman, W. J. 1987. "How Brains Make Chaos in order to Make Sense of the World." *Behavioral and Brain Sciences* 10:161–195.
Skinner, Burrhus Frederic. 1971. *Beyond Freedom and Dignity*, 192–193. Pelican.
Smith, Brian Cantwell. 1996. *On the Origin of Objects*. Cambridge, MA: MIT Press.
———. 1999. "Situatedness/Extendedness." In R. A. Wilson and F. C. Keil (eds.), *The MIT Encyclopaedia of Cognitive Science*. Cambridge, MA: MIT Press.
Smolensky, Paul. 1988. "On the Proper Treatment of Connectionism." *Behavioral and Brain Sciences* 11:1–23.
Smullyan, Raymond. 1992. *Gödel's Incompleteness Theorems*. Oxford University Press.
Sterelny, Kim. 1990. *The Representation Theory of Mind*. Oxford: Blackwell.
Sun, Ron. 1995. "Robust Reasoning: Integrating Rule-Based and Similarity-Based Reasoning." *Artificial Intelligence* 75:241–295.
Teuscher, C. 2002. *Turing's Connectionism. An Investigation of Neural Network Architectures*. London: Springer-Verlag.
Thelen, E., Schöner, G., Sheier, C., and Smith, L. B. 2001. "The Dynamics of Embodiment: A Field Theory of Infant Perseverative Reaching." *Behavioral and Brain Sciences* 24:1–86.
Thelen, E. and Smith, L. B. 1994. *A Dynamic Systems Approach to the Development of Cognition and Action*. Cambridge, MA: MIT Press.
Thomson, William, Lord Kelvin. 1884. *Notes of Lectures on Modecular Dynamics and the Wave Theory of Light*, 270–271. Baltimore, MD: Johns Hopkins University.
Townsend, J. T. and Busemeyer, J. 1995. "Dynamic Representation of Decision Making." In Rober Port and Tim van Gelder (eds.), *Mind as Motion: Explorations in the Dynamics of Cognition*, 101–120. Cambridge, MA: MIT Press.
Turing, Alan. 1945. "Proposed Electronic Calculator (Unpublished Report to the National Physical Laboratory)." Available at: http://www.alanturing.net/proposed_electronic_calculator/.

———. 2004/1948. "Intelligent Machinery." In B. Jack Copeland (ed.), *The Essential Turing*, 410–432. Oxford University Press.
Turing, Alan M. 1936. "On Computable Numbers, With an Application to the Entscheidungsproblem." *Proceedings of the London Mathematical Society* 42: 230–265.
———. 1950. "Computing Machinery and Intelligence." *Mind* 59:433–460.
Turner, J. Scott. 2000. *The Extended Organism: The Physiology of Animal-Built Structures*. Cambridge, MA: Harvard University Press.
Ulam, Stanislaw. 1958. "John von Neumann, 1930–1957." *Bulletin of the American Mathematical Society* 64:1–49.
Van Gelder, Tim. 1991. "Connectionism and Dynamical explanation." In *Proceedings of the Thirteenth Annual Conference of the Cognitive Science Society*, 499–503. Hillsdale, NJ: L. Erlbaum Associates.
———. 1995. "What Might Cognition Be If Not Computation?" *Journal of Philosophy* 92:345–381.
———. 1997. "Connectionism, Dynamics, and the Philosophy of Mind." In Martin Carrier and Peter K. Machamer (eds.), *Mindscapes: Philosophy, Science, and the Mind*, 17–41. Pittsburgh University Press.
———. 1998. "The Dynamical Hypothesis in Cognitive Science." *Behavioral and Brain Sciences* 21:615–628.
———. 1999. "Bait and Switch? Real time, Ersatz Time and Dynamical Models." In R. Heath, B. Hayes, A. Heathcote, and C. Hooker (eds.), *Dynamical Cognitive Science: Proceedings of the Fourth Australasian Cognitive Science Conference*. Newcastle, NSW: University of Newcastle.
Van Gelder, Tim and Port, Robert. 1995. "It's about Time: An Overview of the Dynamical Approach to cognition." In Rober Port and Tim van Gelder (eds.), *Mind as Motion: Explorations in the Dynamics of Cognition*, 1–43. Cambridge, MA: MIT Press.
Vinge, Vernor. 2003. "Technological Singularity." *Whole Earth* Spring 2003 edition. Available at: http://www.wholeearth.com/uploads/2/File/documents/technological_singul%arity.pdf.
Walmsley, Joel. 2008. "Explanation in Dynamical Cognitive Science." *Minds and Machines* 18:331–348.
———. 2010. "Emergence and Reduction in Dynamical Cognitive Science." *New Ideas in Psychology* 28:274–282.
Warwick, Kevin. 2002. *I, Cyborg*. Century.
Warwick, Kevin, Gasson, M., Hutt, B., Goodhew, I., Kyberd, P., Andrews, B., Teddy, P., and Shad, A. 2003. "The Application of Implant Technology for Cybernetic Systems." *Archives of Neurology* 60:1369–1373.
Warwick, Kevin, Gasson, M., Hutt, B., Goodhew, I., Kyberd, P., Schulzrinne, H., and Wu, X. 2004. "Thought Communication and Control: A First Step Using Radiotelegraphy." *IEE Proceedings on Communications* 151:185–189.
Weizenbaum, Joseph. 1966. "ELIZA—A Computer Program for the Study of Natural Language Communication between Man and Machine." *Communications of the Association for Computing Machinery* 9:36–45.
———. 1976. *Computer Power and Human Reason*. London: Penguin.
Wermter, Stefan and Sun, Ron (eds.). 2000. *Hybrid Neural Systems*. Berlin: Springer-Verlag.
Wheeler, Michael. 2002. "Changes in the Rules: Computers, Dynamical Systems, and Searle." In John Preston and Mark Bishop (eds.), *Views Into the Chinese*

Room: New Essays on Searle and Artificial Intelligence, 338–359. Oxford University Press.

Whitby, Blay. 1996. "The Turing Test: AI's Biggest Blind Alley?" In Peter Millican and Andy Clark (eds.), *Machines and Thought*, 53–63. Oxford University Press.

Whitehead, Alfred North and Russell, Bertrand. 1910/1962. *Principia Mathematica to ∗56*. Cambridge University Press.

Wiener, Norbert. 1948/1961. *Cybernetics: or, Control and Communication in the Animal and Machine*. Cambridge, MA: MIT Press, 2nd edition.

Wilde, Oscar. 1890/2008. The Picture of Dorian Gray. Project Gutenberg edition. Available at http://www.gutenberg.org/files/174/174-h/174h.htm

Wilson, Robert A. 2010. "Meaning Making and the Mind of the Externalist." In Richard Menary (ed.), *The Extended Mind*. Cambridge, MA: MIT Press.

Wilson, Robert A. and Clark, Andy. 2009. "How to Situate Cognition: Letting Nature Take its Course." In Philip Robbins and Murat Aydede (eds), *The Cambridge Handbook of Situated Cognition*. Cambridge University Press.

Zednik, Carlos. 2011. "The Nature of Dynamical Explanation." *Philosophy of Science* 78:238–263.

Index

100-step argument, 79, 111

a priori, 19–23
Adams, F., & Aizawa, K., 156–8
algorithms, 36–41, 62, 116
Ashby, W. R., 152

Beer, R., 126–31, 143, 159
behaviourism, 26–7, 121
Block, N., 55
Boole, G., 27–8
brain, 79, 97, 167–8, 175
Brooks, R., 135–6, 142, 145, 171

centrifugal governor, 116–17, 139–40
chess, 48–51, 62
Chinese Room, 69–75
Chomsky, N., 30, 31, 32
Clark, A., 55, 139, 143–5, 151, 162, 164–5
Clark & Chalmers, 153–9
computation, 41
connectionism, 126–9, 142
Copeland, B. J., 36, 42, 53, 67
cybernetics, 12–13, 152
cyborgs, 160

Dartmouth Conference, 14, 166
Deep Blue, 49–51, 62, 173
Dennett, D., 15, 21–2, 55, 60, 62, 66–8, 74, 141
Descartes, R., 5–7, 23
Dretske, F., 1
dualism, 23–4, 167–8, 171
dynamical systems theory, 117–20, 125, 129, 146, 148, 158–9, 174
dynamics, 63, 74, 113, 115ff, 174

eliminativism, 99–102, 104–6
ELIZA, 51–4, 66
embeddedness, *see* situatedness
embodiment, *see* situatedness

emergence, 75, 96, 146–8
explanation, 132–4, 147–8
extended mind, 152–60

Fodor, J., 30, 31, 32, 33, 107
folk-psychology, 99–102, 103–6, 174
frame problem, 15–16
functionalism, 25, 32–5, 54–5, 98, 121–2, 154

General Problem Solver, 22–3, 44, 47–8
Gödel's Theorem, 58–63
"GOFAI", 27ff, 69, 75–6, 84, 86, 88, 92, 95, 101, 107–9, 111–13, 137

Haugeland, J., 6, 8, 9, 14, 27, 29–30, 46, 47, 57–8
Heidegger, M., 164
heuristics, 45–6, 49, 61–2
Hobbes, T., 7–8, 9, 69
Homer, 4
Hume, D., 8–10

Kelso, J.A.S., 125–6, 133, 148–50
Kim, J., 149–50
Kirsch, D., 144
Königsberg, 20–1
Kukla, A., 17, 19, 21, 71, 101

language, 6, 30–2, 51–3, 64, 68, 90–2, 107–9
learning, 81–2
Leibniz, G. W., 11–12
logic, 22, 27–30, 37, 44–7
Logic Theory Machine, 44–8
Lucas, J., 43, 58, 60

McCulloch & Pitts, 77
McLaughlin, B., 112
mentalese, 32

189

mind-body problem, 23–5, 54–6, 96–8, 146–50
multiple realisability, 25, 33–5, 54–5, 154, 168, 173

Newell, A & Simon, H., 19, 22–3, 44–6, 48

paradigm, 113
Pascal, B., 10–11, 173
Penrose, R., 43, 58, 60–2
physicalism, 24–5, 54–5, 96–7, 171
Pinker, S., 32, 61, 108–9
Principia Mathematica, 44–5, 59
propositional attitudes, 34, 101

reductionism, 96–7, 147–50
representation, 34, 83–4, 95, 109–10, 116, 138–43
representational theory of mind (RTM), 34–5, 83, 101

schizophrenia, 93–4
Seager, W., 63
Searle, J., 17, 69–75
singularity, 165–9, 175
situatedness, 129, 131, 134–8
Skarda, C., & Freeman, W., 143
Skinner, B.F., 170–1
Smith, B.C., 135, 173

tactile-visual sensory substitution, 161
Turing, A., 13–14, 30, 37, 40–1, 49, 61, 65–8, 69–70, 77, 165
Turing Machine, 38–42, 122
Turing Test, 64–9

van Gelder, T., 8–9, 113, 115, 117, 121, 122–3, 132–4, 139–42, 146, 147, 150

Warwick, K., 161–3
weak and strong AI, 3, 14–19, 50–1, 95
Weizenbaum, J., 52
Wiener, N., 12, 152